Arthur Latham Perry

Elements of political Economy

Arthur Latham Perry

Elements of political Economy

ISBN/EAN: 9783743346116

Manufactured in Europe, USA, Canada, Australia, Japa

Cover: Foto ©ninafisch / pixelio.de

Manufactured and distributed by brebook publishing software (www.brebook.com)

Arthur Latham Perry

Elements of political Economy

TABLE OF CONTENTS.

CHAPTER I.
On the History of the Science . . 1

CHAPTER II.
On the Field of the Science 23

CHAPTER III.
On Value 33

CHAPTER IV.
On Exchange 74

CHAPTER V.
On Production 89

CHAPTER VI.
On Labor 103

CHAPTER VII.
On Capital 133

CONTENTS.

CHAPTER VIII.
On Land 149

CHAPTER IX.
On Cost of Production 166

CHAPTER X.
On Money 188

CHAPTER XI.
On Currency in the United States 277

CHAPTER XII.
On Credit 314

CHAPTER XIII.
On Foreign Trade 347

CHAPTER XIV.
On the Mercantile System 410

CHAPTER XV.
On American Tariffs 422

CHAPTER XVI.
On Taxation 488

ANALYSIS OF CHAPTERS.

CHAPTER I.

ON THE HISTORY OF THE SCIENCE.

	PAGE
A. Definition of the science,	1
B. Its Basis and mode of Development,	1
C. Its History,	2
a. Oriental traffic. Abraham.	2
b. Greek opinion. Xenophon, Plato, Aristotle.	3
c. Roman opinion. Cicero, Cato.	5
d. Middle-age opinion. The monks and universities,	7
e. The Bullion Theory, and the policy that sprung from it,	8
f. The Mercantile System, and its devices,	11
g. Recoil from the Mercantile System towards freedom,	15
(1) English contributions. North, Hume, Smith, Ricardo, Mill.	17
(2) French contributions. Quesnay, Say, Bastiat.	19
(3) Italian and German writers,	21
(4) American contributions. Rae, Carey.,	21

CHAPTER II.

ON THE FIELD OF THE SCIENCE.

A. Political Economy distinct from Moral Science,	23
B. It is a political, that is, a social science,	25
a. Without society no exchange,	26
b. Without exchange no value,	26
c. Without value no science of value,	26
d. Man in isolation weak, in society strong,	27
C. Some leading definitions of the science,	28

ANALYSIS OF CHAPTERS.

                                                                               PAGE

D. The word wealth useless as a scientific term, . . . 29
   a. First reason of the slow progress of the science, . 29
E. Archbishop Whately's definition, ... 31
   a. Second reason of slow progress, ... 31

CHAPTER III.
ON VALUE.

A. Value not an independent quality of anything, . . 35
B. But a relation of mutual purchase between two things, 35
C. Origin of Value in an exchange of efforts, . . . 37
D. Desires, efforts, satisfactions, the circle of Political Economy, ... 37
E. The simplest case of Value includes all others, . . 40
F. No essential difference between services and commodities, 41
G. This definition of Value final, with manifold advantages, 42
   a. It covers completely hitherto anomalous cases of value, 45
   b. Remarkable aptness of the word Service for a scientific use, ... 45
   c. Ultimate analysis of the phenomenon of Value, . 47
   d. The definition expands Political Economy to its just limits, ... 48
   e. Frees the discussion from previous perplexities, . . 50
      (1) From the notion that value consists in matter, 51
      (2) From some obstinate illusions of language, . 54
      (3) From a mischievous confusion of utility with value, 55
H. Value a different thing from Price, ... 59
I. No perfect measure of value attainable, ... 63
J. Limitations of value in the two elements of efforts, . 64
K. Limitations in the two elements of desires, . . . 66
L. Equation of Supply and Demand, ... 68
M. Every rise or fall of demand tends to check itself, . . 70
   a. Through a consequent rise or fall of value, . . 70
   b. Through action on supply, ... 71
N. Three classes of services in the law of their value, . 71
   a. Those which can be increased without increased difficulty, ... 73
   b. Those increased only through increased difficulty, . 72
   c. Those which cannot be increased at all, . . . 72

ANALYSIS OF CHAPTERS.   ix

CHAPTER IV.

ON EXCHANGE.

	PAGE
A. Principles of human nature involved in exchange,	74
B. Society a hive of buyers and sellers,	75
C. God's will as indicated in diversity of natural gifts,	76
D. Association and Individuality,	77
E. Interest the sole motor in exchange,	77
F. All exchange depends on diversity of relative advantage,	80
G. The greater the difference of relative advantage the more profitable do exchanges become,	80
H. Freedom, association, and invention, essential to just diversity,	80
I. The right to free exchange a natural right,	81
J. Governments formerly unwarrantably interfered with this right,	81
K. But latterly have mostly conceded it within home boundaries,	83
L. Opposed to free exchange are Monopolies,	84
a. Arbitrary prohibitions on the sale of home services,	85
b. Arbitrary prohibitory duties on the admission of foreign services,	85
c. Patents and copyrights are unobjectionable monopolies,	87

CHAPTER V.

ON PRODUCTION.

A. Definition of Production and Producers,	89
B. The beneficent law of production this, that Nature works gratuitously in the service of man,	90
C. The effect on values of Nature's help in production,	93
D. A general glut of products impossible,	95
E. Advantages of the Division of Labor,	98
a. Improved corporeal and intellectual dexterity,	99
b. The saving of time,	99
c. The invention of machinery,	99
d. The more economical distribution of labor,	100

                PAGE
 e. A less waste of material, ... 100
 f. A saving in tools, ... 100
F. Disadvantages of the Division of Labor, . . . 100
 a. Monotonous work becomes irksome, . . . 101
 b. A tendency to dwarf the powers, ... 101
 c. An undue dependence of the workmen, . . 101
G. Limitations to the Division of Labor, . · . . 101
 a. From the extent of the market, ... 101
 b. From the nature of the employment, . . . 102

CHAPTER VI.
ON LABOR.

A. Physical labor consists in moving things, . . . 104
B. Men have sought and found helps in this, . . . 104
 a. The domestic animals, ... 104
 b. The water-wheel and wind-mill, ... 105
 c. Steam, ... 105
C. To apply these capital is needed, ... 106
D. The three requisites of material production, Labor, Power-agents, Capital, ... 106
E. The definition of Labor, ... 106
F. The remuneration of Labor, ... 107
 a. The wages of skilled labor depend:
  (1) On the general action of supply and demand, 108
 b. Are higher than the wages of common labor, . . 108
  (1) From the scarcity of appropriate original gifts, 109
  (2) From the lack of the requisite industry, . 109
  (3) Or of the means of suitable education and training, ... 109
 c. Principles varying all wages, mainly through supply, 110
  (1) Agreeableness or disagreeableness of the employments, . - 110
  (2) The easiness and cheapness of learning them, . 111
  (3) The constancy of employment in them, . 113
  (4) The amount of trust involved, ... 113
  (5) The probability of success, ... 115
  (6) Custom, prejudice, and fashion, . . . 116
  (7) Legal restrictions and voluntary associations, 117

PAGE

 d. Principles determining wages through demand, . 119
  (1) The presence of capital is a demand for labor, 119
  (2) The more of capital the stronger the demand, 119
  (3) Capital a dividend, number of laborers a divisor, and the quotient will express in general the rate of wages, ... 121
 e. Popular remedies for low wages ineffectual, . . 122
  (1) Government can not directly raise them, . 123
  (2) But may indirectly act beneficially upon them, 124
  (3) Public opinion may act usefully in some directions, ... 125
  (4) No legal restraints on population needful, . 126
  (5) Strikes are false in theory and pernicious in practice, ... 128

CHAPTER VII.

ON CAPITAL.

A. Definition of Capital, ... 133
B. How capital arises, ... 135
C. The remuneration of Capital, or Profits, . . . 137
 a. Profits are the reward of abstinence, . . . 138
 b. And are just as legitimate as wages, . . . 139
D. The law of distribution between Capital and Labor, . 141
 a. Labor is directly interested in the success of capital, 143
 b. Capital equally interested in the prosperity of laborers, 143
 c. Increase of capital redounds more to the benefit of laborers as a class than to capitalists as a class, . 144
E. Capital is either circulating or fixed, . . . 146

CHAPTER VIII.

ON LAND.

A. The value of Land and the rent of Land not anomalous, 150
B. The whole earth given to men gratuitously of God, . 150
 a. Till labor has been bestowed on them, or in reference to them, lands are valueless, ... 153
 b. What is sold in land is not the inherent qualities of the soil, but the improvements of man, . . 153

ANALYSIS OF CHAPTERS.

	PAGE
c. God's gifts to the race not interceptible by one generation,	153
d. History here confirms the deductions of reason,	153
C. Lands are subject to the law of diminishing return,	155
a. Through this law the whole earth has been gradually occupied,	156
b. Mr. Carey fails to break down this law,	157
D. Diminishing returns retarded by improvements in agriculture,	158
E. Rent of land the measure of the service rendered by the owner,	158
a. Ricardo's theory too mechanical and rigid,	159
b. Rent partakes of the nature of both wages and profits,	160
F. Approximately equal division of lands, and the tenure in fee simple, the best for production,	161
a. Beneficial operation of the fee simple,	162
b. Free trade in lands, and the consequent natural division best,	162
(1) Because efficient motives are brought to bear more universally,	163
(2) Because there is more of personal supervision,	163
(3) Because the masses are thereby educated and energized,	163
(4) Because it contributes to the national strength,	163
(5) Illustrations from England and France,	164

CHAPTER IX.

ON COST OF PRODUCTION.

A. Foresight an important matter in the sphere of exchange,	167
B. Cost of production one element from which value springs,	167
C. Cost of production made up of cost of labor and cost of capital,	170
a. Cost of labor is made up of three things:	
(1) Efficiency of the labor,	170
(2) The nominal rate of wages,	170
(3) The cost of that in which labor is paid,	170

ANALYSIS OF CHAPTERS. xiii

                    PAGE

  b. Diversity of nominal wages does not prove a diversity in the cost of labor, ... 171
  c. The terms high and low wages ambiguous, . . 173
    (1) Meaning sometimes money wages, . . . 173
    (2) Sometimes real wages, ... 173
    (3) Sometimes relative wages, ... 173
  d. Profits the *leavings* of cost of labor, . . . 175
  e. Cost of capital analyzable into three variables, . 176
    (1) The rate per cent., ... 176
    (2) The time for which the capital is advanced, . 176
    (3) The slow or rapid deterioration of that form of capital, ... 176
D. An enhanced cost of labor will exhibit itself in lower profits, ... 179
E. A general and uniform rise or fall of wages will not affect value, ... 179
F. A partial or unequal rise or fall will affect it, . . 179
G. The same, *mutatis mutandis*, is true of profits, . . 180
H. The amount and durability of machinery an important element in cost of production, ... 180
I. Machinery is not injurious to the wages of labor, . . 184
  a. Because labor is required to make, repair, and work it, 184
  b. Because it makes a broader market, and hence a stronger demand for products, ... 185
  c. Because it cheapens products used by the laborers, 185
J. Manufactured articles tend to decline in value as compared with food and raw materials, ... 185

CHAPTER X.

ON MONEY.

A. Money was devised by men, and hence comprehensible by them, ... 188
B. Barter is inconvenient, and sometimes impossible, . 189
C. Money is a generalized purchasing-power, . . 192
D. It is a medium of exchange, ... 193
  a. It is a small relative part of the values of any country, ... 194

ANALYSIS OF CHAPTERS.

	PAGE
b. Its first function is to help exchange those values,	195
c. It stimulates to exchanges which would not otherwise be made,	197
d. It is a generalized form of capital,	197
e. The amount needed determined by its nature as a *medium*,	198
f. Rapidity of circulation important in this connection,	200

E. Money is a measure of value, ... 201
   a. Importance of some units of measure in this field, 202
   b. Difference between a medium and a measure, . 203
   c. Other tables of denominations fixed and absolute, . 204
   d. Money denominations variable, ... 206
   e. A measure should be as little as possible liable to fluctuation, ... 208

F. Gold and silver constitute the best money, . . 209
   a. On account of their comparatively steady value, . 210
   b. The reasons why their value is so steady, . . 212
      (1) On account of a comparatively steady demand, 212
      (2) On account of a tolerably uniform cost of production, ... 213
      (3) On account of their quantity, ... 214
      (4) On account of their fluency, . . . 216
      (5) Because every rise or fall of their value tends to check itself, ... 219
      (6) Because a temporarily increased demand is neatly met by increased rapidity of circulation, . 220
   c. They are the best money, secondly, because they are self-regulating, ... 221
      (1) Difficulty in a double standard, . . . 223
      (2) Possibility of a universal coinage, . . . 227
   d. Thirdly, because they are conveniently portable, divisible, and impressible, . .' . . . 233

G. An inferior money drives a superior out, . . . 235
   a. Dutch illustration, ... 237
   b. English illustration, ... 239
   c. American illustrations, ... 242

H. A paper money is only tolerable when instantly convertible, ... 246
   a. A paper money is credit money, ... 247

b. It cannot in its very nature well perform the functions of money,	249
c. The French assignats,	251
d. American bills of credit,	254
e. The legal-tender notes,	255
f. The State-bank currency,	257
g. The currency of the new national banks,	259
h. The currency of the Bank of England,	261
I. Gold and silver are an economical money,	265
J. Interest on money is legitimate, and its rate should be free,	266
a. Usury laws are anomalous,	266
b. They are always disobeyed,	272
c. It would be worse if they were obeyed,	273

CHAPTER XI.

ON CURRENCY IN THE UNITED STATES.

A. The colonial currency,	278
B. The continental currency,	280
C. The Bank of North America,	284
D. The first Bank of the United States,	289
E. The second Bank of the United States,	292
F. The State banks,	295
G. The coins,	296
H. The national banking system of 1863,	307

CHAPTER XII.

ON CREDIT.

A. Credit is an exchange in which the return service is delayed,	314
B. The forms of credit are various,	315
a. Book-accounts,	315
b. Promissory-notes,	316
(1) Those of individuals and corporations,	317
(2) Those of governments,	318

xvi ANALYSIS OF CHAPTERS.

	PAGE
c. Bills of exchange,	319
(1) The par of exchange,	322
(2) How restored by natural laws,	323
d. Checks,	325
(1) The clearing-house system,	326
C. The advantages of credit,	326
a. In transferring capital from less to more productive hands,	326
(1) To industrious men who have no capital,	329
(2) Through banks,	330
(3) Through savings-banks,	330
(4) Through life insurance companies,	330
b. In economizing the general operations of exchange,	332
D. The disadvantages of credit,	333
a. "Long sales and large profits." "Quick sales and small profits,"	334
b. It tends to raise prices,	334
E. The general cause of commercial crises,	337
a. The crisis of 1837,	338
b. The crisis of 1847,	342
c. The crisis of 1857,	343

CHAPTER XIII.

ON FOREIGN TRADE.

A. There are no principles peculiar to foreign trade,	347
B. But a separate treatment is needful,	347
C. All exchange depends on diversity of relative advantage,	348
D. National diversities are of God's ordination,	350
E. Relative cost of production — arithmetical illustration,	351
F. The equation of international demand,	359
G. The word "compete" irrelevant in this connection,	360
H. Effect on trade of enhanced facilities for production in either country,	361
I. The costs of carriage,	363
a. Each nation does not necessarily pay its own,	364
b. That will depend upon the new international demand,	364

ANALYSIS OF CHAPTERS. xvii

	PAGE
J. Political Economy demands a free commerce,	366
K. The old Mercantile System gave birth to restrictions,	366
L. Objections to free trade answered,	373
a. A revenue tariff not opposed to free trade,	373
b. A theory?	373
c. Does it diminish wages?	375
d. Why so many men believe in restriction,	379
e. Would manufactures suffer from freedom?	381
f. Would the country become purely agricultural?	384
g. Is there any fundamental difference between commerce and trade?	388
h. Mr. Bigelow's views,	392
i. Every nation ought to be independent,	402
M. The voice of experience on free trade,	404
a. The English example,	405
b. The German example,	407

CHAPTER XIV.

ON THE MERCANTILE SYSTEM.

A. Fundamental principles of the Mercantile System,	410
B. The national policy that sprung from it,	411
a. Its first device, prohibitions,	414
b. Its second device, restrictions for protection,	417
c. Its third device, bounties,	420
d. Its fourth device, colonies,	421

CHAPTER XV.

ON AMERICAN TARIFFS.

A. England's policy towards the American Colonies,	422
a. The "Navigation Act,"	423
b. Prohibitions on manufactures,	425
c. Considerations condemning the colonial policy,	427
B. Want of power to regulate commerce under the Confederation,	428
C. The Tariffs under the Constitution,	429
a. The "Hamilton Tariff" of 1789,	429
(1) Its low duties,	429

		PAGE
(2)	Its steady revenue,	430
(3)	Its principles of tonnage and protection,	431
b.	The "Calhoun Tariff" of 1816,	431
(1)	Unfortunate connection of tariffs with politics,	432
(2)	The restrictive system fairly entered upon,	432
c.	The "Clay Tariff" of 1824,	432
(1)	Higher duties,	433
(2)	Protected interests not satisfied,	433
d.	The "Tariff of abominations" of 1828,	433
(1)	Protection had become unpopular,	433
(2)	Daniel Webster first votes for protection,	433
e.	The "Compromise Tariff" of 1833,	434
(1)	Presidential canvass hostile to protection,	434
(2)	The sliding scale of lower duties,	434
f.	The "Whig Tariff" of 1842,	434
(1)	Average of duties about fifty per cent.,	434
(2)	Factitious character of the industry stimulated,	434
g.	The "Walker Tariff" of 1846,	435
(1)	Low duties, but discrimination,	435
(2)	Increase of revenue,	435
h.	The "Tariff of 1857,"	435
(1)	Lower duties, and increase of free list,	435
(2)	Falling off, and rallying of revenue,	435
i.	The "Morrill Tariff" of 1861,	436
(1)	Duties too high and complicated,	436
(2)	Free list too large, and not honestly framed,	436
(3)	Revenue too small,	437
(4)	It can not be permanent,	437

CHAPTER XVI.

ON TAXATION.

A.	Taxation legitimate on principles of exchange,	438
B.	The Right of Property is the power to render services,	438
C.	Taxes, then, fall properly on exchanges,	439
D.	And should be proportionate to them,	441
E.	Taxes are either direct or indirect,	443
a.	Direct taxes fall on income or expenditure,	444
b.	Indirect on imports or services in transition,	444

		PAGE
c.	An income tax unexceptionable in principle,	444
d.	Taxes on expenditures, special, and hence objectionable,	445
e.	A house-tax, however, less so,	445
f.	General advantages and disadvantages of each form,	446
F.	Taxes and duties, to be productive should be low,	446
G.	Taxes and duties should be simple,	447
H.	They should be collected only just before disbursement,	448
I.	Poorer citizens should be mostly or wholly exempted from taxes,	449

ELEMENTS OF POLITICAL ECONOMY.

CHAPTER I.

HISTORY OF THE SCIENCE.

POLITICAL ECONOMY is the science of exchanges, or, what is exactly equivalent, the science of value. To unfold this science in an orderly manner will require an analysis of those principles of human nature out of which exchanges spring; an examination of the providential arrangements, physical and social, by which it appears that exchanges were designed by God for the welfare of man; and an inquiry into those laws and usages devised by men to facilitate or to impede exchanges. The science of value will be soundly based and properly unfolded when its propositions systematically arranged are shown to be deducible from acknowledged principles of human nature, and consonant with the providential structure of the world and of society; and when, in the light of these propositions, human institutions and laws relating to exchanges are explained and correctly estimated. An attempt to base and to develop the science of value thus will be made in the following pages; but before that work is fairly entered upon, it will be well to give a preliminary glance at the history of the science, and to trace the steps by which successive inquirers have brought Political Economy to its present stage of development.

While labor is as old as the race, and exchanges are as old as society, and while doubtless in all ages individual inquirers have tasked their minds with some portions of the subject, Political Economy as a science can hardly be said to have existed till within a period comparatively recent. Men exchanged among themselves services and commodities, and found their account in exchanging, long before the dawn of authentic history. The first commercial transaction on record dates back about two thousand years before Christ. It was the purchase by Abraham of the cave and field of Machpelah. " And Abraham weighed to Ephron the silver which he had named in the audience of the sons of Heth, four hundred shekels of silver, current money with the merchant." All this implies at that early day fixed conditions of trade. There were merchants as a class. Silver by weight was already a medium of exchange passing from hand to hand. It was current money with the merchant. In the absence of written documents a bargain was made in the presence of living witnesses. It was " in the audience of the sons of Heth, before all that went in at the gate of his city, that the field and the cave were made sure unto Abraham for a possession." An earlier passage in the life of Abraham shows that gold as well as silver was already reckoned an article of merchandise. It is said that Abraham departed from Egypt " very rich in cattle, in silver and gold."

From Abraham's time to the present, traffic has employed a portion of the activity of every people not utterly savage. Nineveh "multiplied her merchants above the stars of heaven." Tyre became "the royal exchange of the world." Athens, Carthage, Alexandria, Venice, Amsterdam, London, and New York, have each in turn not only engaged in domestic exchanges, but also "have ploughed the deep and reaped the harvests of every land!"

The earliest writer known to us who treated economic subjects at any length is Xenophon. In the first half of the fourth century before Christ this accomplished Athenian published two tracts, one " On the Revenues of Athens," and the other entitled " The Economist." These earliest essays, not indeed on Political Economy, but on some of the subjects with which that science has to do, contain, together with much that is fallacious, some sound and liberal principles. In the first of them Xenophon attempts to point out the modes in which the internal resources of Athens, if properly developed, might be made sufficient to balance her expenditures without the imposition of burdensome taxes. He dwells on the abundance of her natural productions, especially her mineral wealth, and her advantages as an emporium of trade. He suggests various ameliorations in the condition of the laboring classes. He would promote commerce, and augment the income from duties by holding out inducements to foreign ships to frequent the ports of Athens, by a more honorable treatment of merchants, by enlarging the public marts and warehouses, and by otherwise facilitating the transaction of mercantile business. He recommends that the government as such should itself undertake commercial enterprises; and especially urges that the silver mines of Laurium should be worked on government account and on a better system, admitting however private persons to a share in the capital stock and its returns. In conclusion he dwells on the importance of a durable peace to the success of every measure of national improvement. In the other little book referred to, there is a discussion on the origin, nature, and value of property; a view of the various parts of domestic economy; and a pretty full treatment of the subject of agriculture.[1]

There is nothing else on economical topics in the whole range of Greek literature that approximates in liberality and soundness to these little works of Xenophon. Plato, in his book called the " Republic," correctly sketches one important principle of the science, namely, the necessity man is in, from his multifarious wants, of uniting in extensive societies, in which each individual may be occupied exclusively with one species of production; but this speculative view is so far from being carried out to its practical application, that he proposes to banish entirely artisans and merchants from his imaginary commonwealth. Aristotle, however, has sometimes been called the father of Political Economy. He was not the father of the thing, but only of the name. He was the first to employ the expression which has ever since been used to designate the science. He wrote a treatise entitled "Economics," on the relation of man towards property; in which he lays down the doctrine that the bounty of nature is the only true

[1] Mure's History of the Greek Literature.

source of wealth, and in which the current prejudices against trading and the interest of money are vehemently maintained. "Interest," he says, "is most reasonably detested." Aristotle, whatever his merits in other directions, can be regarded neither as the founder of, nor a very important contributor to, the science upon which he has the honor of conferring the name.

We should expect beforehand that the more practical Romans, lovers of law and order, and exhibiting to the world many of the high qualities of citizen life, would make some valuable contribution to the science of exchanges. In this we are disappointed. Though in the earlier and better days of Rome, agriculture was highly esteemed, the blighting institution of slavery brought labor, the mechanical arts, and commerce more and more into disrepute. The lands were tilled by slaves. Slaves became the artisans of the country. As always happens under such circumstances, the freemen, the citizens, came to feel themselves above such degrading occupations. It is pitiful to hear Cicero declaim against the noble rights of labor. In the De Officiis there is a whole paragraph of condemnation for those branches of manufacturing and commercial industry which ought to be regarded not only as honorable but as the life and strength of the State. One sweep of his pen pushes out of the pale of respectability the whole class of mechanics. "All artisans are engaged in a degrading profession," says he. Again, "there can be nothing ingenuous in a workshop." Trade and commerce fare no better at his hands. When carried on on a small scale they are to be regarded as disgraceful;

when on a large scale they must not be greatly condemned! When social prejudices and views of labor like these are promulgated by the foremost man of his time, the best educated and the most liberal, there is no longer room for surprise at the lack of Roman contributions to Political Economy.

Moreover, the Roman moralists regarded the accumulation of wealth as pernicious and subversive of those virtues in which they placed the perfection of character. Luxuries and refinements in the mode of living, which are the result of accumulation, found in them uncompromising foes. Old Cato, the censor, in his severe denunciations of wealth, was but a representative of the whole class of moralists. And this ought not to surprise us for two reasons. The stream of the Roman wealth, as it poured in, proved a curse and not a blessing, not because wealth is not a blessing, but because its waters instead of being diffused everywhere, falling like the rain, giving increased comforts to the poor, and adding to every man's enjoyment, rushed at once into a few huge reservoirs. There was no natural distribution. The source of the wealth too was as illegitimate as its consumption. It did not come from the peaceful and gradual development of the national resources. Instead of engaging in agriculture and raising grain or other products of land, instead of building mills and manufacturing useful articles, or by any other class of efforts *producing* something for exchange, it was the Roman method to conquer rich lands, and then subject the inhabitants to interminable tolls and taxes, and thus endeavor to grow rich from the spoils of the industry of others. A comprehensive theory

HISTORY OF THE SCIENCE.

of value will hardly be reached, or be helped forward, in connection with such views of labor and such moral notions as the Romans entertained.

During the Middle Ages, when most of the universities of Europe were founded, the monopoly of knowledge was possessed by the Catholic clergy, and to them was naturally intrusted the regulation of the universities, and the establishing their courses of study. The course of study appointed was as meagre and scanty as the personal culture of the priests. If any one had suggested to those cadaverous and sometimes rope-begirded monks, that they should appoint a teacher to inquire into the nature of value, the laws of property, and the principles of commerce, they would have held up their hands in pious horror! The prejudices against labor and manufactures and commerce were still strong. The monkish ideas that contact with the world, with its practical questions and concerns, was contaminating, was beneath the dignity of the scholar, and altogether unworthy of the Christian, was slow to loose its hold. But the world moves on. The time came when men got a glimpse of the truth that the end of knowledge and science is a practical end, that their utility consists in their power to improve the condition of mankind, and that it is quite as worthy the attention of a rational human being to inquire how poverty may be prevented, the wants of the masses of mankind met, and the sum of human happiness increased, as to spend wearisome days and nights in following the intricacies of disputatious schoolmen, and arriving at last through mazes of metaphysical distinctions at results about as satisfactory as the schoolmen actually reached after a long controversy in the case of the question, "In what consists personal identity?" or, more specifically, "What was it that made Peter Peter and not John, and John John and not Peter?" namely, "that John's identity consisted in his Johnity, and Peter's identity consisted in his Petricity or Peterness!"

In our survey thus far, bringing us down we will say to the year 1600, if we have found little positive light thrown as yet upon the science of value, we have at least discovered some of the reasons why such light could not be thrown. Absence of investigation and discussion however does not necessarily imply the lack of a theory. In truth, there was a theory of value which marks the whole period we have passed under review. This earliest general theory of value I shall venture to call the *Bullion Theory*. From the fact that gold and silver, owing merely to their convenience, came to be the money of all civilized nations, men fell into a curious mistake in regard to them. They came to give to these metals a factitious importance, and to regard them as *the real and only wealth*. They overlooked the fact that these metals are a commodity, precisely like any other commodity, owe their value to labor, precisely like any other commodity, and are bought and sold like any other commodity. With useful products of any kind one can always buy gold and silver. To trade is nothing but to barter one commodity for another, — to exchange corn for silver and silver for corn. Unless the trade is fraudulent, the one is equally valuable with the other; and it would seem as if the simple consideration that men are willing to part, and do constantly part, with gold and silver to buy other things, would have been fatal to the prejudice that the precious metals are the only wealth.

There were however two things that seemed to sustain the Bullion theory. One was, that money is always the measure of value. "How much is it worth?" The answer comes, so many dollars. Dollars are the denomination in which value is reckoned, just as degrees of the thermometer are the denomination by which heat is measured. The difference between value itself and the measure of value — between a bushel of wheat and that round measure by which we determine that there *is* a bushel — seems obvious enough; but money has this peculiarity, it is not only a measure of value, but, so far as this expression is ever true of any one commodity, it has value in itself. There is no heat in a thermometer, and no wheat in a bushel-measure, but a dollar is not only a dollar measure, but a dollar value, and we can see how the fact that dollars both had value and were the measure of all other values, gave some plausibility to the notion that the dollars were all. The other thing that made the Bullion theory plausible was the use of gold and silver as the universal medium of exchange. They came to be such medium simply in consequence of their convenience and their nearly uniform value; and because they were such a medium, everybody wanted them, and whoever had them could get with them whatever else he wanted. Because the great thing was to get money, men seemed to think that money was the only thing to be got!

I cannot find that the Bullion theory had anything better to support it than these two deceptive pillars;

and yet from very early time still long after the discovery of America, it was considered by the whole commercial world to stand on an immovable basis. The commercial policy that sprung from this theory was obvious and universal. If gold and silver are the only wealth, then by all means keep the gold and silver in the country! Get all you can in, and let as little as possible out! Accordingly very early the nations passed laws to prohibit the exportation of gold and silver. We learn from Cicero, incidentally, that this was done repeatedly at Rome. In one of his orations he says, " The Senate solemnly decreed both many times previously, and again when I was consul, that gold and silver ought not to be exported." According to Adam Smith there are ancient acts of the old Scotch Parliament, which prohibit under heavy penalties the carrying gold and silver *forth of the kingdom.* The same thing was done by France and England, and probably by every other nation in Europe. To encourage the importation of the precious metals, and discourage their exportation, seemed to them the high road to national wealth. And indeed it would have been, had the Bullion theory been correct. But the Bullion theory was not correct. The clearness of our views in Political Economy will largely depend upon our thorough emancipation from the prejudice that gold and silver are any more valuable or any more desirable than the products for which they exchange. They constitute a part, but only a small fractional part, of the values of any country.

About the year 1600, there sprung up in Europe a second general commercial theory, which is usually termed the *Mercantile System*. It took its origin somewhat in this way. The discovery of an ocean path to the Indies, the great improvements in navigation, and the general waking up of the spirit of enterprise in the preceding century, gave a vast extension to commerce. The English merchants, particularly, found the prohibitions against the exportation of gold and silver very inconvenient. They found that, by carrying gold and silver to the East Indies, they could bring back articles worth greatly more in England than the specie they carried out; that is, with the imports they brought in they could buy more gold and silver than the sum they had exported. Therefore, in the year 1600, the English East India Company asked and obtained leave of Parliament to export a limited quantity of gold and silver. The adherents of the old theory raised a great storm, alleging that this Company would impoverish the kingdom by gradually draining off the gold and silver, that is, the national wealth.

The advocates of the Company, on the other hand, though they did not venture to assail the doctrine that wealth consists in gold and silver alone, took narrower ground, and asserted that the export of money is advantageous, whenever the articles bought by it and imported, are chiefly reëxported to other countries and sold for as much money as was originally carried out; and also whenever the export of coin, and the consequent import of commodities, occasions, though indirectly, a greater value of exports from home of native products. Thomas Mun, a writer of that period, quoted by Adam Smith, compares the trade of the merchant exporting gold and silver, to the seed-time and harvest of agriculture. "If we only behold," says he, "the actions of the husbandman in the seed-time, when he casteth away much good corn into the ground, we shall account him rather a madman than a husbandman. But when we consider his labors in the harvest, which is the end of his endeavors, we shall find the worth and plentiful increase of his actions." In a word, the Mercantile System reasoned thus: If a country only exports more than it imports, then the balance must come back in gold and silver; and if it keeps exporting more than it imports, and the balance keeps coming back in gold and silver, then the country must grow rich. Hence the great and only care was to preserve the balance of trade, as it was called. A famous phrase this, the balance of trade! The legislation, the diplomacy, the politics of the two centuries preceding the present were full of it.

By the balance of trade was meant the excess of the value of the commodities exported over the value of the commodities imported, which excess, it was supposed, would always come back in the form of gold and silver. Hence unlimited pains were taken to make the exports greater than the imports, and the excess was regarded as the measure of a country's commercial prosperity. Various devices were employed to make the exports great and the imports little. To increase the amount of exports, bounties were offered to domestic producers, to encourage them to sell as much as possible to foreign countries. With the same end in view, the raw materials of domestic manufactures were forbidden to be exported, so that the finished products, thereby rendered greater in amount, might help swell the exports. Colonies were planted with similar intent, that the mother country might find an open market there, and swell her exports. To diminish the aggregate of imports, prohibitions were laid on the bringing in from abroad articles which could be made or grown at home; and heavy restrictions imposed on imports from those countries with which the balance was supposed to be unfavorable, while the same articles, perhaps of an inferior quality, were admitted on easier terms from countries with which the balance was supposed to be better. Thus everything was sought to be regulated in view of an imaginary balance of trade. The Mercantile System was the prolific mother of those commercial restrictions, those attempted regulations of manufactures, those doctrines of monopoly, of corn-laws, and colonies, which have fettered industry almost up to the present time.

The particular fallacies that lurk in the Mercantile System, and the tortuous and cramping policy that grew out of it, will be more fitly discussed at a later stage of our inquiries; this is a proper place to indicate in general that the whole system is based on a misapprehension. It overlooks entirely the mutual benefit to the parties of every act of exchange, without which benefit the exchange clearly would not take place at all, and makes the whole advantage of commerce consist in a certain balance of gold and silver, which comes back to that one of the parties which has managed to part with more of its own commodities. It seems strange that it did not occur to those people, that, if it were worth while to trade at all, the benefits of the trade were rather to be measured by the amount and value of what was received, than by the amount and value of what was parted with! Moreover, the system takes for granted, that traders carry forth goods to foreign countries to receive back goods *and* bullion worth as much, — less goods, indeed, and the balance in bullion. Why on that principle should the goods be carried forth at all? The labors, the risks, and the exchanges all made; the goods and the balance received; and the country just as well, but no better off than before! One thing is certain and obvious. Unless the imports, whether including any specie balance or not, are worth more to the country importing, than the exports, they certainly would not be imported. This difference of value in favor of the imports is precisely the motive for the importation. If they are worth only as much as, or less than, what is exported to pay for them, where is the advantage of the trade? Speaking generally, then, the value of the imports into any country is always greater than the value of the exports, the comparison of course being made in that country and not elsewhere. The whole wisdom of the Mercantile System was to sell as much as possible and buy as little as possible, — a wisdom which is evident folly, inasmuch as, universally applied, it would destroy the commerce of the world.

The leading commercial nations of Europe, nevertheless, fell into the meshes of the Mercantile System. Portugal, Spain, France, Holland, and

HISTORY OF THE SCIENCE. 15

England, all gave their attention to the balance of trade, all laid restrictions on the natural freedom of industry, and all applied the system rigidly to their colonial dependencies. These restrictions on trade, especially on the importation of manufactured goods, and on the exportation of corn and raw materials, to say nothing of the bounties which the people were taxed to pay, were to the last degree vexatious and onerous; while the penalties for their infringement were in many cases cruel and even barbarous. Various writers in the different countries, and particularly in England, where the laws in question were, perhaps, the most oppressive, began to attack the mercantile theory and the policy that had grown out of it. And it is to this series of writers in long succession, some overthrowing one false position, and some another, one establishing a truth here and another there, that we owe the gradual development and present state of the science of Political Economy. The science has gradually emerged from the waves of thought dashing and roaring around the Mercantile System. It is still necessary, at least on the continent of Europe and in the United States, to combat some of the remains of the old mercantile legislation. England is believed to be the only country which has erased from her statute-book the last vestiges of the system. This she has done in direct consequence of the skill and power with which the political economists have guided the public opinion of that country; and it is on account of their success, as well as on account of the superior numbers and weight of English thinkers in this field of inquiry, that it is proper now to consider first the

English contributors to the modern science of Political Economy. We shall then attend to what the French have done towards building up the science; and, with a few remarks on the Italian and German writers, shall close this sketch with a brief recital of American views and writers.

In the last three decades of the seventeenth century, there appeared in England several tracts and treatises, attacking the crooked industrial and commercial policy of the time.[1] Only three writers of that period will here be instanced. The first of these is Sir William Petty, whose views of money in particular are remarkably sound. He fully exposes the current notion that a nation can be drained of its cash by an unfavorable balance of trade. He condemns the laws regulating the rate of interest, observing that there might as well be laws regulating the rate of insurance. He ridicules the idea that tolls and customs and barriers are advantageous to trade. And he was, perhaps, the first to lay down the doctrine that the value of commodities is determined by the labor required for their production. In 1691, Sir Dudley North published "Discourses on Trade." How liberal and intelligent this writer was, how decidedly in advance of his time, may be judged of by the following doctrines, which he lays down as fundamental: That the whole world, as to trade, is but as one nation; that there can be no trade unprofitable to the public, for if any prove so, men leave it off, and wherever the traders thrive, the public, of which they are a part, thrive also; that money is a merchandise whereof there may be a glut as

[1] McCulloch's Introductory Discourse.

well as scarcity; and that money exported in trade is an increase to the wealth of the nation. In his "Essay on Civil Government," published in 1690, at the request of William and Mary, and for the justification of the English Revolution of 1688, John Locke incidentally illustrated the distinction between utility and value, and all but established this one of the fundamental doctrines of Political Economy: that value is the birth of effort, and not the gift of Providence. In the controversy concerning the recoinage of silver money in the same reign, Locke did good service by his tracts on money, in preventing the lowering of the currency standard, and in diffusing sound principles on the nature of money.[1] Locke taught as forcibly as had Petty and North, that it was as absurd for the State to attempt to fix the price of money, as to fix the price of cutlery or broadcloth.

During the next century, that is, the last century, practical questions of taxation, or the rate of interest, or the vexed questions of trade, drew out in England a multitude of tracts and treatises, many of them containing valuable hints and arguments, and the ablest of them all being unquestionably the Political Essays of David Hume. These appeared in 1752. Among them are essays on Commerce, Interest, Balance of Trade, Jealousy of Trade, and Public Credit. His views are enlightened and liberal; not always sound, but always interesting. He did not profess, however, to analyze value, or to ground comprehensively the science of Political Economy. That attempt was first successfully

[1] Macaulay's England, chap. xxi.

made by Dr. Adam Smith, Professor in the University of Glasgow, who published in 1776, his great work on the Wealth of Nations, in which many of the more important propositions of the science are established beyond the reach of controversy. It will be noticed that the publication of this work took place in the very year in which American Independence was declared; and it was itself a sort of declaration of independence of the false principles and foolish policy of the Mercantile System. Like the document of Jefferson, it excited universal attention: like that, it marks an era; and the results in the economical world of the treatise of Smith have been scarcely less striking and beneficent than the results in the political world of the document of Jefferson. Indeed, the merits and originality of Dr. Smith are so great, that he has frequently been called the father of Political Economy. It is hardly just that that title should be given to any man; but if it is to be worn by anybody, it must most assuredly be conceded to him. He exalts labor, shows the advantages of its division, and advocates its unshackled freedom in all departments; he unfolds the benefits of commerce, and demonstrates the absurdity of the restrictive and regulating devices of the Mercantile System; he discusses money, wages, profits, rent, taxation, and public expenditures. The defects of the Wealth of Nations are mainly these: a want of clear definitions; an illogical arrangement; an inconsistency sometimes with its own principles, as when allowing that a State may regulate the rate of interest; a preference, in its theory of value, for material commodities; a want of clear perception of the difference between utility and value, and a consequent partial confusion in the whole doctrine of values; and lastly, a prolixity which is at times tedious. These defects and some others have been pointed out, and valuable additional contributions to the science made, by succeeding English writers. The principal of these are Mr. Ricardo, Mr. McCulloch, Mr. DeQuincey, Mr. Senior, and especially, Mr. John Stuart Mill. The work of the last-mentioned writer, while sharing in the fault common to all these English books, namely, a too exclusive attention to the material over the other forms of value, is the best single treatise on the subject in the English language.

If the French have done less than the English in building up the science of Political Economy, they have done well what they have done. They have the honor of publishing the very first general treatise under the title of "Political Economy." It was issued at Rouen in 1615. To them also is due the credit of having furnished the first writer who undertook a systematic analysis of the sources of value, and whose ingenious speculations gave rise to the first school of Political Economy. This was M. Quesnay, a physician attached to the court of Louis XV., whose book was published in 1758.[1] His fundamental positions expressed the reaction from the principles of the Mercantile System as embodied in the policy of Colbert, the famous finance minister of Louis XIV. That policy gave a decided preference to the industry of the towns and cities. M. Quesnay appeared as the champion of agriculture. His

[1] Adam Smith. Book iv., chap. ix.

system assumes that the physical earth is the only source of wealth, and consequently that labor is incapable of producing any new value except when employed in agriculture. Artisans and merchants are unproductive laborers, because there is no nett produce remaining, as in agriculture, over and above the expenses of production. The system mistook the nature of rent; and falsely though tacitly assumed that wealth consists in matter. The novelty of the theory however, its scientific shape, and the liberal commercial policy coupled with it, gave it for a time a great reputation; and it numbered among its disciples no less persons than Turgot, the financier, and the elder Mirabeau. The disciples of Quesnay were called Economists or Physiocrats. In 1802, appeared in Paris, Say's Political Economy. Say is throughout an eminently skilful expositor of the science, while his own especial contribution is a demonstration of the impossibility of a general glut, — a general over production. He is an able advocate of the freedom of commerce. But the book which has carried Political Economy to its most advanced position, and the most important contribution to the science since the time of Adam Smith, was published in Paris in 1850. Its author was Frederic Bastiat, who died the same year. Its title is "Harmonies of Political Economy." It is the first volume of what was designed to be a larger work; and in it there is a vigorous demonstration of the harmonious mechanism of society, by which, through the agency of liberty and property, God has designed the progressive amelioration of mankind. "All legitimate interests are in harmony," is the key-note of the book. While unfolding the laws of value in their manifold applications, Bastiat incidentally but most effectually demolishes the vagaries of communism, and establishes the right of property upon unassailable grounds. Some of the positions of this book have been claimed by Mr. Henry C. Carey, of Philadelphia, as original with himself; and it seems probable that M. Bastiat did profit by some of the views of Mr. Carey, but the substantial originality and the uncommon merit of the French writer are undeniable.

The Italian and German writers, although voluminous and respectable, have originated comparatively little within the field of this science. The first professorship of Political Economy was established in Italy in 1764; and able men are teaching the subject in most of the German universities at present.

The circumstances of the United States, as well in colonial vassalage as in an independent position, their experience with almost every variety of paper money, the alternations of the national policy in respect to trade, the long continued public discussions on the tendencies and results of a protective tariff, and the efforts — State and National — which have been made towards realizing a healthful currency, have been favorable to the cultivation of economical studies. It is not true, however, that many works of decided merit have yet appeared in the United States. Daniel Raymond's " Thoughts on Political Economy," published at Baltimore in 1820, are remarkable only as being the first formal treatise published in this country. Fourteen years later, John Rae, a Scotchman, published at Boston a book on the subject, which has elicited a strong commendation from John Stuart Mill. He says of it: "In no other book known to me, is so much light thrown, both from principles and history, on the causes which determine the accumulation of capital." The only other American writer whose name requires to be mentioned in this connection, is Mr. Carey, whose economical works have been published at intervals between 1835 and 1860. It is impossible in this place to characterize at any length the peculiar views, many of them original and important, which are brought out in these publications. Among them may be enumerated the following: That it is not so much the cost of production as what would be the cost of reproduction, that determines the value of commodities; that the real interests of classes and individuals are essentially harmonious; that there is a constant tendency to increase in the wages of labor, and to diminution in the rate, though to increase in the aggregate, of the profits of capital; that the well-being and advancement of society correspond to the degrees of association and of liberty which exist in it; and that the prices of land, labor, and raw materials, tend constantly to approximate the prices of finished commodities, and in the closeness of this approximation is to be found the best gauge of advancing civilization.

CHAPTER II.

FIELD OF THE SCIENCE.

WHEN Adam Smith taught Political Economy in the University of Glasgow, it was as a branch of moral philosophy, and the substance of his "Wealth of Nations" was delivered first in the form of lectures, which made up a part of his moral philosophy course. That course was divided into four parts: the first comprising natural theology; the second, ethics, or what Paley terms the science of duty and the reasons of it; the third jurisprudence, or that part of morality which relates to justice; while in the fourth part he examined those political and social regulations which are founded on expediency, and which tend to increase the prosperity and power of a State.

Now, expediency is so radically distinct from duty that there is no need of proving that Political Economy is not to be reckoned a part of moral philosophy at all. The idea of obligation, on which the science of morals is founded, and the idea of value on which the science of economy is founded, are totally distinct ideas. There is one word that marks and circumscribes the field of morals. That word is Ought. There is one word that marks and circumscribes the field of economy. That word is Value. Political Economy does not aspire to place its feet upon the ponderous imperatives of moral obligation. It finds a solid and adequate footing upon the expedient and the useful. As a science, it does and must discuss and decide all questions upon economical grounds alone. As a science, it has no concern with questions of moral right. If it favors morality, it does so because morality favors production. It favors honesty because honesty favors exchange. It puts the seal of the market upon all the virtues. It condemns slavery, not because slavery is morally wrong, but because it is economically ruinous. Moral science appeals only to an enlightened conscience, and certain conduct is approved because it is right, and for no other reason. Political Economy appeals only to an enlightened selfishness, and exchanges are made because they are mutually advantageous, and for no other reason. Each of the two sciences, therefore, has a distinct basis and sphere of its own. The grounds of Economy and morals are independent and incommensurable.

Every science, however, has its points of contact with other sciences; and this is particularly the case with Political Economy in relation to moral science, and is the reason why the two have sometimes been confounded. The sound conclusions of the one are harmonious with the sound conclusions of the other. Both work together for the good of men, for the amelioration of their condition. Their spheres, though distinct, nevertheless touch each other. Duty and interest lie alongside. The ultimate analysis of property, for example, will, as we shall see, lead the inquirer into the higher region of moral science. In legislation also, the question is frequently at the same time an economical and a moral question. Dr.

Wayland has observed that "almost every question of the one science may be argued on grounds belonging to the other." But the grounds themselves, it is important to remark, must be seen to be, and must be kept, distinct.

In the next place, the very name of the science indicates that it is a political, that is, a social science. It relates to men in a state of society, and not to men in a state of isolation. The hermit, who neither buys nor sells, who neither gives nor receives anything in exchange, is not amenable to the laws of Political Economy. So far as men satisfy their own wants by their own efforts without exchange, they stand outside the pale of this science. Under those circumstances the idea of value could neither have birth nor being, and of course there would be no such thing as a science of value. Robinson Crusoe came to lead a very tolerable life upon his desolate island by means of his own industry. He worked, but then he worked to satisfy his own wants directly. He did everything for himself. He had no opportunity to buy anything, sell anything, exchange anything. The whole course of such a life could never have developed the idea of value, and the record of the whole experience of such a solitary individual would require no such word as value. If God had made men so that their varied wants would best be met by applying their own efforts to satisfy these wants directly, without the intervention of exchange, there would have been, there could have been, no such science as the one to which attention is now directed. In that case, men would live, if they lived at all, in perfect isolation. Every man would satisfy his own desires by his own efforts. There would be no society, and no exchange.

But it is evident at the very first glance, that the Creator has not made men thus. Society is God's handiwork. It is the most complicated and the most wonderful, as it was the final, work of his hands. The first man, as he stood alone in Paradise, was indeed a wonderful structure, — wonderful in his body, and in all his mental and spiritual powers. But it was not good that the man should be alone. Society must be provided for; and in providing for a society of human beings, God impressed upon that organization, as upon all others, its own proper and peculiar laws. These laws embrace its entire organization, in its lower, as well as in its higher, parts. They cover the phenomena of exchange, just as they cover the phenomena of morals; and no intelligent observer can watch their working, when left intact and free, without being stimulated and gladdened by the beneficent results to which they lead. If the footsteps of providential intelligence be found anywhere upon this earth, if proofs of God's goodness be anywhere discernible, they are discernible, and are found in the fundamental laws of society. Certainly, if every man could satisfy all his desires as well, by putting forth his efforts to that end directly, he would do it. He would grow his own food, make his own clothes, write and publish his own newspaper, be his own doctor, in one word, perform all needed services for himself. But God has so ordered it that he cannot do this. He cannot, in a state of isolation, with all his efforts, procure for himself one thousandth part of the comforts which he easily procures for himself by less efforts, through exchange. Society and exchange are, under God's ordination, matters of necessity, if men are to rise in a scale of comforts perceptibly above the brutes. And the reason is this. There are obstacles, in all directions, to the satisfaction of men's desires. If the desires are to be met, these obstacles are to be surmounted. But if one man undertakes to surmount any considerable number of these obstacles, he miserably fails. His powers are not adequate to the task; and hence we say, that in a state of isolation, men's wants exceed their powers. But, if he devote himself to surmounting one class of obstacles, as, for instance, those in the way of procuring suitable clothing, his powers are adequate to this, he soon acquires skill in it, he learns to avail himself of the gratuitous help of Nature, and the facilitating processes of art, he is able to realize large products along his line, and is now in position to offer valuable services to society. Meanwhile other men have been devoting themselves each to another class of obstacles, have concentrated effort and skill upon them, have succeeded by the help of Nature and art in surmounting them, and now offer their valuable services to society.

Now, then, these services are mutually exchanged in all directions, and men find, as it is God's clear design that they should find, that, by making given efforts along one line, and exchanging them for corresponding efforts along other lines, they obtain vastly greater satisfactions for their various desires than they could obtain by direct effort. Why? Because there is now a vast increase of useful products in existence. Here we have reached, provisionally, the true explanation of the gains of exchange. It is not so much that by exchange men get better and cheaper articles, as it is that they get more of them. By the division of employments, which is only possible under a system of exchange; by the fact that, under free exchange, men avail themselves of all the varied advantages of Nature and position; the number and variety of useful products created, the number and variety of the services which men are able to render to each other, are immeasurably augmented. More is produced, more is to be exchanged, and therefore there are more satisfactions of all men's desires. Political Economy, therefore, which unfolds the reasons and the laws of exchange, finds its only field in a state of society. It is truly a political, that is, a social science.

In determining now more definitely still the field of our science, we will look at some of the leading definitions of it which have been given by different writers. Mr. Senior defines it " the science which treats of the nature, the production, and the distribution of wealth." Mr. McCulloch regards it "the science of the laws which regulate the production of those material products which have exchangeable value, and which are either necessary, useful, or agreeable to man." Archbishop Whately gives it the name of " catalactics, or the science of exchanges." Among several equivalent definitions which he is at pains to give, Mr. Mill places first,—
" the science which treats of the production and distribution of wealth, so far as they depend upon the laws of human nature." The French writers

give definitions somewhat broader. M. Storch says it "is the science of the natural laws which determine the prosperity of nations, that is to say, their wealth and civilization." M. Sismondi regards "as the object of political economy the physical welfare of man, so far as it can be the work of government." And M. Say defines it as "the economy of society; a science combining the results of our observations on the nature and functions of the different parts of the social body." And lastly, Mr. Carey, in this country, dropping the title Political Economy as a general designation, and adopting the term "Social Science" in its stead, defines it as "the science of the laws which govern man in his efforts to secure for himself the highest individuality and the greatest power of association with his fellow-men."

It will be noticed that in several of the preceding definitions the term wealth is introduced as a part of the definition. This word wealth has been the bane of Political Economy. It is the bog whence most of the mists have arisen which have beclouded the whole subject. From its indefiniteness, and the variety of associations it carries along with it in different minds, it is totally unfit for any scientific purpose whatever. It is itself almost impossible to be defined, and consequently can serve no useful purpose in a definition of anything else. It has been much debated, for example, among political economists, whether the term wealth includes anything more than material products, such as houses, lands, metals, tools, food; or whether the skill of artisans and the services of professional men are also to be reckoned as wealth. Some include under the term only material products; others, as Mr. Mill, widen the signification so as to take in those immaterial services which result in an increase of material products; while others still, with evident violence to the current meaning of the word, include under it all things, whether material or immaterial, for which something may be obtained in exchange. Thus the meaning of the word wealth has never yet been settled; and if Political Economy must wait until that work be done as a preliminary, the science will never be satisfactorily constructed. It is simply impossible, on such an indefinite word as this at the foundation, to build up a complete science of Political Economy. Moreover the word wealth includes the two distinct ideas of value and utility, — ideas which must be kept perfectly distinct, or else there is no sound thinking and no sound conclusions within this field. Men may think, and talk, and write, and dispute till doomsday, but until they come to use words with definiteness, and mean the same thing by the same word, they reach comparatively few results, and make but little progress. And it is just at this point that we find the first grand reason of the slow advance hitherto made by this science. It undertook to use a word for scientific purposes which no amount of manipulation and explanation could make suitable for that service. Happily there is no need to use this word. In emancipating itself from the word wealth as a technical term, Political Economy has dropped a clog, and its movements are now relatively free.

Of the other definitions quoted, against which the objection just considered does not lie, some embrace too little, and others embrace too much. The only one which seems to the present writer to be exactly right, is the definition given by Archbishop Whately, namely, the science of exchanges. This definition, or its precise equivalent, the science of value, gives a perfectly definite field to Political Economy. Wherever value goes this science goes, and where value stops this science stops. Political Economy is the science of value, and of nothing else. To determine with distinctness what value is, to separate it from some things which have often been confounded with it, and thus to lay a foundation for the science at once satisfactory and complete, will be the work of the next chapter. But it is in order at this point to call attention to the second grand reason of the slow advance hitherto made in this field of inquiry. Value is a relative word. It is usually defined as purchasing-power, that is to say, the value of anything is its power of purchasing other things. It is not an independent quality of one thing, as hardness is a quality of a stone, but it is a quality of one thing as estimated in a corresponding quality of something else. It is not a quality, in and of itself, of gold, but a relation which gold holds to other things which gold will buy. The notion of value is not conceivable except by a comparison of two things, and what is more, of two things mutually exchanged. Political Economy therefore is based upon a relative idea, and has to do from beginning to end with a relation. Now in this there is an inherent difficulty, and a difficulty too which can never be obviated. It lies in the very nature of the subject. Men much more readily apprehend an absolute idea than a relative one. They more easily follow a discussion touching the independent attributes of single objects, such as length, breadth, thickness, and many others, than a discussion touching value, which is not an attribute of any one thing, but a relation subsisting between two things. I am not aware that this difficulty has ever been remarked on by any writer, but I am at the same time very sure that it constitutes the principal difficulty in this class of inquiries, and has been the main reason of the tardy progress hitherto made in them. A careful analysis of the nature of value, and copious illustration bestowed upon the elements of the subject, will lessen this difficulty as much as the nature of the case will allow. To this then we next proceed.

CHAPTER III.

ON VALUE.

If I take up a new lead-pencil from my table, for the purpose of examining all its qualities, I shall immediately perceive those which are visible and tangible. The pencil has length, a cylindrical form, a black color, is hard to the touch, is composed of wood and plumbago in certain relations to each other, and has the quality, when sharpened at the end, of making black marks upon white paper. Are then these, and such as these, the only qualities of the pencil? No. It has another quality very important, which is neither visible nor tangible, but relative. It has purchasing-power. It had the power of purchasing from me, two days ago, the sum of ten cents, United States currency; and if I should choose to take it back to the store where the exchange was made, it has doubtless the quality still of being able to purchase again from the storekeeper the same number of cents which it first purchased from me.

This purchasing-power, which the pencil possesses in common with all other articles which are ever bought, sold, or exchanged, is value, and is the subject of Political Economy. It is absolutely essential, in order to engage in any discussions in Political Economy with the least hope of sound results, to determine with distinctness the nature of value, to use the term always in the same sense, and not to confound the thing itself with other things that may be similar. It is convenient to regard value as a quality inhering in a commodity or service. The convenience of such expressions as, "the pencil has value," "gold has value," is so great, that science will not consent to forego the advantage of using them, even though they are not scientifically accurate. She justly prefers to make her language intelligible and popular, and then to explain precisely what she means by it. Strictly speaking, value is not a quality of any one thing, but a relation which one thing holds to another thing. It is not a quality in and of itself of gold, but a relation which gold holds to other things that gold will buy. It is not, therefore, true, speaking strictly, that value is a quality of gold in the sense in which weight is a quality of gold, because circumstances are easily conceivable, and have often occurred, under which gold would have no value at all. To the crew of a boat abandoned at sea, among whom the last biscuit had been rationed out, a bag of gold belonging to one of the men would not purchase a biscuit belonging to another. The inherent qualities of the gold are present. It is still hard, and yellow, and heavy. But valuable it is not. It will not purchase anything. Value, therefore, is not an inherent and invariable attribute, but is the relative power which one thing has of purchasing other things. This power in any one thing will vary according to time and place and circumstances. It may cease altogether, as in the case just supposed, or it may rise under other circumstances to a very high degree; but whenever it exists, it exists with reference to some other thing, which either is, or is supposed to be, exchanged with it. Ten cents had the power of purchasing my pencil, and my pencil has the power of purchasing ten cents. In this transaction the idea of value is developed. A similar transaction first introduced that idea into the world, and the endless succession and variety of such transactions has kept the idea in the world, and will keep it here till the end of time. Value, then, speaking strictly, is not an independent quality of the pencil, any more than it is an independent quality of the cents. Both are necessary in order that the value of either may be conceived of. The value of the cents is estimated, is measured by the pencil; and the value of the pencil is estimated, is measured by the cents. In one word, value is always relative, and never absolute. To say that anything has an absolute value is a simple contradiction in terms.

But why was I desirous to part with good United States money for the sake of the pencil, and the storekeeper to part with a good pencil for the sake of the money? The answer to this question will ground the science of value on the unchanging principles of human nature. I experience a want which the pencil was adapted to satisfy. He experienced a want which the money was adapted to satisfy. But between my want and its satisfaction, both of which were personal to me, there lay an effort, to be made either by myself or by somebody else in my behalf. So, between his want and its satisfaction, both of which were personal to him, there lay an effort, to be made either by himself, or by somebody else in his behalf. If I had chosen to do so, I might have made the direct effort necessary in order to supply myself with a pencil. I might have made the pencil for myself. It would indeed have been a long and tedious process, would have required a learning of two or three trades, a journey to some plumbago-bed, the working and preparation of the mineral, and various other subordinate processes; still, in the course of half a life-time it might perhaps have been done, and I might by direct efforts have supplied myself with a pencil as good as that which I purchased. So, too, the storekeeper, unless the laws had prevented it, might have procured for himself by direct efforts the metal cents which I gave him in exchange for the pencil. He might have dug the ores for himself, refined, alloyed, and minted them. Had we chosen respectively to take this course, and each been able to satisfy his own particular desire by his own unassisted efforts, the processes in either case would have had no relation to Political Economy. There would be in each case a want, an effort, a satisfaction, but there would be no exchange. As a matter of fact, however, we exchanged the efforts which lay between our respective desires and their respective satisfactions. I desired a pencil, he relieved me of the effort necessary to make it, and I experienced the satisfaction. He desired the cents, I relieved him of the effort necessary to procure them, and he again experienced the satisfaction. We each experienced our own desires, and our own satisfactions, but we exchanged efforts. Precisely in this exchange of efforts arose the phenomenon of value. I parted with my cents, which had cost me an effort, in order to satisfy my desire for a pencil, because my effort, represented in the cents, was less than the effort it would cost me to create the pencil. The shopkeeper parted with the pencil, which had cost him an effort, in order to satisfy his desire for the cents, because his effort, represented in the pencil, was less than the effort which it would otherwise cost him to procure the cents. We exchanged efforts, therefore, for our mutual advantage.

The principles of human nature, then, on which the laws of value are grounded, are these: Men have desires, are capable of making efforts to meet these desires, and experience a satisfaction when the desires are met. These three are indisputable and universal facts. But while the desire and the satisfaction are strictly personal to one man, that is to say, belong to him and cannot be communicated to another, it is not so with efforts. Efforts are exchangeable. You have a desire, I make the effort to meet it, and you again experience the satisfaction. On the other hand, I have a desire, you make the effort to meet it, and I again have the satisfaction. We exchange efforts, but experience our own satisfactions. Desires, efforts, satisfactions, constitute the one circle of Political Economy, and value arises in every case from a comparison of two corresponding efforts. Efforts are naturally irksome. Everybody wishes to realize as large a satisfaction as possible from a given effort. If, by making that effort for another, a larger satisfaction will be realized than by expending it directly for one's self, there is an immediate and pressing motive to make the effort for another, and to reach the satisfaction, not directly, but indirectly, that is, by exchange. A precisely similar motive actuates that other person. If his given effort will realize more for himself by being put forth for the first man, and by accepting the first man's effort in return, he too will be anxious to exchange efforts with the first. There is a mutual advantage in thus exchanging. A given effort realizes better satisfactions for each of the parties, and the reason for exchanges is thus seen to spring from the most active and invariable principles of human nature.

Value, then, has reference to efforts, to services; is measurable in and exchangeable for these. And men find by experience — and this is one of the grand harmonies of society — that they gain more satisfactions for less efforts, by thus exchanging efforts. It is because there are obstacles to be surmounted in order that men's various desires may be met; and because any one may choose what class of obstacles he will devote himself to surmounting, and then exchange his efforts along that line with the efforts of other men along their lines; and because by thus doing the satisfactions of all bear a larger and larger proportion to their efforts, that exchange plays so vast a part in the world's affairs.

The exchange of the cents for the pencil, and the pencil for the cents, is a simple case of value, but it is not the simplest. In this case there is an exchange of one commodity for another commodity, the idea of value is instantly developed, and we say that the pencil is worth ten cents, or, what is exactly equivalent, ten cents are worth the pencil. There are two things in every exchange, — that which is parted with and that which is received. Attention should be constantly directed to both. Many errors in science, and numberless mistakes in legislation, have arisen from not attending to this circumstance, as if it were the glory of trade to sell rather than to buy, whereas it is not possible to sell without buying, because the pay must be taken for what is sold. In every exchange, therefore, of commodity for commodity, the value of each is expressed in the other, and the relation between the two purchasing-powers is adjusted. This is the common case. The trade of all past ages, and the present commerce of five continents, presents us, in principle, with nothing different from this. The commerce of the world is substantially barter, that is, the exchange of commodities for commodities; and, though many purchases and sales may intervene, and money may play its part in facilitating the exchange, and many forms of credit may come in, before the transaction is finally closed, these do not alter in the slightest particular either the notion of value or its laws. Each repeated purchase and sale presents us over and over again with the same phenomenon, namely, the estimated relation of two purchasing-powers. And this relation is value.

The simplest case of value, however, will throw light upon the more complex ones, and will be found to include them. Two farmers, who are neighbors, find, on talking over their respective crops, that one has more hoeing and less haying this year than usual, and the other less hoeing and more haying.

A says to B, "Come over and help me hoe in June, and I will go over and help you hay in July." B agrees. It is a mutual advantage. And so, to use the old expression, which is better here than any scientific terms could be, they change works. B does a service for A, and A does a service for B. The two services balance each other. They are mutually exchanged one for the other; and in the very proposal thus to exchange them the notion of value is conceived, and in the exchange itself value is both produced and measured. B's help in hoeing is worth A's help in haying.

This exchange of one service for another service presents the simplest case of value; and I now proceed to show that it essentially includes all other cases. If it can be shown that value is always and everywhere the same thing, that it is always and everywhere THE RELATION BETWEEN TWO SERVICES EXCHANGED, then will Political Economy be seen to possess one grand characteristic of the great sciences, namely, simplicity. This can be shown. There are only three cases of value conceivable. 1st. When a service is exchange for a service, as by the two farmers already supposed. 2d. When a service is exchanged for a commodity, as when the lawyer gives his client counsel and receives five dollars in return. 3d. When a commodity is exchanged for a commodity, which is the common case of commerce. Any cases of value which do not seem, at first sight, to come under one of these three, will be seen after all, on reflection, to come there. For instance, if a man invests money in the national debt, and buys the government bonds, it is exchange of commodity for commodity. The bonds give him a claim on the national property. So with a mortgage. So with any form of credit. These are commodities.

Now, then, what is really exchanged in all these three cases, are mutual services. The client, with five dollars in his pocket, is just as much in position to do the lawyer a service, as the lawyer is in position to do him a service. The counsel is serviceable to the client, and the dollars are serviceable to the lawyer, and so they exchange. Value is the estimated relation between the two. And just so when commodities are exchanged with each other. The hatter serves you with a hat, and the shoemaker with a pair of boots, and you serve them with six dollars each; or if the hatter be in want of boots, and the shoemaker of a hat, they serve each other with their respective products. In every case of value, therefore, without exception, what is really exchanged, whether a commodity intervene or not, are mutual services; and value is then produced, and only then, when two persons are in position to render each other a service; and the respective services being rendered, that is exchanged, and the balance being struck, we have the value of one expressed in the other.

Do I, then, obliterate the old distinction between services and commodities? Yes, I do, as far as the laws of value are concerned. I use the term "service" in a broad sense, which includes the specific sense and something more. I mean by it, *the rendering of anything for which something is demanded in return.* People sometimes do for others what are called services, out of sympathy, from benevolence, from duty; but the characteristic of these is that they are free; nothing is demanded in return. These, therefore, fall in the sphere of morals, and are outside the pale of Political Economy. There is no such thing as proper exchange within the field of morals, and there is nothing else but proper exchange within the field of economy. This principle alone marks the boundary-line between the sciences referred to. A service, then, in the language of this science, and as the word will henceforward be used in these pages, is anything rendered to another in view of a return, and for the sake of a return. The man who furnishes you a barrel of apples, does you, in this sense, a service equally with the physician who attends upon your fever; and you pay them both on precisely the same principles. You render to each an equivalent service in return. To pay them money is to render them a service, just as to furnish you apples and medical advice were a service to you. Whether a commodity, as apples, intervene or not, is, as far as value is concerned, a matter of indifference. The more specific use of the term "service," as opposed to a commodity, is indeed convenient, and will, doubtless, continue to be used: the broader sense is exceedingly useful, and, by its aid, we clear up the whole subject of value.

This ultimate definition of value, namely, that it is the relation between two services exchanged, will never, it is believed, be materially improved. When once a just analysis is made, it is made for all time. And this is the encouragement that men have to labor in the field of science. It is a great thing indeed to contribute even a subordinate truth towards the advancement of any department of knowledge; but that truth, under fuller investigations, may come to be seen in a different light, and may come to occupy a different point from that in which it was put by the contributor. But when a correct analysis is made of the fundamental phenomenon itself, with which any science has to do, and on which it is reared, there is an end. That work will stand just where the fortunate master-builder has placed it. This analysis of value, which I believe to be satisfactory and final, is not mine. The full credit of it is due, as I believe, to the French writer Frederic Bastiat. The reasons why we may feel complete confidence in it will appear in a more and more striking light as we proceed, and until we conclude. Confirmations of it will be seen to come up from every part of the science, and crown it correct. In the first place, this definition covers naturally and easily all those anomalous cases of value which have been so hard to reduce under any other general view. Take for instance the case of the value of the diamond. The English school, and especially Mr. McCulloch, claim that labor is the source of value, and that the purchasing-power of everything is proportioned to the labor which it has cost. But, take care. There must be error in this statement. Value is not always proportioned to the mere labor the thing has cost. Often it is. Frequently it is not. For example, as I am strolling along the sea-shore I accidentally perceive a splendid diamond among the pebbles. It is but a moment's labor to appropriate the prize, but do I on that account sell my diamond for one dollar less to the jeweller or the prince? No. I am now in position to do a great service to whoever wants a diamond. I demand a large service in return, and get it. I say to the man who wants it, give me ten thousand dollars for my prize, and you shall have it. It would be poor mercantile logic for him to reply: Your labor is not worth more than one cent a minute, and it did not cost you but one minute's labor to get that gem, and certainly one cent, therefore, is a fair price for the diamond. He rather reasons in this way: Can I by going myself to the diamond-bearing regions, or in any diamond market elsewhere, procure for myself so good a gem as this by a less sacrifice than ten thousand dollars. He resolves this question mentally; and, if negatively, I am sure of getting my price. In that case I am offering him a service worth at least ten thousand dollars. No one else is in position to render him the same service at so favorable a rate. If, on the other hand, there be other diamond dealers offering gems as good as mine for less than ten thousand dollars, then I have pitched my demand too high; my service is not worth that sum, because there is some other person ready to render the same service for a less sum. The value of my diamond, therefore, is proportioned, not to the labor which it has cost me, but to the service which I am able to render to the purchaser with it, compared with the service which he is able to render to me. I take advantage of his desire for the diamond, and crowd up the price as near as I can to the point at which he will either forego the possession of a diamond altogether, or can obtain a similar one from some other party.

He takes advantage of my desire for the money, and crowds down the price as near as he can to the point at which I can either find another purchaser, or should prefer to retain the diamond myself. The comparison and adjustment of these two, my service to him and his service to me, fixes, for that sale, the value of the diamond.

And here we must stop to notice what an exceedingly good word the English language provides us with, in this term *service*. It explains perfectly all anomalous, as well as all common cases of value. It combines in its own proper meaning all the elements which make up and which vary value. First, it implies always two persons, the person rendering and the person receiving the service. Next, it always implies some effort on the part of the person rendering, and some satisfaction on the part of the person receiving the service. Thus when one service is spoken of there is always implied two persons and two things, and the two things are the effort of one person and the satisfaction of another. But when two services are spoken of as exchanged, as is always the case in Political Economy, there is implied, as before, two persons, each of whom makes an effort for the other, each of whom is recipient of a satisfaction which comes from the effort of the other, and each of whom estimates in the light of his own satisfaction that which is received as compared with that which is rendered. It is this reciprocal estimation alone that constitutes value; and it is the excellence, I may almost say the glory of the term service, that it gathers up in its own signification all the elements which go to determine value, and which ever vary its amount. As here is the very kernel and core of our science, illustration will be well bestowed at this point. Let the parties be A and B, in position to render each other a mutual service. A has a desire which B's effort can meet, and B has a desire which A's effort can meet. Up to the point when the exchange takes place there are only four elements that play any part in the transaction as preparatory to it, namely, two desires and two efforts. In the act of exchange itself two other elements come into being, namely, two relative estimates, A's estimate of B's effort for him as compared with his own effort for B, and B's estimate of A's effort for him as compared with his own effort for A. As a result of the exchange, and as that for the sake of which the whole series took place, there appear two other elements, namely, two satisfactions. Here is the whole of it. Now, then, any change in any one of the first four elements will vary value; and there is nothing else in the world that can vary it. If A's desire for that which B is ready to render be lessened, the other elements remaining the same, A's estimate of B's effort as compared with his own is lessened, and value is at once affected. If A's desire be increased, other things being equal, his estimate of B's service as compared with his own is increased, and value is affected. Just so any diminution or enhancement of B's desire for that which A is ready to render, acts at once upon B's estimate of A's effort as compared with his own, and consequently acts at once upon value. Again, any change in either effort as compared with the other, such as its becoming more or less onerous than the other, will of course affect the estimate of the one as measured by the other, and of course also will vary value. These first four elements then are not only the elements out of which value subsequently springs, but also are the elements any change in any one of which, the others remaining the same, will tend to vary value, and without a change in some one of which, relatively to the others, value never will be varied. The term services expresses just these elements which play and vary as preparatory to the realization of value. Value itself is realized from the adjustment of the fifth and sixth elements, that is to say, from the equalization of A's estimate of B's service with B's estimate of A's service. This adjustment also, together with the remaining elements, the two satisfactions, are all implied in the expression mutual services, or, if you please, two services exchanged. If any of my readers object to this paragraph as abstract, I have only to reply that it is no more abstract than the subject-matter; and if any of them find difficulty in the relative nature of the transaction unfolded, in the fact that the views and comparative estimates of two persons must be kept in mind throughout, I can only say, that this science starts with a relation and has to do with a relation every step of the way to the end. This is the one intrinsic, unavoidable difficulty that lies at the threshold of the science; and whoever, by taking pains at the outset, familiarizes this difficulty to his thoughts, and thus overmasters it, will walk thenceforward with positive pleasure through the whole economic domain. And if there ever was a science grateful for a word, as lessening its inherent difficulties and helping explain its phenomena, Political Economy, which has wandered these twice forty years in the wilderness of wealth, thankfully accepts in the term service its latest and most important gift.

In the second place, the definition of value which is here given expands the field of Political Economy to its natural limits. Even Adam Smith, and the English economists generally, while defining wealth as consisting of material commodities only, have experienced a difficulty in excluding from the domain of the science certain mere services, and in denying that value resides in these services. Some have endeavored to avoid the difficulty in one way and some in another. Some have stigmatized those who render a mere service to society as unproductive laborers, and have gifted with the title of productive laborers all those who bring forward some vendible commodity. John Stuart Mill, as we have seen, enlarged his definition of wealth so as to take in all those sorts of mere services whose action goes directly to swell the volume of material commodities. It is conceded then that value resides in some services; why not then in all services which are put forth for the sake of a return? Why allow value to a service which comes to be embodied in a commodity, and deny the term to another service just as necessary to our comfort that is not thus embodied? Why class the brick-maker as a productive laborer, and refuse the epithet to the hod-carrier, without whose help the bricks would never reach their ultimate destination? The truth is there is no ground for this distinction; and the very difficulty which the various writers have found in trying to make it, is a pretty sure proof that it ought not to be made at all. By making its definitions such that value can only be supposed to reside in tangible commodities, Political Economy excludes itself, without any good reason, from a large portion of its own field. Let us see if there be any good reason. For example, a man buys a spelling-book for his boy, for the sake of his learning to read. He then hires a teacher to teach him to read. According to the usual definitions the spelling-book has value, while the service of the teacher has none. But why has it none? It has to be paid for, certainly, as much as the spelling-book has to be paid for? There are two separate exchanges; first, of money for the spelling-book, and second, of money for the service. Both are made with the same object in view, namely, that the boy may learn to read. The want of a spelling-book and the want of a teacher are the two external obstacles in the way of reaching that object; and the father overcomes them both by similar means, that is to say, by an exchange; and there is no such difference in the two transactions as will justify or even tolerate the distinction sought to be made between them. The teacher sells his service. The shopkeeper sells his book. The father renders a service to each equivalent to that received from each. Political Economy now claims jurisdiction over both transactions alike, and affirms value as truly of the service as of the commodity, and more truly of the service than of the commodity, inasmuch as it stands ready to prove that so far as value resides in any commodity it resides there simply in virtue of the human services which have been concerned in its production and which will be subserved by its exchange. What is ultimate, therefore, in all exchange, is not commodities but services; and the services which are bought and sold in every department of life, the services, for example, of the lawyer, the physician, the clergyman, the teacher, the editor, the musician, fall as much within the province of Political Economy as the traffic of commodities in the market-place. Our science asserts its claim of jurisdiction wherever services are mutually exchanged.

A third advantage of the definition of value now given, and one closely connected with the last, will be seen in the fact that it frees the discussion from a perplexing error which has long infected this class of inquiries, namely, that value is somehow or other connected with matter. This notion has controlled the definitions of wealth; has led, as we have just seen, to groundless distinctions among services; and has taken possession of language so thoroughly that no judicious writer will attempt at this late day to dislodge it from that strongest of the citadels of error. Rather than disturb the current nomenclature of business he will allow such expressions as these to stand: Gold *has* value, strawberries *have* value. Nay, he will even use such expressions himself, because they are short and intelligible. At the same time he will clearly explain and endeavor to make everybody see that such expressions are only allowable as figures of speech. To speak with scientific accuracy it is not true to say that gold *has* value, because there are circumstances under which it has none. Gold has specific gravity and other essential qualities always and everywhere, but it has value only when human services have been employed on it and may be subserved by it; and I now proceed to prove and illustrate the position that value does not reside in matter, or in any form of matter, but only in human services exchanged; and that, therefore, value is never of God's creation, but always of man's creation. We shall see abundantly, before we finish the chapter, that utility is one thing and value quite another. No effort of men can add one particle to the existing matter of the globe, but it has been supposed that the efforts of men, by changing the form of existing matter, impart the quality of value to it, and that thenceforth the value remains fixed in the matter itself. The efforts of a woodman, for example, with the coöperation of nature, can transform the stock of a tree into wooden bowls, and value is now supposed to reside in the vendible bowls, and the current language is, that each bowl *has* a value of fifty cents. Why has it a value of fifty cents? Clearly enough, to reward his *service* who felled the tree, and sawed the block, and then hollowed out the bowl. But the service having been employed upon the matter, and being embodied in it, is not what is really sold now the matter, and not the service? I answer, No. What is really sold is the service, and not the matter. And this, which at first sight might not be thought important, but which is really very important, becomes apparent as soon as we reflect that any changes in the conditions of the service instantly affect the value. Our woodman has on hand a stock of one hundred bowls, which he offers for sale at fifty cents apiece, as fairly rewarding his personal services in their production. But, unknown to him, an enterprising neighbor has invented a machine which enables him to make bowls in every respect equal to the others, and to offer them at twenty-five cents apiece. Whoever now wants a wooden bowl can have that service rendered him for twenty-five cents return. The first man finds that he cannot sell a bowl for over twenty-five cents, and that his stock of one hundred has sunk at once in value from fifty dollars to twenty-five dollars. What is the matter with his bowls? The matter is not in the matter. The matter is all there, and the form of the matter is all there, but the value is just one half escaped, because the service which he can render to a buyer by a bowl has been, by the enterprise of his neighbor, just one half lessened. Value then follows the fortunes of services, and varies as they vary, just as much when they have been employed upon commodities, as when they are independent of them, and we see that the value resides in services compared, and not in matter at all.

I now proceed to indicate the manner in which language came to be used in such a way as gives color to the notion that value resides in the commodities rather than in the services. An instance will bring the whole subject before us clearly. In many parts of the United States delicious wild strawberries may be had in their season for the simple picking. The pastures and meadows are open to every comer, and the strawberries are considered to belong, not to the owners of the fields, but to any one who takes the labor of picking the fruit. Let us suppose that my family are fond of the berries, and that no member of it likes to undergo the labor of picking them, and that I hire some girl, who offers her services for the purpose, to go to the fields and gather some of the fruit for us. When she returns I pay her for her service. She does not conceive of any value residing in the strawberries themselves. Neither do I. She makes a series of efforts for the gratification of my family, and is paid for her efforts. Language recognizes the true state of the case, and she does not say now that she *sells* us the berries, and we do not speak of *buying* the berries of her. She thinks only of her labor, we think only of her labor, she is paid only for her labor, and language is exact in the premises. The next day, as the girl is about to go for us again, my neighbor says to her, "You bring me as many, and I will pay you as much." The third day, a second neighbor makes a similar bargain with her, and she brings strawberries for the three families, and is paid in each case for her service. The girl, on the fourth day, taking it for granted that we shall be likely to want strawberries that day also, does not wait to be sent, makes no bargain for her services beforehand, but goes and gathers the fruit. This time there is a change of language when she comes to my door. She now offers to *sell* me *strawberries*. "How much are they worth?" I ask. She names probably the same sum which she had before received for the service of picking the same quantity. She could not materially increase it, because there are doubtless other girls who are ready to render the service which she before rendered, at the same rate. But attention is now drawn away from the service to the berries, and the idea of value is attached to the berries, and language adopts the illusion, and says, "the *berries* are worth so much." Who does not see, however, that the transaction is substantially the same as before? Who does not see that it is only by a figure of speech, convenient indeed, but still only a figure, that the berries are now said to *have* value? Is it not plain to reason that what the girl really sells in the last case, is just what she really sold in the former cases, namely, her service? The only difference is that she retains in this case the proprietorship of her own service to a later stage of the transaction. In the earlier cases, the berries became mine as fast as she picked them; in this case, they become mine only after she has picked them; but this constitutes no difference in respect to that for which she is paid. The value, therefore, the purchasing-power, resides not in the berries, but in the service; that is to say, in that which she renders as compared with that she receives; and it is only a freak of language which leads us to suppose otherwise. This is but a simple instance, but the principles of the instance are applicable to all commodities whatsoever. It is only mediately and figuratively that commodities can be said to have value at all; and if we use the common language, and say that they have value, we must always remember that they have it simply and solely in consequence of the human services which have been employed upon them, and which may be subserved by them, as related to those other human services for which they may be exchanged. If this be true, and it seems to me certain that it *is* true, it throws a flood of light upon the whole field of value. More attention must be given hereafter, in Political Economy, to persons, and less to things. Man and his wants, man and his efforts, become at once the chief topics, while the material products on which efforts are employed, and which minister to wants, sink in relative position. It follows also from this distinction, that there is not so much difference as is commonly supposed, when a man works for others, and when he sets up for himself,— between a journeyman and a master. The journeyman sells his services, and the master sells nothing more or other than his own services. The services of the master may not be manual, they may be merely supervisory, or they may be connected with the use of his capital; but the finished product, when it is ready for the consumer, represents the aggregate of the human services which have been employed upon it, and whoever sells it, sells those services, and its ultimate value is determined, as all other value is, by a double comparison, the purchaser's comparison of the service of the product to him with that which he renders, and the seller's comparison of the service he receives with that of the product. Service for service, in the last analysis, rather than commodity for commodity, is the rule of value and the law of exchange.

It may be observed, in the fourth place, that a principal merit of the definition of value insisted on in this chapter, is the discrimination which it allows between utility and value. It is absolutely essential that these two ideas be not confounded. But they are confounded in all the earlier writers on wealth. The word wealth itself inextricably confounds them.

Whole discussions in Adam Smith are marred by his not consistently attending to the distinction, which he himself draws in one place, between "value in use and value in exchange:" meaning by the former expression simple utility. Say mixes up the two ideas even more completely than Adam Smith does; and the errors of the two writers in this respect gave rise to the twentieth chapter of Mr. Ricardo's book,[1] in which the difference between utility and value is pretty clearly unfolded. Mr. McCulloch, too, always insists upon this difference, and correctly maintains that the distinguishing characteristic of utility is, that it is gratuitous; although the theory of value of each of these writers is too narrow, unduly restricting the field of Political Economy by assuming that value rigidly inheres in commodities only. The example of these writers shows that the distinction referred to can be made even under their definition of value, but it is not so easily and practically made as under the true definition, because in the true definition attention is inevitably drawn to two persons, instead of to one thing, and utility, which is simple capacity to gratify any desire, is neatly discriminated, even in the nomenclature itself, from the mutual efforts by which the mutual desires are met. The word service enables us to draw the distinction, and to hold it fast.

Utility, then, is the capacity which any thing or any service has to gratify any human desire whatsoever. Political Economy has nothing to do with the estimation in which different desires are held by a philosopher or a moralist. It is enough to consti-

[1] Principles of Political Economy and Taxation.

tute for it utility, if anything will meet anybody's desire or serve anybody's purpose. In this sense, which is the etymological and only just sense of the word, ardent spirits have utility just as wheat has utility. The same thing may have no utility for one man, a low utility for another, and a very high utility for a third; since the first has no desire for it, the second a feeble, and the third a strong desire for it. Desires are personal to individuals. There is no common standard with which they may be compared. They are not exchangeable. Utility is the capacity which anything has of meeting any one of these desires at any time or in any place. But some things have this capacity in a high degree which are never exchanged, which are never bought or sold, and which consequently can have no value. The air we breathe, the light in which we recreate ourselves, the water we drink from the spring or brook, all have the highest utility, but no value. They connect themselves with no service. We give nothing for them. They, and such as they, are the direct gifts of God. They are gratuitous. Utility is, indeed, an element in all value, since it is an element in all service; but the value is proportionate not to the utility, but to the human services. Let us recur to our illustration of the strawberries. The girl brings delicious strawberries to my door in summer. Their utility is great, their capacity to gratify my palate and that of my family is exquisite, but her service in picking and bringing them is relatively little, and therefore it is little that I pay her. She cannot charge me one farthing for all that has been done for the fruit in the wonderful laboratory of Nature, — since Nature works for nothing; she can exchange with me her own service merely for an equivalent service which I may render to her. Her service having been employed upon that which derives its utility from Nature only, the two become, as it were, commingled, but the value is one thing, and the utility a distinct thing. The value has reference to her service, and is measured by it; the utility has reference to the gratification of my family. The one has its birth mainly in efforts, the other in desires. Certainly the efforts would not be made were it not for the desires, but the desires and their gratification is one thing, and the efforts which mediate between them are another thing. Utility is ultimate: value is mediate. Utility is absolute with reference to the individual: value is always relative. Certainly we must believe that utility and value are different things, when we see some things, as air, possessed of the very highest utility and no value at all; and other things, as strawberries, possessed of a very high utility and a very low value.

The history of economy is full to a surfeit of the theoretical errors and of the practical blunders which have come from confounding value with utility; and from not attending to the fact that all utility, until some human service has been mingled with it, is absolutely free. God is a Giver. He gives sunlight, and air, and water, in abundance. He gives the earth, with all its materials, and with all its powers, and with all its spontaneous fruits, gratuitously to man. At the very first, He gave to man, "dominion over the fish of the seas, and over the fowl of the air, and over every living thing that moveth on the earth." So far forth as these gifts minister directly to men's wants, there is utility indeed, but no value. But since, for the most part, human services are required to mould these gratuitous materials, to harness these gratuitous powers, to make these gratuitous fruits and animals available for use, and since services for this purpose are exchanged among men, value springs up in connection with these utilities, but must not be confounded with them. The utilities, disengaged from the service, are free. God never takes pay for anything, and has not authorized anybody to take pay in his behalf; what is paid for is the service of man, and not the bounty of Nature. Even the powers of Nature which men avail themselves of by machinery, such as water, wind, and steam, all work for nothing: water gravitates, and wind blows, and steam puffs, for nothing. These all, and such as these, help to create utilities, but they create no value. Value is in the service which makes the machine, and in the service which tends it, but in the power which moves it, unless that power be human muscle, there is no value.

Value must be carefully distinguished from Price. The price of anything is its purchasing-power expressed in money; the value of anything is its purchasing-power expressed in any other purchasing-power whatever. Price is a relative word, but specific; value is a relative word, but general. When we speak of the price of a service, we mean the sum of money which that service will buy; but when we speak of the value of a service, we mean the command in exchange of that service over other services generally. Thus, we say, " This coat is worth twenty-five dollars;" that is its price. The value of the same coat never could be completely expressed, because it would require a comparison not only with hats and gloves and boots and vests, but with all other things which are ever exposed for sale. Therefore, for convenience' sake, value is commonly reduced to price. By knowing the price of various things, we readily compare their value relatively to each other. Thus, when we know the price of the coat at 25 dollars, and of gloves at 2, of hats at 5, and vests at 10 dollars, we easily determine the value of the coat as estimated in gloves, hats, and vests, namely, that its value as compared with theirs, is respectively $12\frac{1}{2}$, 5, and $2\frac{1}{2}$ times theirs. The value of anything may remain nearly uniform while its price may greatly vary. At the present writing (1865), the prices of almost all commodities are about double the usual rate, because the currency of the country is about one hundred per cent. depreciated; but the value of these commodities, that is to say, their power of purchasing each other, is just about as it was before the depreciation began. All other commodities have risen in relation to the one commodity, money; or, which is the same thing, money has fallen in purchasing-power in relation to all other commodities; and there is in consequence a universal rise of prices; but it would be a total mistake to suppose that values have risen. A bushel of corn, now selling at two dollars, will buy no more labor, or hay, or cloth, than it used to buy when it sold for one dollar a bushel; because the labor, hay, and cloth have risen in relation to money in the same proportion as the corn has; while in relation to each other no changes have supervened. Services and commodities, with few exceptions, exchange with one another at the old rates, — value is unaltered; but exchange for money at about double the old rates, — prices have risen. Moreover it is not possible that there should be any general rise or fall of values, as there may be a general rise or fall of prices. A rise in the value of anything implies a fall in the value of those things with which you compare it; that is to say, if it will buy more of them, they will buy less of it. Its rise in value implies their fall in value, and conversely. Every rise in value of any service involves a corresponding fall in other services; and every fall in value of any service involves a rise in value of other services; and therefore, a general rise or fall of values is impossible. Nothing is more common than a rise or fall of value in particular services. Suppose, for instance, an improvement in machinery by which broadcloth can be made with one half the former effort, and that no change has been made in the efforts requisite to make the gloves, hats, and vests of our former example, and no change in the views of those who wish to exchange them. The coat will sink at once to about half its former value, not only in relation to gloves, hats, and vests, but in relation to everything which does not happen to be affected by a similar depressing cause. It is correct to say that the value of the coat has fallen. As estimated in gloves, hats, and vests, its value now is only $6\frac{1}{4}$, $2\frac{1}{2}$, and $1\frac{1}{4}$ times theirs, respectively. But while coats have fallen in relation to the other commodities, the other commodities have risen in relation to coats; and if similar improvements should be made in the machinery by which gloves, hats, and vests are made, so that one half less effort will bring these also to market, views of parties as before remaining unchanged, they will exchange now for coats exactly in the same ratios as at first, namely, 12½, 5, and 2½, respectively, for 1. As soon as the improvements affect all the commodities equally, value stands just as it did before the first improvement was made. Views of the parties remaining the same, it is only an advantage or disadvantage affecting some services and not others, that will vary their value in exchange: whatever affects them all equally will have no effect upon value. Thus, a universal rise of wages in any country, provided they rise in all departments of effort equally, will have not the least effect upon value; and we have just seen that a universal rise of prices at present experienced in this country, has no effect whatever upon the general purchasing-power of services in exchange, but is only a token that the one commodity, money, has fallen relatively to them.

It only remains in this elementary discussion of value to inquire whether there is, or can be, any measure of value—any standard, by a comparison with which we may determine the general purchasing-power of different services. It has commonly been supposed that there is such a measure, and political economists have expended a great deal of strength in endeavoring to discover what it is. The results have hardly been commensurate with the zeal and patience of the search. Adam Smith seems at one time to regard labor as the best measure of value, that is, the quantity of labor which any commodity will buy as the best gauge of its power to buy commodities in general. At another time he seems to think that corn is a better measure of general exchange value than labor. Others have thought that price furnished the best attainable standard of comparison; in other words, that the quantity of gold or silver which anything will purchase, will best enable us to determine the quantity of all other things which it will purchase. Others still have supposed that the cost of production of any commodity would give the most accurate rule by which to decide the value of the commodity, that is, the degree of its command over purchasable articles generally. But the truth is, a measure of value in the sense in which it has been sought after by these writers, is something impossible to be realized. It never would have been sought after, unless value had been supposed to be a rigid quality inhering in commodities, and, when once placed in them by whatever process, to be invariable. We have seen, however, that value is not a quality inhering in any one thing, but is a relation subsisting between two services which two persons are in a position to render to each other; and that this is not an inflexible relation, but is variable by any change in the views of the two persons, by which either of them puts a different estimate upon the service about to be rendered as compared with the service about to be received. We have seen sufficiently already, that there are four things, and only four, any change in any one of which will vary value; and that these four things are two desires and two efforts, the two desires belonging to two persons, and the efforts made by two persons each for the other. Now these four elements are in their very nature so liable to vary, and as a matter of fact do so constantly vary, that no man who clearly perceives what value is, will waste time and ingenuity in searching for an invariable standard of that which in its nature is variable and relative.

But while no reliable measure of value is possible to be found, there are certain limitations and principles of much importance which ought to be given in this connection. Since the foundation of value lies partly in the effort made by the person serving, and partly in the effort saved to the person served, and since in every exchange each of the parties is reciprocally serving and served, the outermost limitations of value are easily seen. A and B will not exchange services, unless the effort which each renders to the other is less onerous than the effort which each would have to make if each served himself directly. It costs a certain effort for me to bring water from the spring; I am willing to pay a neighbor for bringing it for me, but I should not be willing to make a greater effort for him in return than the effort is to bring it myself; neither should I be willing to make an effort for him which I regarded just as onerous as the bringing the water: unless there is some service which he will accept less onerous to me than that, I shall continue to bring the water for myself. On the other hand, he will not render the service to me of bringing the water, unless it be less onerous to him than the doing that for himself which I am ready to do for him. This principle, applicable to all exchanges whatsoever, draws on the one side the outermost line, beyond which value never can pass. It may be asserted with confidence that no man will ever knowingly make a greater effort to satisfy a desire through exchange, than the effort needful to satisfy it without an exchange. Moreover, within this outermost limitation which is made by the comparative onerousness of the respective efforts, there is a second limitation of a similar kind. To pursue the same illustration, while I should never make an effort for another in return for his bringing the water, greater than that required to bring it myself, the return effort may be very much less than that effort, and may sink down to a point, below which I can get no one to bring the water for me. Suppose I estimate the effort required to bring the water myself as 10; and that there are several persons who would be glad to do that service for me for a return service which I estimate as 8; and that there are two persons who are willing to do it for something which I estimate as 6; and that there is only one person who will do it for a return service which I regard as 5. It is evident that the extreme limits of the value of that service to me are 10 and 5. Higher than 10 it cannot go, lower than 5 it cannot sink. I should render the service estimated as 8, rather than forego having the water brought for me; but I shall render the service estimated as 5, just as long as there is any one person who will make the exchange with me on those terms. If he declines the exchange, I fall back on one of the two persons in the class above him, and value rises now from 5 to 6. It will be steadier at 6 than it was at 5, because there are two persons ready to render the service at that rate. If each, however, in turn should give out, I should then be obliged to fall back upon the larger class ready to serve me for a return service of 8. At this point the value would be very steady from the presence of numerous competetors anxious to serve me at that rate, and it could by no possibility rise above 10. Between 10 and 5 the value may fluctuate, but it cannot overpass these limits in either direction. Therefore we may say that the maximum value of any service in exchange is struck at the point where the recipient will prefer to serve himself, rather than make the exchange; and the minimum value of any service in exchange is struck at the point below which the recipient cannot get himself served. These two limits, it will be observed, are found in the two elements which we have called efforts.

But there are also limitations of value in the two elements which we have called desires. In the foregoing illustration, it is supposed that my desire for the water is all the while of uniform strength, and the desire of each of the three classes willing to serve me for the return service is uniform also, though each class makes a different estimate of the comparative efforts. Let us now suppose that the efforts on either side remain invariable, but there is a change in the element of desire. Any capacity in anything to gratify any desire of anybody is utility. For simplicity's sake, let us look only to the one man who was ready to bring the water for a return service which I estimated as 5, and suppose that he is the only man who will do me the service on any terms. Let now the utility of the water to me be increased, and let him know that fact, all other elements remaining as before, and he can crowd up the value of his service towards 10, according to the intensity of my desire. Of course he cannot crowd it over 10, but the limit below that will now be determined by the relative strength of my desire. On the other hand, if my desire be as before, and the two efforts as before, and his desire for my return service be increased, and I know it, and I the only man who can render him such a service, I can crowd down the value of his service below 5, according to the intensity of his desire. Of course I cannot crowd it down below a point, which we will call 3, at which, rather than continue his service at that rate, he will forego the exchange altogether. But value may vary between these limits, 10 and 3, according to the varying intensity of our mutual desires. If it should so happen that both these desires, my desire for his service and his desire for mine, should increase simultaneously and proportionably, value would not be affected; the exchange would go on at the same rate as before. Or if both desires should diminish simultaneously and proportionably, value would not be affected. The same is true of efforts. If both efforts suddenly become twice as onerous, or twice less onerous, than before, the desires remaining the same, the value of the two services estimated in each other would stand just as before. Thus we see that the natural limits of value, and all the variations in value, are to be sought for and will be found in the play and interaction of the four elements out of which value itself springs.

We shall now be able to understand clearly what

is meant by Market-Value and its variations, and also the action of Supply and Demand. Market-Value is the rate at which services of all sorts are exchanging at the present time in the various departments of society. What determines that rate? What determines that corn is now selling in the market for two dollars a bushel? Two desires come in to determine it, — the desire of people for corn, and the desire of farmers for money. Two efforts come in to determine it, — the effort of farmers to raise and bring a bushel of corn to market, and the effort of people to secure two dollars in money. The presence of corn in the market, or its being ready to be immediately brought there and offered in exchange for money, constitutes what is called a Supply of corn; money offered, or ready to be offered, in exchange for corn, constitutes what is called a Demand. This is commercial language, and is sufficiently accurate, although it must be remembered that each commodity in reality constitutes a Demand for the other, and is a Supply in reference to the other. But, speaking commercially, the money ready to be offered for commodities is the Demand, and the commodities ready to be exchanged for money are the Supply. What, then, is the law of market-value? The law of market-value is the equation of supply and demand: that is to say, the rate of the exchange is adjusted when money enough is offered to take off within the usual times the commodities on hand. Demand and supply are thus equalized, and the current market-rate is determined. If demand for any reason becomes quickened, and the supply not increased, there is competition among buyers for the stock in market, and market-value tends to rise. If demand becomes sluggish, the supply remaining the same, there is competition among sellers to dispose of their stock, and market-value tends to sink. So far it is the action on value of the element of desire, which expresses itself through demand. How far can this action go? Demand being increased, supply remaining the same, value rises: how far does it rise? In the *ratio* of the increased demand, say some; if the demand be one third increased, the value will be one third higher. By no means is this true. The value may rise far higher than that proportion, or it may not rise in anything like that proportion. It depends upon circumstances, and upon the nature of the commodity. We must remember that demand not only acts upon value, but value acts upon demand. As value rises, the number of those whose means or inclinations enable them to purchase at the new rate is constantly diminished. There are ten persons who may wish an article at one dollar, of whom not over four will wish it at two dollars, and perhaps only one at three dollars. Every rise in value then, under the influence of increased demand, tends to cut off a part of that demand, that is, to lessen the number of those who will purchase at the increased price; and the value will rise only to that point, whatever it be, where an equalization takes place between the supply and demand, between the quantity of corn, for example, offered at the enhanced rates, and the quantity of money in the hands of those willing to exchange it for corn at the enhanced rates. Thus we see that every rise or fall of demand, and the consequent rise or fall of value, tends to check itself. An increased demand for any article or service, other things being equal, enhances its value; but the enhanced value in turn lessens the demand by lessening the number of those who will purchase, and the new market-rate is struck at the point of equalization between the old supply and the new demand. Just so, if demand is slackened, value declines; but declining value in turn increases the demand by bringing the article within the range of a larger number of purchasers, and the decline is arrested at the point of equalization between the new demand and the old supply, and a new market-rate is determined. Everything oscillates under the variations of demand, but the point of stable equilibrium, if I may use the expression of anything so unstable as market-value, the point of stable equilibrium is always the equation of supply and demand.

In the preceding paragraph we have supposed supply to remain unchanged, and have followed the law of value through the variations of demand, which, money being invariable, as is here supposed, expresses the element of desire. Supply expresses the element of efforts, and market-value varies with the variations of supply. We have seen that every rise or fall of demand tends to check itself, and will check itself even without variations in the supply; but it is commonly checked at an earlier point by variations in the supply. A brisk demand enhances value, and enhanced value commonly stimulates supply, and increased supply checks the rise. A slack demand lowers value, and lowered value commonly lessens the supply by the action of holders and speculators, — holders withdrawing their stock for a better market, and speculators buying now when the article is cheap, to store away till it shall be dearer. Thus rise of value from increased demand is doubly checked; first, by restricting the number of purchasers, and second, by increasing the supply: the fall of value from slack demand is doubly checked; first, by enlarging the number of consumers of a now cheaper article, and second, by diminution of supply by the action of holders and speculators. This law of the equalization of demand and supply, thus doubly and harmoniously working, is perhaps the most comprehensive and beautiful law in political economy. But we must note the action on value of changes in supply only, demand continuing steady. If the supply be short, and cannot be increased at all, as is the case with choice antiques and certain gems and paintings by the old masters, value may rise to any point, and will be struck, as before, at the precise point of equality of the demand then existing with the supply there offered. The French government paid, in 1852, 615,300 francs for a painting by Murillo, which had belonged to Marshal Soult. The genuine Murillos are comparatively few, and their number cannot be increased, and their merit causes a strong desire to possess them, and their value rises in consequence of the limitation of supply to a point beyond which no one purchaser can be found. When this painting was offered in Paris for sale, many parties were anxious to purchase it, but the equation of demand and supply was reached, and its value was determined only when one party distanced all other competitors and offered a sum greater than any one else would give. There was one painting; there could be but one purchaser; value rose under the influence of demand, and could not be checked by increase of supply; and the equation was complete when the demand was practically restricted to one party, and that the highest bidder. The same principle controls all sales of this sort.

If the supply, instead of being absolutely limited, can only be increased with difficulty, or after the lapse of time, similar but less extreme results will be observed. Suppose pianos are selling in any community at $300 each, and there are twenty persons in that community who wish a piano immediately, and that there are but fifteen pianos on hand, and the number cannot be increased for six months. The value will rise above $300. How much above? To that point, whatever, it be, at which only fifteen of the twenty will be willing to purchase at the new rate. The equation of supply and demand will be reached by a rising value which cuts off five competitors. This is the principle, working only roughly indeed in practice, — working only by the estimates and good judgment of dealers, — but the principle is this. A better illustration of this class of cases is, perhaps, the grains and other products of the earth. When these have been gathered there is no more home supply for a year. Any deficiency in the crops will raise their value, not at all in the ratio of the deficiency, but according to the relations of the diminished supply to a new demand. It will depend on the facility of importation, and other causes, but it has frequently happened that an estimated deficiency of crops amounting to one third has doubled and even quadrupled the usual prices.[1]

In the only remaining, and far more numerous class of cases, in which the supply of commodities and services can be readily and indefinitely increased, every rise and fall of value is speedily checked by the action of supply; and the comprehensive and harmonious law already referred to keeps value in this class of cases comparatively steady.

The general theory of value has now been given. While we shall find no case of value, or its variations, which this theory does not cover and explain, we shall find particular principles which act in certain cases upon demand and supply, and thereby act upon value. We have now seen what value is; how it arises; the elements which alone can vary it; and the universal law which limits it.

[1] Tooke's History of Prices. Quoted by J. S. Mill.

CHAPTER IV.

ON EXCHANGE.

THE strength and safety of our conclusions in Political Economy are derived from the simplicity and certainty of the forces at work. No man has ever denied the great facts that lie at the basis of exchange. That men are possessed of desires, that efforts are necessary in order to meet these, and that satisfactions are the result, are propositions universally admitted. From these simple truths spring all the laws of our science, and all the economical harmonies of society. Let me remind my readers that, while the desires and satisfactions are experienced by one and the same person, and from their very nature cannot be communicated to another, this is not at all true of efforts. Efforts are exchangeable. One man may and does put forth the effort necessary for the satisfaction of another man's desire. But since the effort is not for himself but for another, and since to put forth efforts is not naturally agreeable to man, and never becomes so, except in connection with the satisfaction to which they minister, he will demand for his effort some corresponding effort made for him. This is a simple fact. No man will work for you for nothing. If you think he ought to, there is no law against your trying to induce him to do so.

How now does it happen that society is one vast hive of buyers and sellers, every man bringing something to the market and carrying something off? We speak of the commercial classes, but all classes are commercial. Everybody exchanges. You do something for me, and I will do something for you, is the fundamental law of society. From this results the division of employments, and all the various professions. Every man brings his own product and exchanges with society as best he may. The farmer brings his produce — and exchanges. The mechanic brings the product of his skilled labor — and exchanges. The laborer brings his strength, and the teacher his knowledge, and they are ready to do service — for a consideration. The merchant, the physician, the lawyer, the clergyman, the editor, the lecturer, the singer, the actor, and so on to the end of the list, are all in position to render services to society, and justly expect to receive an equivalent service in return. Indeed, when we look out upon society, the most striking thing we observe about it is, that these exchanges are going on, in a thousand directions at once, determining all employment and professions, reaching everywhere and permeating everything, and all this the more rapidly and perfectly as knowledge and civilization advance. Since, therefore, as a matter of fact, men do constantly put forth onerous efforts to satisfy other men's desires, in order to receive back from them the results of corresponding efforts in return; since this mutual exchange of services is everywhere present in society, not in the market-places only, but in every department of life, there must be in this exchange some great GAIN. We now inquire particularly what this gain is. What is the motive that leads men universally to exchange?

The answer to these questions will bring us to the gratifying conclusion that the laws of exchange are based on nothing less solid than the will of God. The desires of men are not only various in kind and indefinite in degree, but also tend to increase in variety and extent by the progress of knowledge and freedom. To the gratification of almost all these desires, however, there are obstacles interposed, some of which are physical and some moral; and these obstacles are so great in all directions, that the powers of the individual man are utterly incompetent to surmount them. They mock at his weakness, and throw him back upon his destitution. Without association with his fellow-men, there is no creature so helpless, so unable to reach his true end, as is man; and therefore it is, that the impulse to association is one of the strongest of our natural impulses. Men come together, as it were by instinct, into society; and, associating themselves together in a society, it is very soon discovered, not only that there are various desires in the different members of the community which are now readily met by coöperation and mutual exchange, but also that there are very different powers in the different individuals in relation to those obstacles which are to be surmounted. There is a vast diversity in natural gifts. One man has physical strength, with no mechanical ingenuity; another combines with a feeble body a wonderful knack for contrivance; a third has a philosophical turn, liking to examine into the laws of nature; and a fourth has a bent and genius for traffic. Now, then, Nature speaks in this diversity of gifts in as loud a voice as she can utter, in favor of such a degree of association and exchange as shall allow a free development of these varying capacities, while they work upon the obstacles to the gratification of men's wants which are appropriately opposite to them. Mr. Carey is right in his principle that the degree of individuality depends on the degree of association, each advancing hand in hand with the other; but he seems to me to be wrong while he lacks confidence in the natural forces at work tending to the highest degree of association and consequently to the highest degree of individuality. There is no social force stronger than interest, and interest is driving society continually to exchange, and to a wider and wider application of the principles of exchange, that is to say, to a higher and higher degree of association, which allows of course a continually freer development of individuality. When interest fails as a motive power, at least in this department, it is vain to appeal or to trust to an inferior and factitious motor.

It is interest that leads men to exchange. It is because a given effort put forth for another, in view of a return, realizes more of satisfaction than when put forth directly for one's self, that exchange ever takes place. Why does it realize more? BECAUSE THERE IS DIVERSITY OF ADVANTAGE BETWEEN DIFFERENT MEN AND BETWEEN DIFFERENT NATIONS, IN DIFFERENT RESPECTS. All exchange depends on diversity of relative advantage; and diversity of relative advantage exists by God's appointment among individual men, and among the nations. Reserving this national diversity for a later discussion, it is very clear that a diversity of advantage in different things displays itself as between the individuals of every community large and small. There is no village in which one man has not an advantage over his neighbors in the making of coats, another in the shoeing of horses, another in the curing diseases, another in the keeping a school; while each of those neighbors may have an advantage over each of these in some other art or avocation. This diversity of advantage in various directions depends, in every advanced state of society, partly upon diversity of original gifts, partly upon concentration of personal effort upon the one set of obstacles that lie in the path of a single branch of business, and partly upon the use, and familiarity in the use, of the gratuitous forces of nature which lend their aid towards overcoming these obstacles. As the result of one or two or all of these, one man comes to have a legitimate advantage over others in his own branch of business, whatever it is; and the others come to have a legitimate advantage over him in their own branches of business, whatever they are; and if he has desires which their efforts can satisfy, and they desires which his efforts can satisfy, nothing more is necessary to a profitable exchange between them than this relative advantage at different points. The tailor and blacksmith can profitably exchange their respective efforts just as soon as each has a relative superiority to the other in his own trade, provided of course each has a desire for the product of the other; and the greater the relative superiority of each to the other, the more profitable is the exchange to both. This is a point of considerable consequence, and will repay some pains in illustration. If the blacksmith can shoe horses only a little better than the tailor could shoe them, and the tailor make coats only a little better than the blacksmith could make them, there will be only a slight advantage in their mutually exchanging efforts. For the sake of definiteness, let us say, that the tailor's capacity in making coats is 6, and his capacity in shoeing horses is 5; and the blacksmith's capacity in shoeing horses is 6, and his capacity in making coats is 5. Each has a relative superiority to the other of 1, and if they exchange, there is an advantage of 2 to be divided between them. Now let us suppose that each, by exclusive devotion to his own trade, by developing his latent skill and ingenuity, and by availing himself of all the forces of nature at his command, comes to have a capacity in his own business of 15, his capacity in the other business remaining as before at 5. Each now has a relative superiority to the other of 10, and when they exchange there is an advantage of 20 to be divided between them. The motive to an exchange, and the gain of an exchange, are ten times greater than they were before. Therefore we lay down the principle, as universally applicable to all exchanges, that the greater the relative superiority at different points, the more profitable do exchanges become. If this principle is just, and I flatter myself that it will be found to be just, it follows, that every man who has anything to exchange, is directly interested in the success of his fellow-citizens, that every trade finds its advantage in the increasing development of other trades, and that all discoveries and inventions by which Nature is made to pay tribute to any art is, restrictions apart, so much clear gain to the world at large. In the light of sound principles, what has been sometimes called the jealousy of trade is simply silly.

All exchange, then, depends on difference of relative advantage, because without some difference of relative advantage, each party could serve himself directly just as well as he could be served by the other party, and there would be no motive at all for an exchange. As soon as there is any difference of relative advantage, there begins to be a motive for an exchange, and a gain as the result; and the motive and the gain become stronger and greater as the difference increases; so that the gains of exchange are the greatest in that state of society in which the freest opportunity is allowed to every individual to employ his peculiar powers in work for which he is best fitted, in which desires are so various and employments so diversified as to give a chance for all kinds of efforts, and in which men avail themselves to the utmost of those natural advantages and gratuitous powers which lie open to their disposal. Freedom, association, and invention, are the three things which make exchanges as profitable as they can become, and which will carry society, so far as exchanges can do it, to the highest pitch of prosperity. Of these by far the most important is freedom, because, where freedom is conceded, association and invention follow in time by laws of natural sequence. By freedom is meant the right of every man to employ his own efforts for the gratification of his own wants, either directly or through exchange. Each man's right of freedom is limited of course by every other man's right of freedom which he is not at liberty to infringe; and also, in certain respects, by what is called the general good, of which the judge must be the government under which he lives. Under these limitations, which limit in common all other rights, the right of exchange is just as much of a right as the right of breathing. It stands on the same unassailable ground. Every man has a natural, self evident, and inalienable right to put forth efforts for his own well-being; and whenever two men find that by exchanging efforts with each other, they can better promote their own happiness, they have an indisputable right, subject only to the above limitations, to exchange; and it is a high-handed infringement of natural rights, a blow aimed at the life and source of property, when any authority whatever interferes to restrict or prohibit the freedom of exchange, except that act be justified by a solid proof that other private or public rights which are as well based as the right of exchange are infringed thereby.

Happily, since governments have become more enlightened than formerly, they perceive for the most part that they have no right to interfere with this natural right of their people, and also, that, by interfering with it, they would do them an incalculable injury. The only motive to a mutual exchange of services, is always and everywhere the mutual benefit of the parties. After every fair exchange, each party is richer than before, has more satisfactions, otherwise there would be no exchange. I esteem the service

I receive more highly than the service I render, otherwise I should not render it. The man to whom I render it esteems that service more highly than the service he renders to me. We are both gainers. And since almost everybody in every community has something to exchange, — either service or commodity, and nobody exchanges except in view of a gain, it is clear that free exchange benefits everybody, and harms nobody. Moreover, under a system of free exchange, every man is allowed, under the stimulus of self interest, to follow the bent of his own mind, to work away at those obstacles to the gratification of human desires which he feels himself best able to overcome, and to avail himself of all those helps in his work, of which Nature offers to him a full store. Under these circumstances, obstacles give way in all directions: the amount of material products produced and offered for exchange is vastly augmented; the number and variety and excellence of the services proffered is indefinitely increased; the diversified and rapidly increasing desires in such a community are readily met by exchange; all peculiar facilities are taken advantage of, and the difference of relative advantage becomes great in all directions, and a new day of industrial and commercial prosperity is ushered in. Under freedom all men have the greatest possible motive to produce, because they can dispose of their efforts to the best advantage. They can purchase with these efforts what they will, and when they will, and where they will. Thus freedom leads to extended association, and, speedily also, to the invention of machinery and all labor-saving appliances. Therefore, since free exchange indefinitely multiplies, in number and variety, the services which men may render to each other; since, by means of it, men's satisfactions bear a larger and larger proportion to their efforts; and since the only possible motive to an exchange is a mutual benefit of the parties, no reason can be given, no good reason ever has been given, why exchanges should not be the freest possible.

After long centuries of meddlesome and vexatious interference with the freedom of industry and the rights of exchange, by limiting the number of apprentices to each artisan, by dictating what should and what should not be manufactured or grown, by attempting to determine what should and what should not be imported and exported, and by arbitrary burdens on certain classes, and arbitrary privileges granted to others, the more enlightened nations of the world have come at length to perceive that wealth and power and progress are dependent on free exchange, at least within their own boundaries. Common sense reigns now, for the most part, in this thing, within the limits of the individual nations. When Bonaparte brought half of Western Europe under French dominion, the previously existing custom-houses and toll barriers of the interior fell as by a stroke, and free trade became the rule between French, Dutch, Germans, Italians, and Spaniards,— all who were subject to his sway. But when his vast empire was dissolved into its original independent kingdoms, up shot the custom-houses again, around all the petty frontiers, and each State was busy to reimpose on itself the fetters which his powerful hand had broken.[1] Just as if the benefits of exchange depended on the accident that the parties to it are subjects or citizens of the same government!

Opposed to free exchange are monopolies. A monopoly is a legal restriction imposed by the government upon the sale of certain services or commodities. This restriction is ostensibly laid for the benefit of certain persons or classes, and limits of course the competition to which they would otherwise be subject in their business, and tends therefore artificially to raise the value of that which the privileged few offer for sale. If the view be limited to these persons alone, monopolies would certainly seem to be advantageous, but what of the purchasers and consumers of their wares? They all are obliged to pay a higher price for what, were it not for the monopoly, they could obtain at a cheaper rate, since the only object in laying the restriction, is to enhance the price for the benefit of those possessing the privilege. Monopolies, therefore, infringe the right of exchange, are unjust and odious in their nature, and are in practice abominable. Nearly all governments have been chargeable, at times, with successful attempts to make things thus artificially dear to the mass of the people. Queen Elizabeth called the power of granting patents of monopoly to her favorites "the fairest flower of her garden." Towards the close of her reign, her abuse of this power had reached an intolerable height, and some of the most necessary articles of life, such as salt, iron,

[1] Senior. Page 177.

calf-skins, vinegar, lead, paper, and many others, were in the hands of patentees, and could only be procured at exorbitant prices. In 1601, the House of Commons met in so angry and menacing a mood, in consequence of this abuse, that Elizabeth was obliged to promise at least, that the monopolies complained of should be abolished. Up to 1834, tea was a close monopoly in England, in the hands of the East India Company. To this day tobacco is a government monopoly in France. Salt and opium have been, and for aught I know still are, monopolies in British India. For governments to confer a power of this sort on an individual, a company, or any set of persons so few as to enable them to combine, is to give them a power to levy any amount of taxation on the public, for their own especial benefit, which will not compel the public to forego the use of the monopolized article. Monoplists, however, do not find it for their interest to crowd up the price beyond the reach of the mass of the ordinary consumers, especially if they can command a full supply, because their aggregate income would be lessened by the falling off of buyers from the highest price. They adjust the price at that point at which they suppose they will realize the largest aggregate gains; a price which is still considerably above what it would be under free exchange; otherwise the monopoly would be of no benefit to them.

A second form of monopoly is that in which governments by prohibitory duties exclude foreign competition in certain articles, leaving the domestic dealers open only to home competition. One of two things is sure to follow upon such exclusion. It sometimes happens the hope of extra gains from dealing in an article whose foreign supply is thus prohibited, seduces capital and labor from other profitable channels and concentrates them upon this business; and the home competition, thus artificially stimulated, becomes feverish and intense, and the whole business is overdone, and they in whose behalf the prohibitory duty was laid, have reason to pray to be delivered from their friends. Their profits for a time sink below the current rate from the eagerness of others to share in their expected gains; the weaker houses are ruined, and an element of distrust and unsteadiness is introduced into the whole business. Only the stancher firms weather the depression consequent upon overdoing, and they will now control the market for a time at a monopoly price. But their prosperity has been purchased at too dear a rate; the losses of home competitors, and of those who would otherwise have been foreign competitors, and of those who would have exchanged with those foreign competitors, but whose market is also cut off by the duty, overbalance many fold these factitious and precarious gains. This series of results has several times been witnessed in this country under the stimulus of high protective duties, as, for instance, in the iron business after the tariff of 1842. More commonly, however, competition is less active after the foreign competitors have been thrust off; those who are in fair possession of the home field control the markets at a monopoly price. Relieved in great measure from the stimulus of competition, the manufacturers and dealers are less on the alert for improvements and inventions, they are less attentive and compliant to their customers, and the consumers are obliged, not only to pay a tax levied for the benefit of the monopolists, but also an additional tax on account of their want of enterprise and spirit. At this present writing, there is in this country a virtually prohibitory duty on foreign paper, and the few paper-makers are not only growing immensely rich out of their monopoly, but are able so to combine and influence the action of Congress, that a very popular and widespread combination among paper users to induce Congress to lower the duty, is likely to founder on the single opposition of the paper-makers. A similar monopoly is enjoyed by the manufacturers of carpets. This form of injustice cannot abide a fair and full discussion. It is bound to disappear with other abuses of the past.

Very different in character is the third form of monopoly, that involved in the granting of patent-rights and copyrights. That the originator of an improved process should enjoy for a limited time the sole right to employ and to sell his improvement, is a very proper way to compensate him for the thought, the pains, the expense, involved in his invention. This mode has the merit of graduating the compensation according to the real benefits of the invention. The same is true of copyrights. Society does well in protecting by law inventors and thinkers in the sole use of their respective productions for a limited time. Otherwise men would have less motive to think and to invent; since in that case only the public spirited and the rich would or could devote themselves to an important branch of the public progress. A patent or copyright is merely a return service which society renders for a service received. It violates no man's right of property, as an ordinary monopoly does, but is a provision to protect a right of property. In the United States a patent right extends for fourteen years, and may be in certain cases extended further by the Commissioner of Patents, or by act of Congress. A copyright extends for twenty-eight years, and may be renewed by the author, his widow, or children, for fourteen years longer.

CHAPTER V.

ON PRODUCTION.

WHILE it is impossible to make discussions in Political Economy amusing, it is also impossible intelligently to conduct them without constantly coming to conclusions which are most cheering. We shall find a gratifying law underlying the operations of production, which demonstrates that God designed man to be a producer, and to produce under conditions of constantly increasing advantage. The world with its forces, and man with his motives, are so admirably constructed, that these conditions of increasing advantage cannot fail, under freedom, to redound to the benefit of the masses of men. We will first determine what production is, and then the cheering law that underlies it.

Every man who puts forth an effort to satisfy the desire of another, with the expectation of a return, is, in the language of Political Economy, a Producer. To produce is to render a service for an equivalent. A Product is a service rendered. The hod-carrier is as much a producer as the man who makes the bricks. Unluckily, Adam Smith, who is sometimes called the father of this science, used these terms in a restricted sense, and thereby almost unfitted them to do their proper work. He confined production to the occasioning of changes in material objects. He gifted with the title of producer the farmer, the mechanic, the miner, the hunter, and fisherman, because they bring to the market a material commodity; and refused the honor of the term to those who render simple services, however essential. This is wrong. It proceeds from an inadequate analysis of value. That which is produced, that with which we have to do, is not matter but value. He who creates value is the producer. But we have seen that value is not an attribute of matter, but of services exchanged. The service may be employed upon matter, may be embodied in it, but what is really sold is not the matter, but the service; and services are all the time being sold, as those of the singer, the teacher, the clergyman, which have no connection whatever with matter. These services have purchasing-power, these persons create value, and therefore, they are producers. Certainly, in an inventory of all values, a large portion would be found connected with material objects, but by no means the whole. Our language must be broad enough to cover all the cases. Therefore, Production is the rendering of any service for which something is demanded in return.

Now, then, as to the beneficent law that underlies it. Production is effort. But efforts are irksome. Is there, then, no way to lessen efforts, to make them less onerous, and, at the same time, more productive? Yes, thank God, there is! We may bring to our aid the gratuitous help of Nature! The world is full of powers which we may employ to facilitate our work. For example, at first people ground their grain by hand; and it was a weary, weary task to sit cramped at the mill all day, and turn, and turn, and turn.[1] The effort was great, and the result was small. At length it occurred to somebody that the weight of water would turn a wheel, and that the wheel might turn the mill-stones. Once thought of, the water-wheel was soon an actual fact. Instead of human strength, Nature works now, and what is better, works for nothing! Man's service is still needed, he feeds the hopper, tends the bags, but he does not ache so bad! Nor is this all. One day's labor is now vastly more productive. More grain is ground, bread comes easier to the poor, and the wheel which free water turns blesses its millions with a cheapened product!

Let us take another illustration. The old hand-loom was the only means antiquity knew of for procuring clothing. The shuttle was thrown by human muscle. Every thread cost a throw. This work was mostly done by women. The word wife comes from the word to weave. The wife, then, was primarily the weaver. While the slave woman sat on the ground, and turned the handle of the mill to grind the grain, the wife was exalted to the dignity of the loom, and worked away at the monotonous task, thread by thread, thread by thread. Doubtless the hand-loom was a great improvement on the earlier processes, and was itself gradually improved as the centuries went by, each improvement being the substitution either of a gratuitous force of Nature for an irksome human effort, or an easier process of art for a more laborious one. Every step of improvement was a lessening of obstacles with reference to a given satisfaction. All the way up to

[1] Exod. xi. 5; Isa. xlvii. 2.

our present admirable machinery — the power-loom, which weaves, as if by magic, while a child can tend it — every step has marked a lessening of efforts relatively to utilities. The utility, the satisfaction, the yard of cloth, has cost less and less of human effort, not only to the producer, but, through exchange, to everybody. Accidental causes in this country have interrupted this progress for a little, at least in the case of cottons, but it will go on again in the good time coming. And this progress, thus briefly illustrated in the two cases of flour and cloth, has been going on, and is constantly going on, in all directions; more strikingly, perhaps, in the production of material commodities, in which the powers of Nature may be indefinitely applied by machinery, but at the same time there are no services of any kind which are not facilitated in some degree by the progress of knowledge and experience; and the benefits of this increasing advantage come home, through exchanges, to everybody; and, consequently, the satisfactions of all bear a larger and larger proportion to their efforts.

This, then, is the underlying and benevolent law of production, that God has placed freely at men's disposal such materials and forces in Nature, that, availing themselves skilfully of these, onerous efforts bear a less and less proportion to realized utilities. Men have a strong motive to substitute, whenever they can, force for muscle, machinery for labor. The farmer who used to cut every spire of grass with a hand-swung scythe, then rake it up with a hand-drawn rake, and then pitch it into the loft with a handfork, now mows and rakes and pitches with a machine. And it is a beautiful consequence of this law, that all improvements in machinery, all inventions, all substitution of Nature's forces for human labor, soon become the common property of mankind. Patent rights speedily expire by their own limitation, secret processes are sure to become known, and the competition of the different men who, under a system of freedom, will be sure to use these gratuitous helps, will compel each of them to sell their product at a rate graduated only by the actual human service rendered; so that, the liberal gifts of Nature, though seemingly monopolized at first by ingenious men, are not long intercepted in their descent towards the masses of mankind. An invention of great merit even at first does not benefit the patentee alone; as a patentee, his interest leads him to lower the price of his product, to bring it within the reach of a wider circle of consumers; and so soon as the patent has expired, the benefit has at once a wider reach. The steam-engine, for example, has long been common property. There are, indeed, certain features of the more perfect engines still restricted in their manufacture by the rights of individuals, and this will always be so while invention continues busy, but the perpetual tendency in all inventions is from individual property towards a common right. And it is here in place to remark, that the application of machinery to all departments of production, and the introduction of improved processes of every name, can hardly in the first instance be prejudicial to any, and are sure ultimately to be beneficial to all.

What is the effect on values of these processes now made easier in all directions? Clearly, since value is nothing but the relation between two services exchanged, no effect at all is produced on values, if the improvements have gone on equally in all directions. Everything exchanges just as before. If the improvements have not gone on equally, then the value, that is, the purchasing power, of those products is diminished in whose production the improvements have been relatively greater. As the service has now diminished, the value, other things being equal, has diminished along with it. For such a service less can be demanded in return. The utility of the product, on the other hand, that is, its capacity to gratify desire, remains as before. A less effort produces the same utility. The portion of effort thus set free, however, is not probably idle. It will be still put forth to create a larger number of products of the same kind, each one of which indeed has less purchasing power than before, but the aggregate value of which is much greater than before. For example, when machinery is employed in the making of gloves, which before were cut and stitched by hand, the value of a pair of gloves, estimated in anything whose production has not been altered by a similar improvement, will infallibly decline; but the aggregate value of all the gloves made in the establishment will be greater than before, because otherwise there would have been no motive to introduce the machinery. Does, then, the machine create value, contrary to the doctrine in the chapter on value? Not strictly. The machine creates utilities, since each pair of the now increased number of gloves has the same utility as a pair of the former fewer number; and the maker is able to render a service to a greater number of persons than before; and it is true, that, for a time, especially if the process be not yet generally applied in glove-making, before value has a chance to adjust itself to the new state of things, he will realize extra gains; he will obtain, in part, the old price for his product, and it would seem, in this case, as if the machine created value. Nevertheless, it is only a transitory state of things. Just as soon as machines come to be generally employed in the business, value adjusts itself, through competition, to the real human service rendered, and the extra gains of the first operators are cut off. The gain of the reduction has now become permanent to all consumers of gloves. It is this interval between the old price and the new which gives to producers the margin for their enterprise, and a sharp spur to invent and adopt improvements. The improvements once become general, the gain redounds to the whole community. The value then of all services which have been facilitated by improved processes, is constantly being lessened relatively to services not equally facilitated; and here we gain the first glimpse of a truth, which will afterwards appear in the clearest light, namely, that the value of commodities tends to decline as compared with human labor, and therefore, that there is inwrought into the nature of things a tendency towards the elevation of the masses of men in a scale of comforts.

A leading proposition of production is the following: — *Production may go on indefinitely in all directions without ever a fear of reaching a general glut of products.* This proposition was first fully developed by Say, in the fifteenth chapter of his well-known treatise on "Political Economy," and the proof of it, and some of the consequences of it, are well worthy of our attention. I shall put the proof of it in this form: the desires of men which the efforts of other men can satisfy, are unlimited in number and indefinite in degree; and therefore, mutual efforts can continue to be put forth in exchange, until these unlimited and indefinite desires of all men are all met — a goal which never can be reached. This proposition demolishes at a stroke the fallacy which pervades Dr. Chalmer's book on "Political Economy," namely, that the universal market is limited, and therefore, were it not for the unproductive consumption of the rich and luxurious, and the equally unproductive consumption of wars, there would soon be a general glut, and production must cease for the lack of a vent for its products. What constitutes a market for anything? This, that somebody desires the service thus offered, and is willing to render a return service acceptable to the offerer. Only two things can limit the universal market, first, a lack of desires, and secondly, a lack of return services. But there can be no lack of desires at any time, and there will be the greatest plenty of return services where production is most busy and most universal. Therefore, again, no general glut of products, is possible to occur. A truth which we have already seen in another connection, reappears here as a consequence of this proposition, and will reappear again and again, namely, that all persons are interested commercially, as well as morally, in the prosperity of other persons, and each nation which has anything to exchange, is directly interested in the prosperity of all other nations; because the more production everywhere, the better market everywhere. A market for products is made by products in market.

But while no such thing as a general glut of products ever did, or ever can occur, a glut in respect to certain services is very common. Through want of foresight, or miscalculation, particular services are offered in too great abundance, or of a kind not adapted to the demand, and in respect to these the market is truly said to be glutted. This frequently happens with editions of books; more copies are printed than can be sold at remunerative prices. Also when fashion changes, the goods which were fashionable, but are so no longer, are apt to be in excess of the demand. The only precaution that can be taken to avoid losses of this character, is the cultivation of foresight, by studying as accurately as possible the nature of human desires, and the changes that have been observed to take place in them. This constitutes mercantile sagacity; and the most successful producers in all departments are those who best develop this sagacity, who adapt their services to the existing and coming demand, who, to excellence in the substance of their services, add taste and attractiveness to their form, who tend rather to lead the fashions for the many than follow in their wake. The field of production is like the billowy and heaving sea: to navigate most successfully requires foresight, a wise courage, a power of adaptation to varying circumstances, skill to veer and tack when the wind changes, and a will to scud before a favoring breeze with all sails set. Production, as a general rule, is no dead level of monotonous exertion; since its sphere is life with its wants, man with his desires; and there is scope for the development of ingenious mind in almost all of its departments. Since all exchange is due to the diversity of relative advantage, whoever develops his powers of observation, of application, of adaptation, to a higher point, and avails himself more skilfully of all peculiar facilities, will reap a larger share of the harvest of exchange.

The immense increase of production, and the superior perfection of products consequent upon what he calls the Division of Labor, was first pointed out by Adam Smith. The chapter in which this author treats of the division of labor, has always been the most famous, and is still one of the most interesting in the "Wealth of Nations." We have already seen how exchange is stimulated and made profitable by the diversity of employments, and by the application of all peculiar gifts to the corresponding obstacles which lie in the path of production: this is the more general truth of which Adam Smith's principle of the division of labor is a specific part. He means by this term the dividing up of a process or employment into particular parts, so that each person employed can devote himself wholly to one section of the process. The proposition is, that by means of the division of labor, the processes of production are vastly facilitated. He cites, as an illustration, the manufacture of pins. One man draws out the wire, another straightens it, a third cuts it, a fourth sharpens the points, a fifth grinds it at the top for receiving the head. The making the heads consists of two or three distinct operations, each confided to a single person. The remaining processes are similarly divided up, and the result is, according to Dr. Smith, that in a single establishment, employing only ten persons, 48,000 pins are made in a day, while if each man went through all the processes himself, he could hardly make twenty pins a day, or two hundred for the whole establishment. Perhaps a more striking illustration of the division of labor may be found in the art of watchmaking. According to evidence brought before a committee of the British House of Commons, there are one hundred and two distinct branches of this art, to each of which a boy may be put apprentice; and when his apprenticeship is expired, he is unable, without subsequent instruction, to work at any other branch. The watch-finisher is the only person, out of the one hundred and two, who is able to work in any other department than his own. The causes of increased efficiency imparted to production by the division of labor are reduced by Dr. Smith to three: —

1. The improved dexterity, corporeal and intellectual, acquired by the repetition of one simple operation.

2. The saving of the time which is commonly lost in passing from one species of work to another, and in the change of place, position, and tools.

3. The invention of a great number of machines which facilitate and abridge labor in all its departments. Because the simple task which complete division of labor gives to each operator is precisely what machinery may most easily be made to per-

form, and what the operator, if intelligent, will be most likely to devise machinery for. Add to these advantages of the division of labor these other:—

4. The saving of the waste of material, which is unavoidable when a person learns an art, but which is much less when he learns one process, than all the processes.

5. The more economical distribution of labor by classing the operatives according to their strength, skill, and experience. The easier parts may be performed by women and by children, whose labor is less expensive; the ruder parts by ruder hands; and only the more difficult processes by the most skilful workmen, who must be highly paid. Next to the first, this advantage is the most important.

6. There is a saving in tools. The various implements, being now in constant use, yield a better return for their original cost; and therefore their owners can afford to have them of a better quality, and this, too, facilitates production.

7. It brings the producers and consumers into more intimate and safe relations. The division of labor between the wholesale and the retail trade is of great advantage. The retailers know their local markets, and supply them without loss or waste from the wholesale reservoirs. The wholesale reservoirs neatly control the various streams of production, according as demand is slackened or intensified. Thus, for example, a large city is daily supplied with fresh meat, without the loss, perhaps, of a hundred weight.

There are some disadvantages resulting from this division of labor:—

1. The work becomes in some departments monotonous and irksome, while some variety of occupation would afford relief by employing different muscles, or different faculties of the mind.

2. There is some tendency to dwarf the mental and corporeal powers, through exclusive attention to one part only of a complicated process.

3. When this part has been learned, and long made the means of a livelihood, a person has less power to adapt himself to change of circumstances, and becomes too much dependent on the continuance of the business in that form.

The degree to which the division of labor can be carried, depends in part upon the extent of the market, and in part upon the nature of the employment. To recur to Dr. Smith's illustration of the pins: if the market would only have received 24,000 pins a day from that establishment, instead of 48,000, the division of labor could not have been carried to the same extent, because if it had been, the men would be idle one half the time. In that case, some of the men would be dismissed, and some of the separate processes be combined, and production would be less efficient from the limitation of the market. (Production, therefore, is most profitable when the market is broad enough to allow a full division of labor, and complete employment to all the operatives; and, the market being presupposed, is more likely to be profitable in large establishments than in small; because, (1) the division of labor can be carried to a fuller extent; (2) more perfect machinery can be afforded; (3) relatively less superintendence is required; and (4) the scraps and ends of a large business are frequently of sufficient importance to justify one or more subordinate branches of business in connection with the main business. For example, a large saw-mill may profitably furnish lath as well as lumber, since the refuse boards and slabs may go to lath. A wholesale butchering establishment of neat cattle might profitably have, in connection with the sale of meat, a tannery to dispose of the hides, a comb manufactory to dispose of the horns, a glue manufactory to dispose of the feet, a stall for the hair, which is useful in plastering, while the offal might be chemically disposed of in fertilizers.

The nature of the employment also limits the degree to which the division of labor may be carried. Agriculture, for instance, allows less of this division than most other departments of production, because its various operations cannot, from the nature of the case, become simultaneous. When the sowing is once done, the producer must wait some months upon Nature, till his agency is again required in the reaping. This fact, that agriculture can be less facilitated by the division of labor, and by the use of machinery, than most other departments of material production, constitutes one ground of an important truth, which we shall hereafter perceive stands also on another and firmer ground, the truth, namely, that agricultural products tend constantly to rise in value as compared with other commodities.

CHAPTER VI.

ON LABOR.

It is a curious thing, and one that draws after it very important consequences, that physical labor consists simply in moving things. When a man works with his hands, all that he does, or can do, is to produce a series of motions. Human muscles are only capable of two things, namely, producing motion, and resisting motion. All the marvellous results of human labor in all the world, have flowed from so simple a matter as the contraction and expansion of muscle. Work is motion, and weariness is weariness of muscle. The world of materials is so cunningly constructed, that, when they are moved into right position the powers of Nature do the rest, and objects of utility are the result.

When the pioneer fells a tree, he moves his axe through the trunk, and then the power of gravitation seizes the tree, and brings it to the ground. He produces a series of motions upon the tree, but the final motion, by which the century-girdled oak comes crashing to the earth, is not of his producing. Nature does that. Wool, cotton, and flax, have by nature a certain tenacity of fibre. Man moves these fibres in certain relations to each other by an instrument called a spindle, and the result is thread. Then the threads are moved in certain relations with each other by an instrument called a shuttle, and the result is a web of cloth. The tailor moves his shears through the cloth, and then his needles, and the result is a coat, — the object of utility for which all these processes were gone through with. The farmer first moves the ground, then moves his seeds into it, moves his sickle through the standing corn, moves his corn to the granary and mill, moves his meal from the mill to the larder, at which last point he surrenders the product to the official who acts as his secretary of the interior. She moves the meal to the kneading-trough, and, having well moved it there, moves it to the oven, and, from the oven, after due interval, moves it to the table, at which point production ceases, and consumption begins.

Physical labor, then, is, and can be, nothing but this, *an effort, by which materials or implements are moved with reference to a given result.* Nature furnishes all the materials, and all the primary qualities of which we avail ourselves in production. She coöperates at every step. We pay her absolutely nothing for all she does. All we can shirk off our own shoulders, and throw upon hers, is so much clear gain. And it is a most happy circumstance that this is being done more and more completely in the production of nearly all commodities. Nature is good, to use a commercial term, for all she can be made to carry.

Now, since motion is the only thing which man is required to furnish in the production of commodities, he naturally looks around for helps in this matter. The first thing he lighted on, as a help to produce motion, was the domestic animals. The ox, the ass, the horse, were doubtless domesticated in the very beginnings of society. Men want these animals to produce motion for them — simply that. And as they can be used in so many different places, and for such a variety of purposes, and are so cheaply reared, they are exceedingly convenient as a motive power, and will probably never be superseded. The discovery and application of the great motive powers of water and steam have scarcely occasioned a lessened demand for the earlier and humbler motors, oxen and horses. Some of my readers will probably remember the time, when the introduction of railroads was opposed by some people, on the ground that the value of horses, and the business of teamsters would thereby be destroyed. Experience has demonstrated in this case, as it does in all similar cases, that improved machinery, and improved facilities of all kinds, so far from harming any class of persons permanently, are likely to be a gain to all classes of persons. At least, they only are harmed, who stupidly hold on to the old methods.

Labor, having employed from a very early time as a motive power the domestic animals, secured after a while, as inanimate auxiliaries, the water-wheel and the windmill; and, much later, the steam-engine. It is a point that has scarcely been noticed, even if it has ever been noticed at all, that all these auxiliaries, whether animate or inanimate, produce simple motions of the same kind as, and only supplemental to, the motion produced by a human arm. The most ponderous engine merely reduplicates that which the arm of a child is capable of; while in point of delicacy and firmness of touch, perhaps no machinery has yet been devised which can subdivide and apply this motion as skilfully as the human fingers can. It is said, that some of the lace made wholly by hand, is finer and more delicate than any yet woven by machinery, although the introduction of machinery into lace-making has cheapened the product, according to Dr. Ure, to about $\frac{1}{50}$ of its former cost. What we call power, then, however produced, is simple motion. But in order to subdivide these motions and apply them to the various purposes of production, implements of all sorts are needed, and implements, as we shall see in the next chapter, are always the gift of capital. But no power however mighty or however delicate, and no implements however perfect, can ever dispense with some portion of human labor. Not until machinery can be taught to think, to adapt means to ends, will human labor cease to play a chief part in production. These therefore, are, and always will be, the three requisites of material production: LABOR, POWER-AGENTS, CAPITAL.

Besides physical labor, there are the various forms of mental efforts put forth by men to satisfy the desires of other men, and with reference to a return. So far as exertion, physical or mental, is put forth for amusement, or for a pure benevolent motive, it has nothing to do with Political Economy. *It is only exertion which demands for itself something in exchange, that is technically labor.* Labor, which is primarily mental, such as most professional labor, the labor of the editor, the teacher, the architect, has of course little connection with motion or with commodities. But it is not on that account less useful or less valuable. The exchange of simple services depends on the same principles, gives rise to the same phenomena, and is amenable to the same science as all other exchanges. One man, as the violin-maker, offers services in which a commodity intervenes; another, as the violinist, offers services in which no commodity intervenes; each has gained in his own art a point of relative advantage as compared with other men, and these doubtless have gained some point of relative advantage as compared with them; each, by the sale of his respective service, meets some desire of the buyer, and is paid on the same principle as the other. The violin-maker of Cremona, who sold his instruments for five hundred francs apiece, was no more and no less a laborer, in the language of our science, than Paganini, who sold an hour's playing in the theatres for five thousand francs.

Having now seen what labor is, let us pass to the principles that determine its remuneration. I can see no reason why the purchasing-power of labor is not determined in the same way as the purchasing-power of all other things; and, if so, there is no difficulty in pointing out the general law of wages. I go back constantly to first principles, because I believe that first principles really control everything. Chance effects there most certainly are; but, as they happen now on one side and now on the other, they balance each other, and leave all the great working forces unaffected. For the sake of convenience, a distinction may be made at this point between professional and common labor, — a distinction which is not indeed very definite, but which is sufficiently so for the purpose in hand. The wages of professional labor of all sorts run up and down upon a scale whose extremes are much wider apart than the extremes of the scale which marks the variations in the wages of common labor, while at the same time the principle that determines the value of both forms of labor alike is the principle that determines all other value, namely, the law of Supply and Demand. The wages of professional labor, however, are so far different from the wages of common labor as to demand a somewhat distinct treatment. Why could Daniel Webster demand a fee of a thousand dollars for attending to a single case in court, Paganini a like sum for an hour's playing on a violin, and Jenny Lind at least as much for an evening's singing in a concert? Because there was in each case a strong demand for a peculiar service, and only one person in the whole world who could render that service, at least in the same perfection. The demand was large, the supply was small, and the value consequently great. The highest efforts of professional skill will always receive a high reward, whenever there is one person even, who, together with a strong desire for the product, has also the power to give a service in return; and especially whenever there are many persons who have a similar desire and power, to whom, as in the case of Paganini and Jenny Lind, the service can be rendered in common without lessening the satisfaction of each individual. That the supply is small in these higher regions of skilled effort, is due partly to the fact, that Nature is not lavish in her gifts of peculiar talents, and partly to the fact, that those who have received have assiduously cultivated them, and have reached in consequence a high point of relative advantage. These persons have what may be called a natural monopoly in their respective fields of high effort, because there are few others who have the natural gifts and the acquired skill which enable them to come in competition with them. But the objections which lie with such force against artificial monopolies, cannot be urged at all against a natural monopoly; for, if the road to excellence be open to all, and no artificial obstructions thrown in the paths of any, there is no blame but rather praise for him who distances all competitors, and demands for services of peculiar excellence a large remuneration. John Sartain is a superior engraver: he enjoys a natural monopoly in the highest walks of that art; the wages of his labor are very high; yet nobody can complain of this, since he has had no factitious privileges, but has fairly attained his excellence under freedom. Exchange rejoices in all diversity of advantage that is the birth of freedom, but reprobates with all her force advantage that is gained by artificial restrictions, because artificial restrictions always infringe on somebody's right to render services for a return; and the right to render services for a return is the fundamental conception in the right of Property. The wages of professional labor, then, are determined by the relations between the demand for such labor and the supply at hand; and are usually higher than the wages of common labor, because the supply of such laborers is restricted by the lack either (1) of appropriate original gifts, or (2) of the requisite industry, or (3) of the means of suitable education and training.

Within the great law of supply and demand, there are several important subordinate principles, which go to vary the wages of both professional and common labor, principally through their action upon supply; and it is now in order to consider these, before we pass to consider the wages of common labor. In common with all the writers who have succeeded him, I shall avail myself freely at this point of the labors of Adam Smith. That writer considers that there are certain circumstances in the employments themselves, which either really, or at least in men's imaginations, make up for a small pecuniary gain in some, and counterbalance a great one in others.

1. The agreeableness or disagreeableness of the employments will have an influence in determining the rate of wages paid to those who engage in them. The more agreeable employment will attract the larger number, and will experience in consequence the press of competition, and the rate of wages will be lessened by the increased supply of laborers. The more disagreeable employment will feel less the pressure of numbers, and will secure, other things being equal, a higher rate of remuneration in consequence. Among the elements which, in spite of the diversity of natural tastes, make any employment agreeable or disagreeable to the laborers, are (1) the less or greater exertion of physical strength required, (2) the healthfulness or unhealthfulness of the labor, (3) its cleanliness or dirtiness, (4) the degree of liberty or confinement in it, (5) the safety or hazard of the employment, (6) the esteem or disrepute of it in public opinion. To illustrate

each of these in order, the stone-mason, the glass-blower, the scavenger, the factory operative, the worker in a powder-mill, the smuggler, will each receive a larger compensation owing to the peculiar element of disagreeableness involved in his employment; and he will be able to demand and secure it through the action of the disagreeableness upon the supply of such laborers. Of all these elements, public opinion is perhaps the most operative; and if this be favorable to an employment, and some social consideration be attached to it, and only common qualifications be required for it, the wages in it will infallibly be low. This is probably the main reason why so many young women prefer to teach, rather than be employed in mills, shops, or offices, and why the wages of female teachers are so pitifully low; although each of the elements of agreeableness specified above may also contribute something towards the same result. If a business be decidedly opposed to public opinion, it must hold out the inducement of a large reward, or nobody will engage in it. This explains the abnormal gains of the slave-trade, the liquor-business, of gambling-houses, and of lotteries.

2. The easiness and cheapness, or the difficulty and expense, of learning different employments, will have an influence on the rate of wages paid in them. The more quickly and cheaply one can learn to perform the duties of a place satisfactorily, the less, so far forth, will be his wages; because there will be many who will compete with him in rendering such services; the more time, difficulty, and expense involved in learning a business, the larger, so far forth, will be the wages secured by it;

because fewer persons have the means, the foresight, the patience, to prepare themselves for such an avocation. This is the principal ground of the difference in the wages of skilled and unskilled labor. The artisan has, at least, given time, and the professional man has given both time and money, to fit themselves to render the services which they now offer to society; and it is right, therefore, for them to demand a higher rate of compensation than is accorded to operatives and common laborers. But a right to demand does not always carry along with it an ability to secure: in this case it does, through the reduction of numbers which these obstacles at the entrance occasion, and the consequent weakness of competition. To put a boy apprentice to a trade, requires on the part of the parents a foresight, an ability to get on without his immediate help, and sometimes an amount of money for his board and clothes, which all parents do not possess; and consequently, the number of skilled artisans, who must learn when they are young if at all, are relatively few compared with common laborers, and are able to realize a much higher rate of wages than they. In the professions, if we confine our attention to those persons who are thoroughly trained for them, we shall find a higher rate of compensation still, and one made higher on the same principles; although we must here bear in mind the counter-working influences which tend to increase the competition in the professions, namely, the respectability which attends them, the desire of knowledge for its own sake which is gained in connection with them, the instruction wholly or in part gratuitously offered to those in course of preparation for them, and the desire to do good, without regard to pecuniary reward, which actuates many who enter upon them.

3. The constancy or inconstancy of employment is a consideration that affects wages. If the employment be such that it can only be carried on during nine months of the year, the wages of the day or month will be greater than they would be if it could be carried on during the twelve months. The laborer looks to the aggregate earnings of the year, and will hardly take up a trade which affords employment but a part of the time, unless some compensation can be found in the higher wages for that time. This is the chief reason why the day's wages of the mason and the house-painter, in this climate at least, are higher than those of the carpenter or smith. The coachman, also, may stand by his horses half the day or night, with no call for his services, and must have, therefore, a proportionably higher fare from those whom he does transport. In general, it is found that men prefer a constant employment with a lower rate of wages, than an inconstant one, with a prospect of higher pay for the particular jobs actually done, and because they prefer that, those who take up with the other are able to secure a higher rate of pay in their less eligible vocation. Counter working this, however, are the desires which many men have, for intervals of leisure in their business; and the opportunity to make these intervals subservient to another branch of business or means of livelihood.

4. The amount of trust involved affects wages. Men in responsible positions secure a higher rate of

pay for their services than can be accounted for, except by a reference to the unwillingness of people to intrust great interests to others, unless they are men of established character for probity. Such men, men who combine all the other requisites for an important post, with a well-known honesty, are comparatively rare; and, when they are found, will receive a very high compensation for their services. Treasurers of corporations, cashiers of banks, and holders of trust-funds generally, are examples in point. Shall we say, then, that men offer their honesty in the market, as they offer their skill, and are paid for the one as for the other? No! Their skill has been acquired to sell, and for no other reason; but their honesty, if it be genuine, has another basis altogether; and he who is honest, simply because honesty is the best policy, is not honest at all! The very characteristic of honesty is that it cannot be bought! It has a moral, and not a mercantile foundation. In point of fact, a man who has the full confidence of his fellow-citizens, as an honest man, and at the same time all the other qualifications requisite for a post of high pecuniary trust, is in position, partly on the ground of his honesty, to render a high service, and will receive for that service a high reward; but I protest, in the name of morals, against the notion that honesty is a marketable article: it is rather an underlying element of moral character, which fits men indeed to render certain services, but the honesty is maintained, not for the sake of the service, but has an independent basis of its own. So, also, most people would prefer a deeply religious man for a preacher and spiritual guide, but it is a perversion of language to maintain that in rendering these services a clergyman sells his religion. It is true that he sells services to the appropriate rendering of which his personal piety contributes one element; but the piety is not nourished for the sake of the services, but for its own sake, and it must not be confounded with that which is sold. Accordingly, while the clergyman's vocation is sacred, and belongs to the sphere of religion, his salary belongs to the sphere of exchange, and its determination is wholly a business transaction. This distinction ought to be better understood than it is; and both clergymen and people need to be reminded that the spiritual things belong to one sphere, and the carnal things to another. The amount of a clergyman's salary, and the time and mode of its payment, are matters of pure business; and the clergyman himself is to blame if he does not attend to them, and insist on them, on business principles.

5. The probability of success in any employment is a circumstance that has some influence on the rate of wages paid in it, through the action of this probability on the numbers of those who enter upon it. If success is problematical, fewer will engage in such a business, and those who do engage in it and succeed, will reap a very high reward. Ten boys, for example, put to the blacksmith's trade, ordinary capacity being presupposed, will probably every one succeed in becoming a tolerable workman; but of ten boys of the same capacity put apprentice to an engraver, probably not over three would ever reach any high degree of skill and success; and therefore,

the pressure of numbers will be felt much more in the former than the latter art. So also, those who take jobs by contract, and who consequently assume some risks, are usually paid at a higher rate than those who do work by the day. It is true that this is owing partly to the fact that the contractor commonly uses his own capital, and must therefore be paid profits as well as wages, and also that the wages of superintendence are due to him as well as ordinary wages; still there is a residuum of difference which can only be accounted for by the risk he runs of a successful issue. The difference in wages from this fifth cause of variation, would be greater than it is, were it not for the overweening confidence which most men have in their own good luck. This confidence is seen in the rush which is always made for newly discovered mining regions, and in the facility with which even yet lottery tickets are sold. It is demonstrable beforehand, on the doctrine of chances, that no lottery ticket is worth so much as it is sold for, and yet men buy on in spite of the demonstration; and experience in California and at Pike's Peak, has sadly taught how excessive was the confidence in their own success of the men who flocked to those new El Dorados.

6. Custom and prejudice and fashion, have something to do with the determination of wages in some departments. Custom, especially in former times, has been very operative. The current fees of lawyers and physicians have been largely dependent on custom, competition merely coming in to decide how many such fees a man should get, rather than lessening the amount of each particular fee. Cus-

tom determines the wages when men take farms on shares. But competition is now breaking down custom in all directions, and will soon, I think, reign supreme over the economic field. Prejudice is closely allied to custom, and has some voice still in adjusting wages, as may be seen, perhaps, in women's wages, crowded down to a point unreasonably low, as compared with the wages of men. Custom and prejudice may yield the field, but fashion, which is one form of competition, will always have an influence over wages. They who lead the styles in any department whatsoever, will always offer their services to society at an advantage to themselves, and their rate of compensation will be legitimately higher than the average rate.

7. Legal restrictions and voluntary associations are another cause acting on wages, by acting on the supply of laborers. Laws inhibiting or promoting immigration, laws appointing the fees and salaries of officials, tariff laws, whether prohibitory or only restrictive, unequal taxation, and so on, all have an agency in adjusting wages. Governments are coming, however, much more freely than formerly, to leave everything except the wages of their own servants, and those things which they choose to tax, to the simple and safe action of supply and demand. The guilds of the Middle Ages, and the trades' unions of our own day, are examples of voluntary associations for the sake of regulating the wages of the members by combined action. The restrictions in the old guilds, limiting the number of apprentices to each artisan, determining the time a man should serve before he could become a master, and

so on, were very onerous, and have mostly passed away. The trades' unions in this country have never been very popular or successful. The Printers' Union in the principal cities has just been dissolved amid universal contempt. The spirit of Political Economy, which is the spirit of freedom, is against such associations for such purposes. If any man has a service to render, let him offer it freely, and make the best terms he can with whoever wants it.

Having looked at the principles that determine the compensation of skilled labor, and also at some causes tending to vary the wages both of skilled and common labor, we pass now to a consideration of those principles more particularly applicable to the wages of common labor. All value, as we know, is a resultant of two desires and two efforts, and is variable by any variation of either desire or either effort. When the laborer offers a series of efforts to another person, he does so in virtue of a desire for something which that other person has to give, for food, clothing, money; and the other person has a desire for the efforts of the laborer, and is willing to give in return the food, clothing, money, or whatever it may be. The more laborers there are who offer their service to this person, the more likely he is to obtain the service at a cheap rate, since there is a competition among the laborers to secure that food, clothing, money, and so on, which he offers in return for the service: the more persons, on the other hand, who offer food, clothing, money, and so on, to the laborers there present, the more likely are the latter to receive a high rate for their efforts, since there is a competition among employers to secure such efforts. The number of employers and the amount of that which they offer as return for such efforts, constitutes the demand for laborers; the number of laborers willing to render service for what is thus offered in return, constitutes the supply of labor: the current rate of wages of common labor is determined by the adjustment, that is, the equalization of the demand and supply. In what we have said thus far in relation to wages, we have referred chiefly to causes acting on the supply of laborers, rather than on the demand for labor: we must now look in the other direction, and anticipate the discussions of the next chapter, so far as to say, that all capital constitutes an immediate and pressing demand for labor. Whoever desires a service which a laborer can render, and lays by something to pay for that service, creates that instant a demand for labor; and especially, whoever accumulates raw materials which laborers are to work up, builds, buys, or keeps machinery which laborers are to tend, or puts himself in position to suffer loss by the ownership of lands, ships, or other property whatsoever, unless laborers be employed to make them productive, creates thereby an instant demand for labor. All such accumulations whatsoever, destined in the owner's mind to be employed in further production, all implements, buildings, and improvements, designed to assist labor, and raw materials which labor must work up, are capital; and capital must be constantly united with labor, or the owners will suffer an inevitable loss. The presence of capital anywhere constitutes a demand for labor. The more capital there is anywhere, the stronger the demand for labor; and capital, therefore, is the poor man's best friend. Mr. Carey regards the laborer as at a disadvantage compared with capital, because the laborer must at once dispose of his product, or starve; which seems to me a superficial view of the relation, because capital submits to an instant loss when it declines to employ labor. Capital does not like to lose its profit any more than the laborer likes to lose his bread. In a true and general view, the one is under just as much pressure to employ laborers, as the other to get employment. They come together of necessity into a relation of mutual dependence, which God has ordained, and which, though man may temporarily disturb it, he can never overthrow.

Labor, then, takes itself to the market to effect an exchange with capital. It is only capital that employs labor. Now, the terms of the exchange, that is to say, the average rate of the wages of common labor, will depend on the number of laborers compared with the amount of capital there present. The aggregate of all the forms of capital there present, helps to make up in the mind of the capitalist his motive for employing labor, because the more he has invested in buildings, machinery, and materials, the more urgent is the necessity to employ laborers, in order to make the investment productive; although only a part of the capital is free to be offered in payment of wages. Demand for labor is constituted, strictly speaking, by that part of the capital which is available to be offered in the form of wages, but it is clear, that, as a rule, demand, that is, the portion of capital set aside for the payment of wages, may increase under the influence of increased desire for laborers, and an increased desire for laborers is a necessary consequence of the increase in the aggregate of capital. Whether the portion set aside for wages *will* increase or not, on an increase of capital, will depend on the number of laborers. It is certainly possible that capital may go on increasing, while the wages-fund (the portion set aside for wages) may remain stationary, or even diminish, owing to the competition of an increased number of laborers, and the diminished compensation going to each. The number of laborers remaining the same, and intelligently comprehending their position, the size of the wages-fund will necessarily keep pace with all increase of aggregate capital. This point of connection between the two, this influence of the whole capital on the desire for laborers, and consequently on the wages-fund, is a point which I do not remember to have seen noticed by anybody, yet which is obviously of much importance in unfolding the relations of labor to capital. Now, wherever there is capital there is a wages-fund, and we have just seen what the connection is between the whole capital and that portion of it which is ready to be devoted to the payment of wages. If we call this portion of capital, or wages-fund, a dividend, and the number of laborers a divisor, the quotient will be the general average rate of wages at that time and place. This principle invariably determines the current rate of wages in any country. If the laborers are few relatively to the amount of capital, there will be a large dividend, and a small divisor, and infallibly a large quotient. In the reverse case, when laborers are many as compared with the capital that seeks to employ them, the large divisor and small dividend will surely give a small quotient. In the first case, capitalists will compete for laborers, and wages will go up. In the second case, laborers will compete for employment, and wages will go down.

We see now what we are to think of many remedies popularly recommended for low wages. When wages are very low in any country, or in any department of labor, there are some who think that the government ought to interfere to better them, at least to designate a minimum below which wages shall not go; others propose that strong public opinion be brought to bear upon employers, to induce them to give sufficient wages: others still maintain that combinations among the workmen themselves, for the purpose of dictating the rate of wages to the employers, would be an appropriate and effective remedy. Every one of these is a delusion, and so is every other proposal that ignores the law of wages just established. That which pays for labor in every country, is a certain portion of actually accumulated capital, which cannot be increased by the proposed action of government, nor by the influence of public opinion, nor by combinations among the workmen themselves. There is also in every country a certain number of laborers, and this number cannot be diminished by the proposed action of government, nor by public opinion, nor by combinations among themselves. There is to be a division now among all these laborers of the portion of capital actually there present. Suppose there has been free competition on both sides, and that the average rate of wages as thus determined, is one dollar per day for each laborer. Suppose that everybody thinks that this is insufficient, and that government accordingly issues a decree that wages thereafter must be one dollar and a half per day to each laborer. This decree has no tendency to increase the size of the wages-fund; *that* is determined by the general productiveness of labor, and by the division, under free competition, between wages and profits; if the decree, therefore, were carried out, as it never could be, the result would be that only two thirds of the laborers there present could be employed at all, and the remaining third must be supported by charity, or starve. The wages-fund is only sufficient to give to all the laborers a dollar a day, and if the government enforces a new distribution at a rate one third higher, then one third of the laborers cannot be employed at all. There is no use in arguing against any one of the four fundamental rules of arithmetic. The question of wages is a question of Division. It is complained that the quotient is too small. Well, then, how many ways are there to make a quotient larger? Two ways. Enlarge your dividend, the divisor remaining the same, and the quotient will be larger: lessen your divisor, the dividend remaining the same, and the quotient will be larger. All accessions to capital, all investment of profits in an enlarged business, all saving from expenditure for the sake of further production, will increase the dividend, and, the number of laborers continuing as before, the rate of wages will rise. Or, if there be no accessions to capital, the wages-fund consequently standing as before, and the number of laborers be diminished, as by emigration to new fields of effort, or by enlistment in armies, the divisor will be lessened, and the rate of wages will rise. The reversed suppositions will give, of course, reversed results, and wages will go down.

Though not in the way proposed, there is a way in which government may act most beneficially upon this matter of wages. By faithfulness to its peculiar trust, that is to say, by making the rights of person and property as secure as possible, it gives an impulse to enterprise, a spur to industry, makes the desire of accumulation effective, and thus indirectly but most powerfully contributes to the increase of capital, to the fund out of which wages are paid. Also, by fostering the means of education, and by the diffusion of knowledge among all classes, government acts beneficially upon the laborers, to make them intelligent, to impart to them that character and self-respect which fits them, in exchanging services with capital, to demand and secure their full rights in the exchange. It is not denied that capital takes advantage of the ignorance and immobility of laborers, and sometimes secures their services at a less rate than the just relations of capital to labor then and there would indicate, but the remedy for this is not in arbitrary interference of government in the bargain, but in the intelligence and self-respect of the laborers which shall fit them to insist on a just bargain. In this whole sphere of exchange, the just and comprehensive rule always will be, that when men exchange services with each other, each party is bound to look out for his own interest, to know the market-value of his own service, and to make the best terms for himself which he can make. Capital does this for itself, and laborers ought to do this for themselves, and if they are persistently cheated in the exchange, they have nobody to blame but themselves. Government should give them all facilities for intelligence: they should give themselves a character, and cherish a hearty self-respect, which there is nothing in their position to diminish: towards such laborers, capital occupies no vantage ground in an exchange of mutual services.

Public opinion can do something towards bettering the wages of labor, in countries where they are low, by organizing means to assist the laborers in distributing themselves at points where their services are most in demand. Societies in our seaboard cities, whose object it is to aid immigrants to pass on from those cities where labor is very abundant, to the country towns and to the West, where it is relatively much less so, are commendable in their purpose and spirit. So also are emigration societies, in countries situated as Ireland has been, where centuries of misgovernment combined with centuries of ignorance, produced a temporary pressure of population on the means of support. Where such pressure exists, as it does also in China, it is a good thing for public opinion to be favorable to emigration to newer and more fortunate countries, and liberally to assist in the distribution of labor to those points, wherever they may be, where capital is ready and anxious to employ it.

It may surprise some who are familiar with books on Political Economy, that I do not here adduce the influence of public opinion in restraining population as favorable to wages, and inveigh against the force of that spring of population which the Creator has coiled up in the nature of man, as compared with the weakness of that power by which the earth produces sustenance for man. In respect to the law of population and of human fecundity, I have only to say, that it is just that with which God saw best to endow the race; that experience has shown that it is not too strong for the purpose for which it was given; that under it, men are bound to act rationally and religiously, as accountable to God; that the same law of population which produces laborers, produces capitalists as well, and that the restraints on population, which economists have been at such pains to commend, are as likely to keep capitalists out of the world as laborers, which would be a disadvantage to the latter; that every human being is as much constituted by nature to receive services as to render them, and therefore, until it is demonstrated that the earth can no longer support the population that is in immediate prospect, no sound commercial reason can be given for artificial restraints on population; and finally, that Political Economy, as the science of exchange, presupposes the actual existence of men in society, and therefore, that it is without its province to discuss the laws under which they are born into society, and especially without its province to discuss the future possible contingency, nowise likely to happen in actuality, when the broad bosom of mother earth shall be unable any longer to nourish and support her children. In saying this, I would not be understood to deny that in certain states of society, in certain parts of the earth, population has pressed heavily upon food; or that poverty and improvidence do sometimes stimulate population, or that intelligence and self-respect are needful to order that marriages may be well and wisely contracted. What I affirm is, that, under freedom to receive and render services, to which freedom all men have a natural right, and under intelligence and morality, which all men are bound to possess, this matter of population will perfectly regulate itself; that there is no prospective and calculable danger that population will ever outstrip the means of supporting it; that the population of the world, as a whole, was never so well fed and clothed and housed as it is to-day; that the alleged laws of nature in respect to the increase of population and of food, which are said to be in antagonism, have never yet been proved; and that, in any actual case of persistent pressure of numbers on the means of life, it is, to say the least of it, quite as reasonable to look for the causes in the miscalculations and maladministrations of men, as in alleged colliding laws of God.

But will not strikes accomplish that for the raising of wages which neither government nor public opinion can effect? A strike is a combination among workmen for an increase of wages. They agree to stop work altogether until their employers shall comply with their terms, and raise their wages to a certain definite sum. It is not to be denied that workmen thus possess, under many circumstances, a very considerable reserved power which they can bring to bear upon their employers. When the processes of production are going briskly forward, when the manufactory is thoroughly furnished with competent hands, and profitable orders are in waiting, it is no laughable thing for the owner to be told, of a cloudy morning, that his hands have all stopped work, and refuse to lift a finger, until he shall agree to pay them wages at a rate which they themselves dictate. Of course, his first impulse is to discharge every man of them, and endeavor to fill his factory with new hands. But this he cannot always do. At best it will take time. Meanwhile his wheel or engine must be idle, customers be lost, orders unfilled, and profits nowhere. And so, many an employer has surrendered to a strike, when he felt that it was all unjust, rather than undergo a still greater loss. It is admitted that workmen may sometimes strike and gain their point, but it is none the less true for all that, that strikes are false in theory and pernicious in practice; that they spring from utter misapprehension of the true principles of wages; that they embitter relations between employers and employed which ought to be cordial and free; and that they rarely or never are permanently advantageous to the workmen themselves.

In the first place, then, strikes are false in theory. It is a very old adage, that it takes two to make a bargain. Express this in the language of Political Economy, and it will take this form: When two men have mutual services to exchange, let them come to a fair agreement as to the terms on which they will exchange. Certainly, let each make the best terms he can, but let the bargain always be free. If one party, who happens to have the power to do it, uses compulsion upon the other, it ceases to be a bargain at all, and becomes a sort of robbery. If, driving with my good horse along a lonely road, I meet another man driving an inferior one, and he, being the stronger man, compels me to exchange horses, it may be all very well for him, but I protest that it is no bargain. It is robbery. Now, workmen bring a certain valuable service to the market, just such a service as the capitalist wants, and he has to offer just such a service as they want, namely, wages. Now let them come to a free and fair agreement on the terms of their exchange. Let the workmen by all means make the very best terms they can; let them insist to the last penny on all which they can get elsewhere, for the value of their service is determined, as the value of every other service is determined, by what it will bring. Let the employer do the same. Let a fair bargain be struck. There is no objection to this kind of striking; and the more intelligence and skill and self-respect a workman has, the better prepared he is to strike the bargain and secure his just due. If the employer will not yield him this, let him have done with it at once, and go elsewhere. Or, if a just bargain has been struck, and afterwards circumstances shall so alter that he thinks he can rightfully demand more, let him frankly demand it, remembering always that it is an exchange he has to do with, and that it takes two to make a bargain. If he does not get for his service what he thinks he ought to get, let him quit. He has a perfect right to quit. All this is legitimate and fair and above board.

But a strike is wholly different. This brings com

pulsion into play. A combination among workmen to leave an employer in the lurch, and especially a combination which forces into its ranks by cajoling or menaces, those who are unwilling to join it, is of itself a confession of the injustice of the claim. If the claim be just, there is no occasion to extort it. If the value of the service rendered be equal to the sum demanded, if this can be obtained elsewhere, there is no need of consultation and conference, combination and conspiracy. Let each man go quickly where he can get the most for his service. The fact that this is not done, that means are brought to bear upon the employer which are not ordinarily used in bargains,— means of the nature of a threat — that the justice of the claim is not relied on in a case where, more than anywhere else, justice can enforce itself, that full and free explanations are not had, that no notice is given, that great damage is expected by their action to accrue to the employer, all this seems to forget that the transaction between employers and employed is a case of pure exchange, a simple bargain of one service against another service. Therefore, I say, that strikes are false in theory.

But this is not the worst of it. Strikes are pernicious in practice. And the grand reason for this is they tend to lessen the wages-fund. The production of all material commodities is a joint process. Capital and labor both conspire in it. The gross returns belong wholly to the capitalists and the laborers. The profits of capital and the wages of labor are paid out of these returns and from no other source. It is for the interest of both capitalists and laborers that these returns be as large as possible, because they are wholly divided between the two, and if the whole be large the parts will also be large. Profits being taken out, the rest is wages-fund; or, more strictly speaking, wages-fund being taken out, the rest is profits. It makes no difference practically that the wages have been advanced to the laborers while the production was still going forward, since the wages really come out of the proceeds of the joint process. The capitalist never means to pay wages out of his previous accumulations, and ought not to be expected to do so, and were he obliged to do so, it would soon be worse for the laborers, since these accumulations are the only stock which supports labor. It is not only just but needful for the laborers, that wages shall be paid out of the proceeds of that on which labor is now expended. Whatever, then, tends to lessen these proceeds, necessarily lessens the wages-fund. Any interruption of the process of production by strikes, any want of full and hearty coöperation between the two parties to the joint process, will, if continued, infallibly make the wages-fund smaller.

Suppose it takes three months to realize the returns in some branch of manufacture. If, when the workmen are paid off at the end of one three months, they all strike at the beginning of the next, and both parties hold out for three months, what is now the chance for higher wages? It shall go hard even if they get as much as before. And why? Because the mill has stood idle, and the fund out of which alone wages are paid has not been created. The capitalist has lost all his profits, and they have lost all their wages for three months, and now when they come to begin again, wages are to be advanced, not out of a fund already in existence as it would have been, but out of a fund not yet created. The employer is by no means in as good position to raise the wages as before the strike. He has lost profits which he might have put back into his business as a part of a new wages-fund. He has lost customers by the strike, and his business relations are all disarranged. His workmen by inflicting a loss upon themselves have found an opportunity of inflicting a loss upon him. Their loss is undoubtedly the greater of the two. Therefore, I say, strikes are commonly, and almost necessarily, a disadvantage to the workmen themselves. The case just put is a strong case to show the principle involved, but all interruption whatever to the processes of production by strikes, all consequent embittered relations between employers and employed, all want of hearty working together of the labor with the capital, tend to diminish the gross returns, and consequently, both the wages-fund and profits. As far as this point is concerned, there is no sense or reason in the common jealousy of workmen towards employers. There is no real antagonism between them. Their interests lie along the same line. They are partners in the same concern. Workmen who are intelligent, prudent, skilful, will infallibly get their due. Employers who are humane, urbane, fair, will find their account in it.

CHAPTER VII.

ON CAPITAL.

THE three requisites of production are labor, power-agents, and capital. Of the first we have now learned what can be learned, without attending in turn to its counterpart — capital; of the second we have learned already that all the powers of Nature work gratuitously in the service of man; and of the third, we are now to learn what it is, how it arises, how it works, and what its influence is upon the progress and amelioration of society. Political economy is able to show that there is no natural opposition of interest between capitalists and laborers; that capital is just as dependent on labor as labor is dependent on capital; that each is equally interested in the prosperity of the other, and that thus a deep and admirable harmony subsists in this part, as in every other part, of the social organism.

Capital is any product reserved to be employed in further production. This definition will be found to cover all the cases, to obviate many difficulties, and to take the life out of many disputes. Mr. Carey defines capital as the instrument by means of which man obtains mastery over Nature, including in it the physical and mental powers of man himself, and thus needlessly confuses the boundaries between capital and labor. It is much simpler and better to define labor, as has already been done, as physical or mental exertion for the sake of a return, and to define capital, as is now done, as any product outside of himself reserved by man for further production. There are many products devoted to immediate consumption; that is to say, to the gratification of present desires, without any reference to the rendering of future services by means of their help. Such products are not capital. They are a portion of the wealth of the community, they are valuable, but capital they are not. All capital is wealth, but all wealth is not capital. Only that portion is capital which employs, assists, and pays for labor. All raw materials are capital, all machinery is capital, all funds destined to purchase these, and all funds destined for wages, are capital. As all values reside in services exchanged, so all capital resides in services accumulated with reference to an ultimate exchange. It is only in the intention of the owner that capital can be discriminated from other products destined by him for the gratification of himself and his family, or for benevolent purposes. Take a hardware manufacturer, for example, and he has a stock on hand of finished hardware, a part of the proceeds of which he will put back into his business in the form of materials, tools, and wages, and another part will go in the form of personal and family expenditure, and it is only his intention that discriminates the first part, which is purely capital, from the second part, which, as far as he is concerned, is not capital at all. It may indeed become capital in the hands of those to whom he pays it out; and will become so, in case they destine it as an aid to further production in their several lines of business. The whole mass of capital, then, in any country, is the whole mass of those products, of whatever kind, which are destined in the mind of their owners to be retained as an aid towards rendering future services to society.

How does capital arise? We have seen that there are obstacles which lie in the way of the gratification of men's desires in all directions, and that these obstacles can only be removed by human effort. When a man devotes himself to one set of these obstacles, with a view to surmount them, he is not long in discovering, that if he had certain tools, his work would be greatly facilitated; and having discovered that, it will not be long before he will attempt himself, or induce others to attempt, to invent such tools. The beaver gnaws down the tree with his teeth, from generation to generation; but man is a being more nobly endowed than the beaver, and no sooner had he occasion to fell trees, than something of the nature of an axe suggested itself to his ingenuity. It is true, that his earliest attempts at axe-making were probably of the rudest sort, but just as soon as anything was devised, whether of flint or shell or metal, that rendered easier the labor of felling a tree, capital made a beginning along that line of obstacles. Among the more gifted races, progress in this direction was perhaps more rapid than we are wont to think it was, since Tubal-cain, even in the times before the flood, is said to have been "an instructor of every artificer in brass and iron." At any rate, we are at no loss to explain the origin of capital: it is found in the motive that exists everywhere, and that always existed, to lessen, if possible, a given irksome effort that is the condition of a given satisfaction. And this origin of capital gives the key-note to its universal use and indefinite expansion. Tools are invented and employed for no other reason than this, that, by means of their help, the human effort is lessened relatively to a given satisfaction. The powers of Nature, which grow the grain, which brings down the tree, which turns the wheel, which impels the locomotive, which sends the message round the world, all stand ready to slave in the service of man; but in order to make their aid available for human purposes, there must be a plough, an axe, a wheel, an engine, an electric machine. These, and all other implements whatsoever, from the tiniest needle to the most ponderous engine, are products created and retained for the sake of further production. They are capital. They are not capable of yielding in themselves an ultimate satisfaction to human wants, but they mediate between the powers of Nature, which they enable us to make available for our purposes, and those ultimate satisfactions. Nature furnishes all the powers, and all the natural qualities of objects, but labor can go but a very little way towards making these available for the satisfaction of human wants, without the aid of implements and contrivances which are produced by labor; and which, being retained as an aid to future labor, are capital. Since it requires tools to make tools, the progress of capital at first was very slow; but, since every advance in mechanical contrivance makes still further advances easier, there is a natural tendency, which facts abundantly exemplify, to a more and more rapid progression in the number and perfection of all implements of production. The same motive that impelled to the first invention, has impelled to the whole series of inventions since, and will constantly impel to further inventions till the end of time. This motive, — and there is no motive that actuates man more universal, — is, to lessen the onerous effort of human muscle, and to throw upon the ever-willing shoulders of Nature more and more of the burden of production. Every step of this progress gives birth to a larger and larger proportion of satisfactions relatively to efforts; marks an increasing control on the part of man over the powers of Nature; and gives promise for the time to come of greater advantages still in both these two directions. And it is because capital brings gratuitous natural forces into service, and the more so as capital progresses, that the value of those things created by the aid of capital tends constantly to decline as compared with the value of those things, in whose production capital less conspires; and in the chapter following the next will be developed from this point one or two important laws of value.

Now, then, having seen what capital is, and the human motive that brings it forward in production, we next inquire after its remuneration. *The remuneration of capital is technically called profits:* just as wages are technically the remuneration of labor. The present proposition is, that profits are the legitimate reward of a service, just as much, and in the same sense, as wages are the legitimate reward of a service. The distinctive service of the capitalist as such, as distinguished from the service of the laborer, consists in his voluntary *abstinence* from the use and enjoyment of that which he contributes in aid of further production. If a man puts a thousand dollars, which he might spend upon his immediate gratifications, into a machine to be used in his business, the money immediately becomes capital; the owner practices abstinence, and for this abstinence justly expects a reward. This reward we call profit. The expected profit is the only motive for the abstinence. He will not be content simply to get his thousand dollars back, for that he has now: he must have his thousand dollars with a profit. Suppose A to be a manufacturer of flax fabrics, B to be a farmer in his neighborhood, and C an expert mechanic acquainted with the current modes of spinning and weaving flax. A has a capital of $10,000 invested in his business, in buildings, machinery, materials, and wages-fund, which nets him $1000 a-year clear profit. At the end of the year, the question with him is, whether he shall spend this $1000 unproductively in immediate gratifications, or, adding it to his capital stock, increase his business with it. If he concludes to do the latter, he must forego the use and enjoyment of his $1000 for the present, he must practise abstinence; and this he will not do, and ought not to do, except in view of increased profits to accrue from his business at the end of the next year. If more flax is to be spun and woven in his factory, more money must be invested to buy more materials, to pay more laborers, or to pay for more or better machinery. His contribution to the prospectively increased production is $1000, transformed by his intention from simple property to capital, devoted to production by a voluntary abstinence from its present use and enjoyment, in view of a future reward or profit. It is a service rendered by one man to a joint process to be performed by many, and gives him a just claim to a portion of the product. Is exertion irksome? So is abstinence. Are wages legitimate? So are profits. B as a farmer might devote all his fields to growing food and fruits for the gratification of himself and family, but since A now wants more flax fibre for his factory, he gives up a part of his acres to growing flax, and this becomes a part of A's capital in the form of raw material; and the money received for it may become capital in B's hands by being spent either in agricultural improvements, or in buying additional land. The mechanic C, by giving time, exertion, and money to the work, may invent an improved machine for spinning flax, to be introduced into A's factory. The machine becomes a part of A's capital, and the money paid to C for his machine is partly wages, a reward for the labor bestowed on its construction, and partly profits, to replace to C the money used in making the machine, together with a reward for his abstinence from the use of this money until the machine was sold. Thus we see that capital, whether in the form of wages-fund, materials, or implements, is always the result of abstinence; and that whoever abstains from the present enjoyment of anything, in order that that something may contribute to a future production, renders an essential service; and, consequently, that the reward of such abstinence, or profit, is just as legitimate as are wages. This is very clearly seen in the common case in which one man loans capital to a second, to be used by that second in his own business. Brooks has a thousand dollars in hand which he is at liberty either to enjoy unproductively, or to employ himself productively, with the assurance of a profit; but is willing to forego the use of it for a year in favor of Smith, who is anxious to enlarge his business. Brooks' abstinence is a clear service to Smith; and at the end of the year, therefore, Smith not only refunds the thousand dollars borrowed, but also sundry other dollars besides as a specific reward for this specific service. If Smith keeps the money ten years or twenty, it is no more than just that he should pay this sum every year till the principal is refunded, because the service is every year repeated, the abstinence is still practised in his favor. Therefore, capital once acquired by abstinence, becomes, if the abstinence be continued, a legitimate source of perpetual revenue to the owner, as well as a perpetual source for the maintenance of laborers. Whoever transforms his property into capital, establishes thereby a permanent fund whence he may draw an income, and laborers support, in perpetuity; because the capital, though constantly disappearing in production, as constantly reappears in products, with profits added: a fact which shows the folly of the popular opinion which regards more favorably the man who spends his money freely and unproductively, than the man who, turning his money into capital, building a mill, or making other permanent investments, creates by that means a fund in the community, out of which permanent wages and permanent profits can be paid. The strength of the motives to abstinence in any country will depend largely upon the character of the government, and the organization of society there; these motives being generally strongest where liberty of action, equality of privileges, and security of property are the greatest.

We turn now to the relations of capital to labor, and to that law of the distribution of the products between capitalists and laborers, which was first promulgated by Mr. Carey, and which of itself fully justifies his claim to be regarded as an important contributor to the science of Political Economy. As I regard some of the positions of Mr. Carey as fundamentally erroneous, and shall freely animadvert on them in that view, I wish at this point to bear testimony to his great merit as the original discoverer of the beautiful law of distribution, in the light of which the future condition of the laboring classes in all countries, if they are only true to themselves, seems hopeful and bright. Capitalists are interested in profits, and laborers are interested in wages; is there, then, as is commonly supposed, a deep-seated antagonism between them? None whatever. No profits can be realized unless labor be united with the capital, because it is labor alone that works up the raw materials, tends the machinery, and disposes of the products. Capital not united to labor remains barren, giving birth to no profit, nay, itself commonly becoming less. At any rate, the idle mill and hoarded gold yield no profit. Without the profit there will be no capital; since no man will practise abstinence without the hope of a reward: but without the labor there will be no profit; and therefore the very presence of capital in any community, constitutes of itself a demand for labor. The more of capital in any community, the greater the demand for laborers, since it is through laborers alone that the profits are realized. But the greater the demand for laborers, the greater the reward of labor; and, therefore, laborers as such, are interested in nothing so much as in the increase of capital, and in the strength of those motives to abstinence, out of which capital springs.

Capital must have laborers. Laborers desire remunerative employment. It is the old case of values over again. Labor offers a service to capital, and capital offers a service to labor. They exchange to the mutual advantage of both, and one is as independent as the other. Hold up your heads, workmen! You offer an honorable service, on which capital is absolutely dependent for its existence. You offer a service as legitimate and as respectable, as that of the clergyman who preaches your sermons and baptizes your children, and are paid on precisely the same principles. Do not feel too much stuck up towards your workmen, employers! The money you render them is no whit better than the work they render you. The exchange is honorable, and the parties to it on the same level of advantage. They are as necessary to you as you are necessary to them. As a capitalist, you cannot exist without them; as laborers, they cannot exist without you. You are one blade of the shears, they are the other blade, and it takes both blades to cut. It is absurd to ask which blade cuts most, because there is no cutting at all, unless both blades work together.

More than this. Capital and labor are not only essential to each other, but also each is bettered by the prosperity of the other. If capital realizes a good round rate per cent., every capitalist is anxious to enlarge his business, whether as lender or active operator, and employ as much of his wealth as possible, as capital. This process increases capital. If men constantly put their profits only back into their business, which, under a high rate per cent., they will be pretty sure to do, capital rapidly increases. But increase of capital is, in its very nature, an increased demand for laborers. An increased demand for laborers, other things being equal, infallibly raises wages; just as an increased demand for anything else raises its value. Therefore, laborers are directly interested in the prosperity of capital, because the prosperity of capital leads to its increase, and its increase leads to higher wages. As a matter of fact, high profits and high wages, so far from being incompatible, usually accompany each other.

But is the capitalist equally interested in the prosperity of laborers? I think so. That he has to pay high wages is not necessarily a dead loss to him. This is no game of grab, in which what one gains another loses; it is a case of joint production, in which two parties conspire, and in which whatever helps to enlarge the gross amount produced, helps to increase the share falling to each party. If then, as they undoubtedly do, high wages tend to make the workmen more intelligent, industrious, frugal, and inventive, they are not a loss to the capitalist, but a gain. Larger gross returns are thereby secured.

Improved intelligence and skill of workmen affect production, just as improved machinery, secured by the aid of capital, affects it. Both alike enlarge the aggregate of products to be divided between capitalist and laborer. Now, in the division of products thus rendered larger in amount, what hinders capital from getting a fair share? When a firm is prosperous, are not all the partners benefited? All that is produced is to be divided; if more is produced, more is to be divided. Intelligent, industrious, skilful workmen, are best for production, are best for the capitalist, and therefore, high wages, which tend to make them so, and which are a consequence of their being so, are to be paid without grudging. When the matter is sifted to the bottom, it is seen that capital is as much interested in the prosperity of labor, as labor is interested in the prosperity of capital. All legitimate interests are in harmony.

I am now prepared to prove that all increase of capital, while it redounds to the benefit of capitalists, redounds in a still higher degree to the benefit of laborers. The demonstration is Mr. Carey's, and is the law of distribution above referred to. The proof is this. The rate per cent. of profits invariably goes down as a country grows older and richer. This is a simple fact of history, which no one will dispute. It has been exemplified alike in ancient and in modern times, so that one is at a loss whence to take the best examples, when all the examples are so good. In England, three centuries ago, the legal rate of interest was ten per cent., while now the average rate is barely four in that country, and lower still in Holland. During the first years of mining operations in California, from eight to fifteen per cent. a month, with security of real estate, was paid for the use of money, which enormous rates have now declined to rates not much higher than those paid in the States along the Mississippi River, and in these also the rates are constantly approximating those current in the older Eastern States. It may be assumed, therefore, as an indisputable fact, that, as capital increases, the rate per cent. for its use tends steadily to decline; but, while less profit is received on every hundred, there are also more hundreds, and consequently, there is an absolute gain to capitalists as a class, and both an absolute and relative gain to the laborers. Let us take to figures. While capital stands at $100,000,000, let the rate of profit be six; when it rises to $500,000,000, the rate goes down, say, to four. The value of the products to be divided at the end of the year, will be represented respectively by $106,000,000 and $520,000,000. In the first case, $6,000,000 is profits, and $100,000,000 is wages. In the second case, $20,000,000 is profits, and $500,000,000 is wages. Here is an absolute gain to capitalists. Profits have gone up from six to twenty millions, are more than three times as great as before. But wages have gone up both absolutely and relatively. They have risen from one hundred to five hundred millions, and are *five* times as great as before. Profits have risen in the ratio of one to three, but wages in the ratio of one to five. This arithmetical example is put for the sake of illustration, but the principle holds good in every case where the rate per cent. goes down in consequence of the increase of capital, and therefore the advantages of ever enlarging capital are even greater to the laborers as a class than to the capitalists themselves. Most assuredly, if capital now takes less out of every hundred, more is left to labor. Profits and wages are reciprocally the *leavings* of each other, since the aggregate products created by the joint agency of capital and labor are wholly to be divided between them. This demonstration is extremely important; for it proves beyond a cavil, that the value of labor tends constantly to rise, not only as compared with the value of the material commodities which, by the aid of capital, it helps to create, a truth we have seen before, but also as compared with the value of the use of its co-partner capital itself; and therefore, that there is inwrought in the very nature of things a tendency towards equality of condition among men. God has ordered it so. Self-interest is indeed the mainspring of movement in the economic world; but no man can labor intelligently and productively under its influence, without at the same time benefitting the masses of men. His very savings, productively employed, are the poor man's wealth.

It only remains to speak of the forms which capital assumes, and to divide these, in general, into circulating and fixed capital. Circulating capital comprises all those products which, in rendering aid to further production, are capable of but a single use in their present form. Such are (1) all raw materials; (2) funds destined for wages; (3) products on hand for sale, whose proceeds are destined as an aid to further production; (4) products loaned or rented, or retained for that purpose. Fixed capital comprises all those forms of capital which are capable of repeated use in the processes of production. Such are, (1) all tools and machinery; (2) all buildings used for productive purposes; (3) all improvements upon land; (4) all investments in aid of locomotion, such as railroads, canals, ships, and everything subsidiary to these; (5) the national money. " The test of fixed and circulating capital is the inquiry, Are returns secured by the retention, or by the transfer, of the particular product? Tools in the hands of him who uses them are fixed, in the hands of him who manufactures them, circulating capital." [1]

As civilization advances, and the aggregate of all forms of capital enlarges, there is a tendency towards a relative increase of fixed capital, as compared with circulating. There may, indeed, at times, be a transformation of the one kind of capital into the other, too rapid for the general interests of production, as was seen both in this country and in England about the year 1847, when such an amount of money was permanently invested in railways and similar improvements, as to drain unduly the loan markets in both countries, as to bring on a commercial crisis in each, and as greatly to depress the value of these permanent investments, thus multiplied beyond the immediate wants of business, whose activity was besides curtailed and disturbed by the necessary expenses of their construction. It has been estimated, that at the present time, the proportion of circulating capital to fixed in France, is one to eight; in

[1] Bascom's Political Economy, p. 71.

England, one to three; in the United States, three to five; proportions which are believed to be much higher in favor of fixed capital than formerly obtained in those countries.[1]

[1] Carey's Social Science, iii. 56.

CHAPTER VIII.

ON LAND.

THE crucial test of a definition, a generalization, a theory, is found in those seemingly anomalous cases with which all science has to do, and which come with such apparent reluctance under her painstaking classifications. If a definition given, or a generalization propounded, reduce into order these outlying cases without violence, as well as cover easily the more central phenomena, there is at once created a strong presumption of their truth. Does it cover all the cases? Does it account for all the observed facts? These are tests of definitions and of theories. The questions relating to the value of land and of its products have been among the most vexed questions of Political Economy, have exercised a vast amount of ingenuity, have led to careful and commendable observations and investigations in the whole field of agriculture, while the diverging views that have been taken, the arguments adduced, the conclusions drawn, and the spirit manifested, in these discussions, form the most unrefreshing portion of the history of the science. These questions, however bitterly debated in the past, are approaching, even if they have not already reached, a satisfactory solution. The value of land and of the products of land have been almost uniformly regarded in the theories of wealth as anomalous matters, to which peculiar principles are applicable, and from which certain conclusions are deducible, which color and modify results and prospects in the whole field of value. Adam Smith, Ricardo, McCulloch, Senior, and Mill hold substantially one set of views on land and its rent. Carey and Bastiat hold views on that subject almost totally at variance with the English writers; it seems to me that the means are at hand for combining what is true in these opposing views in a clear and consistent manner, and for settling the dispute. I feel sure that both parties are right in many respects, and are wrong in some respects, and am not without some hopes of being able in this chapter to reconcile the difference, and to show that the value of land and the rent of land are not anomalous cases of value, but arise from human services rendered and exchanged, just as all other value arises, and vary under the same laws as vary all other values.

A series of propositions, and discussions under them, will bring out what seems to be the truth in this whole matter.

1st. The whole earth with all its productive powers was given to men gratuitously of God under the simple direction that they replenish and subdue it.

No provision was made for particular ownership. The whole earth, thus bestowed without partiality upon a whole race, had in all its spontaneous products a great utility, but, for a time, no value whatever. The spontaneous fruits, when gathered by any person, might become thereby possessed of value from his effort expended, but to the land itself, on which no human efforts had been expended, the idea of value could not have attached. No man would have *thought* to say to another under such circumstances, This field is mine: give me something for it, and you shall have it; and if he had, that other would not give it; because such fields were open on every hand to his occupation gratis. It is not in human nature to render anything for something which may be gratuitously obtained; value has no place in a sphere where everything is free. But it is well worth while to notice, that under God's command, the earth was not only to be replenished but *subdued*. Under this word subdue, and under the work implied in that, came in the first idea of ownership in land. When a family commenced this work of subjugation upon a piece of land, when they enclosed it, settled on it, tilled it, in any way whatever improved it by an expenditure of their own toil, then first dawned upon their minds the idea of possession, then first began the land to be possessed of *value*, since now the family would justly say to another, If you want this field, you must give us an equivalent for what we have expended on it. If the transfer took place, is it not very plain that what was sold, was not the inherent qualities of the soil, but the services which had now been expended in its amelioration? The first family received the soil and its powers gratuitously, and then expended a series of efforts on its improvement; but a similar series of efforts bestowed on other gratuitous land in the neighborhood would make it as eligible as this now is; if, therefore, the family insisted on more than an equivalent for their exertions actually bestowed on the land, the other would reply, For as much labor as you have given to your land, we can make other free land as good as yours, consequently we can give you no more than a fair equivalent for your efforts. The *value* therefore of the parcel sold, would be determined, not by the gratuitous elements involved, but by the onerous elements involved, that is to say, by the efforts already made by the first family in connection with the land, as compared with the efforts of the second involved in the remuneration offered. It is not possible in the nature of things that God's bounty to the whole race should be thwarted by any number of individuals through exclusive appropriation on their part of this bounty. What they received gratuitously, they must gratuitously transmit; what they have wrought of permanent improvements on the land, they may justly demand a recompense for, and can secure it. By their expenditure of efforts they have saved to the purchaser a like expenditure of efforts, and for these they can demand, and he will be willing to concede, a recompense; but if they go further, and demand pay for the natural qualities of the soil which God gave and they have not improved, for the sun that shines, and the rain that falls on it, the demand is blocked at once by the common sense of the purchaser. He replies: There is land enough in its natural state, with inherent qualities as good as yours, the same sun shining on it, and just as much blessed rain falling on it, which I can have for nothing. I cannot give you something for that which costs you nothing, and which I can get for nothing.

As long as there is abundance of land still open

to occupation, everybody will concede that this line of argument is just, and that the general value of land cannot rise above the estimated measure of the human efforts actually bestowed on its improvement. Though less obvious at first, the principle is just as true after all the land has been taken up. Improved farms are always for sale in every country, lands once appropriated and ameliorated are perpetually changing hands, and men enough are always found willing to part with land, as with everything else, for what it has cost them. If some proprietors are unreasonable enough to try to intercept God's gifts bestowed alike on all the generations, and endeavor to exact a price for their land made up of compensation for what they and their predecessors have done upon it, together with something added for what God has done for it, their cupidity is instantly thwarted by the readiness of others to dispose of their land for a fair equivalent of their onerous exertions. Human motives are such, and everything is so providentially arranged in this department, that men cannot sell God's gifts; it would be derogatory to the Giver, if they could.

What might be thus inferred from the nature of the case, is abundantly confirmed by facts. As a matter of fact and experience, lands are absolutely *valueless* until some portion of human effort has been expended on them, or in reference to them. They may have utility, but they have no value. Nobody will give anything for them. The United States government has been selling for years some of the best lands in the world for one dollar and a quarter an acre, and this after the lands have been surveyed at government expense, local governments provided for the settlers, and mail facilities and other privileges guaranteed to them. The same government is now giving away similar lands in homesteads to actual settlers, merely taking a nominal fee for the title-deeds, whose aggregate amount does not begin to meet the expenses incurred in connection with these lands. If lands had value, independent of human exertions, then would the English companies and individuals who received grants in the seventeenth century of vast tracts of as fertile land on this continent as the sun ever visited in his diurnal revolutions, have become rich as Crœsus; but these companies and individuals did not become rich at all, but rather poor. The amount realized from the sale of their lands fell far short of reimbursing the expenses of colonization; and, after incurring debts and endless vexations, most of the companies and proprietors were glad to be rid of their lands at any price. It is a current proverb now in regard to wild lands at the West, that the more a man has of them the worse off he is; and it is a maxim also in the newer settlements everywhere, that improved lands are worth the present value of the improvements and no more. And Mr. Carey is at pains to prove at great length that the value of lands in all old countries is now vastly less than they have cost of actual human efforts in their subjugation and improvement; less, because the progress of capital and inventions enables similar work to be done now at much less outlay. We conclude, then, that the value of land follows the law of all other values; that it arises only in connection with human efforts; that men cannot appropriate God's gifts in the soil, and then dole them out to other men for pay; that land is no monopoly; that landed property, violence aside, rests back, like all other property, its ultimate defence upon the right of making efforts for one's own welfare, and of not parting with these efforts except for an equivalent; that land and the use of it have value because the proprietor can by them render a service to somebody else; and finally that the value and the rent of land vary, like all other values, under the law of supply and demand.

2d. *The powers of all land, under more laborious culture, agricultural skill remaining the same, are subject to the law of diminishing return; in other words, increased labor upon it, though increasing the aggregate return of produce, does not secure an increase proportioned to the increase of labor.*

This is the fundamental proposition on which Ricardo, and the English writers generally, lay such stress, and on which they found the law of Rent, and the necessity of restraints on population; while Carey and Bastiat, impliedly if not expressly, deny the proposition, and of course, the inferences deduced from it. In my judgment, the proposition cannot be logically denied. The law of diminishing return from land is a law of Nature, and has played a very important part in the occupation and culture of successive portions of the earth's surface. The proof of the proposition is all the better for being short. If by doubling the labor on a piece of land, double the produce could be secured, and by quadrupling it, quadruple, and so on, there would be no reason why any man should ever cultivate more than a square acre, or even a square rod. He has a strong motive to confine his culture to a small space, just so long as the amount of produce is in the ratio of the labor expended, because there is less locomotion of tools and fertilizers and crops. The fact that he extends his culture from one acre to another, and then to distant acres, notwithstanding the inconveniences and expense of transportation, is an irrefragable proof of the proposition in question. Increase of agricultural labor and expenditure on a given space of land will secure a larger amount of produce, but as a general law, the increased amount will not be proportioned to the increased expenditure. If it were thus proportioned, if the law of diminishing return did not exist, then, for purposes of agricultural production, a square acre is as good as a continent.

It is through this law of diminishing return, that the Creator has secured the gradual occupation by men of almost the whole earth. There is a strong tendency to leave the old acres to advance upon new, the old countries to emigrate to new, whenever the returns begin to bear a more unfavorable ratio to the labor bestowed. The farmer will advance from the first to the second acre as soon as he thinks that more produce can be obtained from it by a given amount of labor than can be got by a like expenditure of additional labor upon the first acre, allowance being made for the increased inconvenience; and so, cultivation has gradually extended itself, and men have become dispersed over the whole earth. Other principles leading to dispersion have undoubtedly coöperated, but this is the fundamental one, operative at all times, changing the course of population, and consequently of empire.

Mr. Carey seems to think that this proposition is dependent on another, and endeavors to break down this by an attempt to break down that other. That other proposition is, that in the course of occupation the best lands are entered upon first, and that afterwards recourse is had to the poorer soils. He attempts to prove that the exact reverse of this is the historical fact, that cultivation has always been begun upon the poorer soils, and that afterwards the river bottoms and strong lands have been drained and cleared and tilled. This discussion, however interesting in itself, is irrelevant as far as the law of diminishing returns is concerned, because that law is nowise dependent on the order in which soils of different productive power are entered upon in cultivation; it is true of all soils, whether rich or poor, whether entered upon in the order of their fertility, or in the inverse order; and I cannot help thinking that Mr. Carey puts upon this matter of the order of occupation, which he asserts has always been from the poorer to the richer soils, an estimation altogether disproportioned to its importance. Whenever men have entered upon new countries, they have undoubtedly selected those lands first which seemed to them most eligible, reference being had of course to their present means of subduing them; and whether these lands proved ultimately to be better or worse than other parcels which they might have chosen, is a point, which, however determined, has no effect to disturb the fundamental proposition in hand.

3d. The operation of the law of diminishing returns is retarded by all improvements in agriculture.

The discovery of new and more available fertilizers, the invention of better agricultural implements, the light thrown by chemistry upon agriculture, the consequent adoption of better methods of culture and rotation of crops, the more perfect adaptation to the various soils of the kinds of produce sought to be raised from them, all these and similar improvements tend to increase the ratio of the produce to the labor, and disguise the law just established. The lands that are now under cultivation may be made, under more skilful modes of culture, to yield indefinitely more than at present, and the vast still uncultivated lands of the world may come to render an incalculable quantity of food to the world's population; but yet, as improvements are naturally less continuous in this than in some other departments of production, as invention has less play, as there is less opportunity for the division and coöperation of labor, as nothing can materially shorten the time during which the fruits of the earth must ripen, the value of agricultural products tends to rise relatively to manufactured products generally. Labor, for a reason already given, and produce, for the reasons now given, have risen and tend steadily to rise, as estimated in general commodities.

4th. The rent of land is the measure of the service which the owner renders to the actual cultivator, and does not differ essentially in its nature from the rent of buildings in cities, or from the interest of money.

Mr. Ricardo's famous doctrine of rent, is for substance, this: there are some lands in every country whose produce just repays the expenses of cultivation, and consequently yields no margin for rent; and the cost of production on these rentless and poorest lands under cultivation, will determine the price of the produce; and as there can be but one price in the same market, the produce raised on more fertile lands will be sold for the same price, and this price, besides paying the cost of production, will yield a rent rising higher according as the land is more fertile; so that the rent paid on any land is always a measure of the excess of productiveness of that land over the least productive land under paying cultivation; and therefore, an increased demand for food in consequence of increased population, and the higher price resulting, will force cultivation down upon still poorer soils, or else compel a higher culture for less remunerative returns on the old soils, according to the law of diminishing returns, which in either case will raise the rents on all the soils above that grade that just repays the expenses of cultivation, and no more; so that it is the sole interest of landlords, as such, that population should be dense and food high, their interest being directly antagonistic to that of the other classes of community.

This very ingenious and complicated theory, which is supported by many other authoritative names besides that of its author, is too mechanical and rigid to be applied to any existing state of facts. There is much truth in it, and some error; and I believe that a few simple statements will embody the truth and eliminate the error. It is not true that there is but one price in the same market; prices vary in the same market, and are shifting perpetually in all markets. Produce is not always sold for money, but is frequently exchanged directly against other commodities and services. The theory makes no allowance for the food imported, or which may be imported, from abroad. As I understand it, the whole truth in regard to rent is nearly this: Land is an instrument for certain productive purposes; has been prepared to answer these purposes by human efforts. These efforts only are to be remunerated from the use of the instrument; if the owner allows another the use of it, he justly demands a recompense for the use of an instrument which has cost him efforts; this recompense is rent; it is the reward of a service rendered, just as profit is; there is no gauge by which to measure the amount of rent except the degree of service rendered; this is very variable in lands, owing to various causes, such as proximity to markets, natural fertility, state of improvements, and so on; the rent of land then depends on the quality and situation of the instrument; it differs nowise in principle from the rent of other instruments which are wholly made by labor; the range of landed rents is up and down, a quite extended scale, simply because, from accidental causes, the service which the owner is in position to render the lessee varies greatly; the rent of mines and of oil lands presents no new principle; the right to rent stands on ground as unassailable as the right to wages and to profits; rent partakes of the nature of both these two; and varies, just as they do, under the action of supply and demand.

5th. *That division of land is best for purposes of*

production, which gives farms approximately equal in size to the cultivators; and the best tenure is the fee-simple.

Taking the last part of the proposition first, the fee-simple is better for production than any other tenure, because when one owns the land he tills, he takes a greater interest in it, it is his own, he has a constant motive to improve it, to make the production from it as great as possible, since all it produces is his own. If men work from motives, and if the energy and persistence of the work be proportioned to the constancy and press of the motives, then will the fee-simple most certainly make the aggregate of produce greater than any other tenure of land. Moreover the fee-simple immeasurably improves the character of the cultivators. The masses of men are educated and developed by nothing so much as by the ownership of land. It tends to make them industrious, thrifty, independent, hopeful of the future, anxious to give their children better privileges, as well as better lands, than they themselves had. The testimony on this point is abundant from many countries, and it all goes to show that the peasant proprietor is a happier and more virtuous, as well as a more industrious and productive man, than the mere tenant and farm-laborer; while similar testimony, as well as common observation, proves, that lands under the copyhold tenure, or leased at will, are far inferior in point of improvements and production, to contiguous lands held in fee-simple. The zeal of absolute ownership, especially if it be a limited ownership, has been observed to produce almost magical effects, as well upon character as upon lands, transforming after a while the poorest into excellent lands, and thriftless and desponding laborers into frugal and enterprising proprietors.

The practical play of the fee-simple draws after it such a division of lands into farms moderately large and approximately equal, as can be shown to be most favorable to the largest aggregate production. Wherever there is no primogeniture and no entails, and owners can consequently sell a part or all their lands, whenever it is their interest to do so, lands naturally fall into those hands which are most capable of using them productively, because such persons can afford to pay more for them than anybody else; and the division that follows this impulse of self-interest and this freedom of exchange is likely to be into farms tolerably equal in extent and moderately large. Such a division has naturally taken place in New England, in the Middle States, and at the West; while in the South, the institution of slavery led to the system of large plantations and few land-owners, which system, I believe, will now, under the auspices of freedom, give way to the better system of small farms and numerous proprietors. That the latter system is more profitable in reference to production, as well as advantageous in point of national character and a broadly based and sound development of the national resources, is evident from a few considerations, and has been exemplified distinctly in the diverse experience in this respect of France and England. 1. When the mass of the agricultural population are owners of the soil they till, the motives to productive cultivation are brought to bear most universally. These motives are interest and hope. There is a high pleasure in possession, and in self-guided exertion, a strong stimulus to get as much as possible from the land, and at the same time to keep good and ever improve its condition. When the great body of the land of any country comes under the action of such motives as these, then will the amount of production be the greatest. 2. Dr. Franklin used to say that the best manure for the land was the foot of the owner; and wherever the system of small farms prevails, there will be the most of what is so essential to successful farming, the personal supervision and exertion of the owners. Personal supervision, to be most effective, must be limited in its sphere; and the best agricultural knowledge and skill becomes comparatively weak when it attempts to exhibit itself on too broad a surface. Because a man can cultivate one hundred acres better than any of his neighbors, it does not prove that he will cultivate fifty acres additional to them better than a neighbor of inferior skill, who is the owner of those fifty and no more. 3. The possession of small freeholds educates and gives energy to the masses. That educates a man which calls forth varied efforts of intelligence and will. To protect and advance his own interests, to attend upon the seasons, to watch and wait, to foresee and plan and labor, all this will secure that a nation of freeholders will never be a nation of ignorant, indolent barbarians. 4. National strength is best secured and maintained wherever there is a broad basis of independent yeomanry to lean back upon when heavy taxes are to be raised and strong blows of battle are to be struck in behalf of the nation.

France and England are instructive examples in this whole matter. In France, since the abolition of all entails and primogenital rights by the revolution of 1789, and under the action of the law requiring the equal partition of a man's landed estate among his children, the lands have become subdivided into small parcels, averaging perhaps from ten to thirty acres, and out of a population of about 37,000,000, nearly 6,000,000 are proprietors of land, either in town or country. Undoubtedly more than half of the total population of France belong to families which own some portion of the soil. As we should expect from the considerations already urged, the results of this division have been most happy in all respects; in point of the increase of agricultural products, the statistics show an annual average increase, from 1813 to 1840, of 1,000,000 francs; in point of an industrious, frugal, cheerful peasantry; in point of a very general desire and ability to purchase land; in point of showing that subdivision ceases as soon as the lands, if divided further, would be less profitable in production; in point of pauperism; in point of national strength and weight, in spite of a centralized and repressive government; the results of such division of the lands have been such as we should expect, and such as we should wish. In England, on the other hand, the monster-farm system prevails, the small proprietors have mostly disappeared, the law of entails and leases ties up the landed estates from sale and division, about 2000 persons own one third of all the lands in England, Scotland, and Ireland, five noblemen own about one fourth of all Scotland, and the total number of all proprietors of land in the three kingdoms will not reach 50,000, in a population of 28,000,000. The results are seen, in part, in what has been justly called the irretrievable helotism of the laboring classes; in an annual poor rate, raised by taxation, of over $42,000,000; in unmeasured inequality in fortunes and comforts; in the lack, felt alike in war and peace, of a large class of sturdy yeomanry, the strength of a State; and in a consequent sinking of relative position, power and influence, former times being held up with the present, as compared with France and the other first-class powers. No degree of merit in the other parts of the English system, can ever compensate the want of just and broadly liberal laws of land.

CHAPTER IX.

ON COST OF PRODUCTION.

WE are now in position to be able to analyze the cost of production, and to bring forward some supplementary matters relating to value, which could not be properly discussed, until the subjects of labor, capital, and land, were, at least in their ground principles, understood. While we were inquiring, in the chapter on value, whether such a thing as a measure of value were possible, it was remarked that some political economists have thought that the cost of production of any commodity is the most accurate measure of its general purchasing-power; and it might have been added, that these writers consider that there is such a thing as *natural* value distinct from market value, that natural value is the cost of production, and that market value oscillates perpetually around that, and tends constantly to return to it. How far these views are just, how far cost of production constitutes a law of value within the all-comprehending law of demand and supply, is the point to which attention is now directed.

It is noticeable, that while almost all people put forth onerous efforts to satisfy the present and immediately prospective wants of other people, in view of receiving back from them corresponding efforts to satisfy their own present and immediately prospective wants, there are some people, who have both foresight and capital, who set to work to make preparations in reference to services which they expect to render some time in the future; and it is evident that this matter of the cost of production has an especial bearing upon those classes of production in which permanent investments are made, looking to future rather than to present exchanges. It becomes necessary to attend to cost of production simply because cost of production is sometimes an exact measure of one of the elements out of which value springs, namely, the element of effort. When a surgeon, for example, charges fifty dollars for cutting off a man's leg, cost of production is an impertinent phrase in relation to such a service, and is no measure of the effort; but when a capitalist invests $20,000 in a cutlery establishment, hires all his labor, and at the end of the year has produced 5000 knives, cost of production has a definite meaning as applied to each one of the knives, and is an accurate measure of the one element of effort, which goes, together with other elements, to determine its value. It is not true at all that cost of production alone determines the value of the knife, or is a measure of the value of the knife, but it *is* true that, in this case, and in all cases in which a commodity is produced by a definite capital invested for a fixed time, and by labor wholly hired, or estimated as hired, the cost of production is an exact measure of one of the four elements which go to determine value, namely, of one effort. Now let us suppose that when these knives are exposed for sale, no such return efforts are offered for them as are estimated by the maker as compensatory and remunerative. He may, in order to avoid a still greater loss, sell his knives below the cost of their production, but it is evident that he will not go forward at present in his enterprise of making knives. He will suspend operations, or withdraw from the business; and his action in this respect will affect the supply of knives to lessen it; and the next equalization of demand and supply will be likely to adjust a market value more favorable to knife-makers. Or if, when the knives are exposed for sale, they meet with an exchange at very remunerative rates, our capitalist is now stimulated to increase his production, to put back his profits into his business, and perhaps to invest in it additional principal. His action in this respect will affect the supply of knives to increase it; and the next equalization of demand and supply, or if not the next, some subsequent one, will be likely to adjust a new market value less favorable to knife-makers. Thus it is seen, that absolute cost of production influences value not directly, but remotely, through its influence on supply. To suppose and to say that the cost of production of one commodity determines its value in an exchange with another, is to perpetuate the old mistake of ignoring the second commodity, is to reiterate the fallacy that value is an independent quality of one thing, is to confuse the whole subject of value. When the writers referred to speak of the "natural value" of any commodity, they mean its absolute cost of production; but, at this stage of our inquiry, it surely cannot be necessary to repeat the thought already so often expressed in substance, that an analysis of one component part falls far short of determining the resultant of four component parts. I do not think the expression "natural value" is calculated to be useful. From the very meaning of the word "value," if it is to have any consistent meaning at all, there can be no other kind of value than market value, that is, value in exchange.

But while all this will doubtless be conceded to be just, there are other points of view in which the cost of production of any commodity comes to be a very important matter. From its obvious relations to supply, already exemplified, it is constantly, though indirectly, influencing the value of the commodity itself; and in respect to permanent investments, looking solely to future production, it becomes the main inquiry; because, while the cost of production can never determine the purchasing-power of the product, it is always one element in determining it; and also, especially, because the improvements which are all the time being introduced into the mechanical and other processes of such production, which improvements always tend to lessen the cost of the product, have the effect to lessen the value of all permanent investments, unless similar improvements be inaugurated in connection with them. The march of improvement is so constant, that old machinery and old processes are rapidly depreciated; and a calculated cost of future production in one establishment is almost sure to be disturbed by new labor-saving inventions in other similar establishments, which will be able in consequence to offer the commodity at a lower rate than the rate estimated; in which case the value of the product will not conform to the estimated or even actual cost of production in that establishment, but will pitilessly fall to the point at which similar commodities are offered by the more fortunate producers. For these reasons we must inquire carefully after the elements of cost of production.

These elements are two: cost of labor, and cost of capital. These are the only onerous elements that enter into production. Assisting the processes are, indeed, the natural powers of land, water, wind, steam, electricity, and so on, but as these are always gratuitous, they form no element of cost. Labor must have its wages, and capital must have its profits, and also a sinking-fund from which to replace the original capital when worn out or expended. It will be in vain to search for any other ingredient of cost than these two.

1. By cost of labor is meant, of course, its cost to the employer, and not to the laborer himself, in reference to whom the phrase would have no definite meaning. Now, if we make an exhaustive analysis of the cost of labor to the employer, we shall find that there are three things, and only three things, that go to determine its cost. 1. Efficiency of the labor. 2. The rate of nominal wages paid. 3. The cost of that in which the wages are paid. To illustrate each of these in order:— If a capitalist hires two men to work for him at the same rate of wages, and if the one is twice as efficient a laborer as the other, the cost of his labor to the capitalist is one half less than the cost of the other's labor. The first element of the cost of labor is its efficiency. If a capitalist, accustomed to pay one dollar a day, is

now obliged to pay one dollar and a half a day to his laborers, their efficiency remaining the same, the cost of labor to him is just one half increased. The second element is nominal wages. If that commodity, whether money or other, in which wages are paid, varies in cost to the capitalist, the cost of the labor compensated by that commodity, nominal wages and efficiency remaining the same, is varied thereby of course. We shall discover in the next chapter that the value of money is by no means invariable, as we have already learned the variable nature of all other values, and accordingly the third element of cost of labor is the cost of that in which the labor is paid. It is easy to see that there is nothing else, aside from these three things, that can ever affect the cost of labor. This analysis is not given here for its own sake merely, but for some ulterior purposes, of which the first is to show, how various are the ingredients that enter into the computation which men ought rationally to make before engaging in extended enterprises of production. They must make calculations on the prospective cost of production, since that is one element that will determine the value of their future product. In doing this they must calculate the cost of labor, and the cost of capital; and the cost of labor alone involves, as we have just seen, three variables, no one of which can be safely neglected in the supposed estimation.

The second purpose is to explain from the analysis, that a great diversity of nominal wages may exist in different countries without necessarily affecting the cost of labor. If English wages, for example, are, nominally, one half wages in the United States, it is very poor logic to jump to the conclusion, that the cost of labor in England is one half less than in the United States. That will depend partly on the efficiency of the labor, and partly on the cost of that in which the respective labor is paid. If English laborers are only one half as efficient as American laborers, then a difference of one half in nominal wages, cost of money in the two countries being the same, will occasion no difference at all in cost of labor. Because nominal wages in England are lower than with us, many people think and maintain, that the English have an advantage over us, whereas it is notorious, and admitted even by themselves, that American labor is more efficient than English labor, and therefore there is no such difference in cost of labor as the difference in nominal wages would indicate, even if there be any difference in cost of labor at all. Just at this point great confusion has existed in the popular mind, and some by no means harmless fallacies are still current, arising from the want of a due analysis of the cost of labor. It is probable, all the elements being allowed for, that the cost of labor in one country is not very widely different from its cost in other countries; because, if there were much difference, there would be a greater difference than is actually observed in the rate per cent. of capital; and this conclusion is strengthened, when it is remembered, that in those countries in which the cost of labor is supposed to be low, as in England, the rate per cent. of capital is also low; and in those countries, as the United States, in which the cost of labor is supposed to be high, the rate per cent. is also high. Before leaving this point, I wish to remove one or two causes of misapprehension, which have frequently infected discussions of wages. The terms "high and low wages," are often used ambiguously; some meaning by the words, a high or low nominal rate; others, a high or low degree of comforts enjoyed by the laborers, as the fruit of their wages; others, still, as Ricardo, using the words high and low in relation only to profits, in which last sense, if wages are high, profits are low, and conversely. In the first two senses, wages and profits may both be high, or both be low, at the same time and place, but not in the last sense. When the first sense is meant, the expression should be *money wages;* when the second, *real wages;* when the third, *relative wages.* Had this nomenclature been adopted and consistently employed, many an angry dispute and many a false conclusion would have been avoided. Also, it has been thought by some, that high money wages create high prices of commodities, that is to say, that things are dear because laborers have been paid a high price for their agency in producing them. This does not follow. Their labor may be very efficient, and may be assisted by first-rate machinery, and the price of the commodities may be low, although the money wages may be high. Money wages must not be confounded with cost of labor, because it is only one element of cost of labor. A higher cost of labor in any department of production, other things being equal, will tend to raise the price of the product, but not higher money wages alone. Price is value expressed in money, and general rise or fall of prices is usually due to changes in the currency. An inflated currency produces universally high prices, as well of labor as of commodities, and for the same reason of labor as of commodities, and it is a superficial view which supposes, that, of these two effects of a common cause, one is a cause of the other. On the other hand it is sometimes supposed, that the exact reverse of this takes place, and that money wages become high simply because the commodities which the laborers consume have become high. This is an error similar to the other. If an inflation of the volume of the current money of the country has supervened, then the price of labor rises by the same impulse that carries up the price of commodities. Both are effects; neither is the cause of the other. But if the currency has remained sound and stable, a high price of any of the commodities consumed by the laborers, has no tendency, that I can perceive, to raise the rate of money wages. The higher price of those commodities may have arisen from deficient harvests, or from a higher cost of labor in those departments, from inequality of taxation, or other similar causes; but no one of these enables capital to share the gross proceeds of production on better terms with labor. Neither money, nor real, nor relative wages can rise, as I see, merely from high prices of the commodities which the laborers consume. It seems to me, accordingly, that much clear light is thrown from this analysis of the cost of labor upon the whole vexed question of wages.

The third ulterior purpose of presenting this analysis is briefly to unfold the principles according to which the division between wages and profits is practically made. It was Mr. DeQuincy who first called profits the *leavings* of wages; but this is only true when by wages is meant the *cost of labor*. The gross products created by the combined action of capital and labor belong in common to the capitalists and laborers, and are to be divided between them in some way, and the analysis in question enables us to perceive just how they are divided. Cost of labor being deducted, the rest goes to capital as a matter of course, and the proportion of this part to the whole capital determines the rate per cent. of profit. If this part falling to capital is large for every hundred invested, the rate per cent. is high; if small, low. The efficiency of labor and the state of the currency being as before, a rise of money wages will lessen profits, but no rise of money wages accompanying increased efficiency of labor, or resulting from inflated currency, has a tendency to lessen profits at all. The capitalist as such is interested in having cost of labor low, but not in low money wages necessarily, because a low cost of labor is consistent with high money wages, and with high real wages too. Very efficient labor may be very highly paid, and yet leave to capital a high rate per cent. We here see again from another stand-point, and from a deeper view, a truth we have seen before, that there is no real antagonism but a real harmony of interests between capitalists and laborers. Both are alike interested in the combined efficiency of capital and labor, that is to say, in the amount of gross products created; and, in respect to the division of this gross amount, there is no more collision of interest than in making the dividends of the year among the partners of a commercial house. The cost of labor must first be defrayed; and this depends on its efficiency, its nominal rate of remuneration, and the present purchasing-power of money. What is left is gross profits, and the relation that this bears to the whole capital invested decides the rate per cent. So far of cost of labor.

2. The second element in the cost of production is the *cost of capital;* and this also must be analyzed into three variables, no one of which can be safely neglected in a computation which has for its object to decide a prospective cost of production: — 1st, The rate per cent.; 2d, The time for which the capital is advanced; 3d, The form of the capital as liable to slow or rapid deterioration. We must look at the influence of each of these elements on cost of production.

(1.) Let us suppose that the rate per cent. at Amsterdam is 3, and the rate at New York is 7, that the cost of labor is equal in the two cities, that the time of advance is one year, and that there is no liability of the capital to wear out; a commodity made at Amsterdam with an outlay of $100 can be sold for $103, while the same commodity made at New York with the same outlay cannot be sold for less than $107. The current rate per cent. is one element of the cost of capital, and through this, of the cost of production.

(2.) The effect of the time of advance on cost of capital is more striking. Let the same supposition be continued, except that the time of advance in New York be extended to four years. The commodity will sell in Amsterdam, as before, at $103, but in New York for not less than $131. This principle is well illustrated also in the case of wine, which to reach its perfection requires to be kept a number of years. Even under the same rate per cent. which we will suppose 6, a commodity made in six months with an outlay of $100 may sell for $103; while wine grown in the same six months at the same outlay, kept five years, cannot be sold without loss for less than $133. If the period of advance be long, and the rate per cent. be high, the cost of capital from the two causes enhances enormously the cost of the product; so that, it is only countries like England and Holland, in which the rate per cent. is very low, which can successfully engage in enterprises requiring a large capital to be invested for long periods before returns are realized. This accounts for the fact that mining operations in Mexico and South America have been largely carried on by foreign rather than American capital. One million of Dutch capital at three per cent., expecting to realize returns only after twenty years, will be remunerated by a product selling for $1,806,111; but under like circumstances, American capital at seven per cent., must have a return of $3,869,685, or lose.

(3.) Most forms of capital, especially that invested in buildings, machinery, and the like, more or less rapidly wear out, and a sinking-fund must be reserved from gross profits in order to replace the principal. This is the third element in cost of capital, and through this cost, influences the cost of production, and through cost of production, affects, in the manner already pointed out, the value of the product. Suppose there are two commodities A and B produced in two establishments, in each of which is invested a capital of $11,000, in one of which is a machine costing $1000, which is wholly worn out by one year's use, and in the other a machine costing the same sum, which will last however for ten years. Let the rate per cent. be ten, and the time consumed in completing the products be one year. There is a difference in the cost of capital in the two establishments, and this difference indirectly but immediately appears in the value of the respective products. To A must be charged not only $1100, the interest on the capital at the current rate, but also another $1000, wherewith to replace the machine already worn out by the year's production. A cannot be sold without loss for less than $2100. B however will cost less. To it must be charged, as before, $1100, current rate of profit on the capital invested, and only $100 to replace after ten years' use the machine. B therefore can permanently sell without loss for $1200.

Now, then, if my readers are willing to follow me a little further along this dry and dusty road, we shall be able to draw some important conclusions in respect to value as depending on wages and profits. While we have been seeming to attend to only one of the four elements out of which value springs, namely, one effort, of which cost of production is always an exact measure whenever the effort is embodied in a commodity made jointly by paid labor and capital, we have really been attending to the other effort also whenever that effort is similarly embodied; and since gold and silver money is a commodity, like any other, we have incidentally, in this analysis of cost of production, taken some steps towards determining the value of money. Now, cost of production is made up of cost of labor and cost of capital, and the first general conclusion is, that if the cost of labor for any reason be enhanced, nothing can prevent this higher cost from taking effect and exhibiting itself in lower profits. The second conclusion is, that money-wages, or any rise or fall of them, provided they are uniform, or uniformly rise and fall, in those departments of production whose commodities exchange with each other, have no effect at all upon value, since they are common factors in two costs of production, and like all common factors, cancel each other; but any inequality of money-wages in these departments that affects the cost of labor, will have an indirect but controlling influence on the value of the commodities. The same is true of profits. So far as the rate per cent. is common to all branches of production, the capital advanced for the same period, with a similar risk of deterioration or loss, and so far as any one or all of these advance or recede uniformly and together, they do not affect the value of any of the commodities produced. But inequality in any one of these points, varies the relative cost of capital, and consequently, the cost of production, and consequently the value of the product. It is at this point precisely that there is opened up to us a clear view of the influence of machinery upon values. So far as machinery brings into play, as it always does, a gratuitous natural force, it is outside the pale of value; but since the machinery itself is one important form of capital on which rate per cent. must be paid, the more machinery employed relatively to labor in the production of commodities, the more do profits enter into the cost of production, and the more powerfully do changes in the rate per cent., in the time of advance, and in the risk of deterioration, tell upon the value of commodities so produced, as estimated in other commodities. This whole matter is exceedingly well put by Mr. Mill in the fourth chapter of his third book, and I shall here enrich my own pages by transcribing two or three paragraphs from his. .

"All commodities made by machinery are assimilated, at least approximatively, to the wine in the preceding example. In comparison with things made wholly by immediate labor, profits enter more largely into their cost of production. Suppose two commodities A and B, each requiring a year for its production, by means of a capital, which we will on this occasion denote by money, and suppose to be £1000. A is made wholly by immediate labor, the whole £1000 being expended directly in wages. B is made by means of labor which cost £500, and a machine which cost £500, and the machine is worn out by one year's use. The two commodities will be of exactly of the same value;[1] which, if computed in money, and if profits are twenty per cent. per annum, will be £1200. But of this £1200, in the case of A, only £200, or one sixth, is profit; while in the case of B there is not only the £200, but as much of £500, (the price of the machine,) as consisted of the profits of the machine-maker; which, if we suppose the machine also to have taken a year for its production, is again one sixth. So that in the case of A only one sixth of the entire return is profit, whilst in B the element of profit is not only a sixth of the whole, but an additional sixth of a large part.

"The greater the proportion of the whole capital which consists of machinery, or buildings, or material, or anything else

---

[1] Better; the two commodities have exactly the same cost of production.

which must be provided before the immediate labor can commence, the more largely will profits enter into cost of production. It is equally true, though not so obvious at first sight, that greater durability in the portion of capital which consists of machinery or buildings, has precisely the same effect as a greater amount of it. As we have just supposed one extreme case, that of a machine wholly worn out by a year's use, let us now suppose the opposite and still more extreme case, of a machine which lasts forever, and requires no repairs. In this case, which is as well suited for the purpose of an illustration as if it were a possible one, it will be unnecessary that the manufacturer should ever be repaid the £500 which he gave for the machine, since he has always the machine itself worth £500; but he must be paid as before a profit on it. The commodity B therefore, which in the case previously supposed was sold for £1200, of which sum £1000 were to replace the capital, and £200 were profit, can now be sold for £700, being £500 to replace wages, and £200 profit on the entire capital. Profit, therefore, enters into the value of B in the ratio of £200 out of £700, being two sevenths of the whole, or 28$\frac{4}{7}$ per cent., while in the case of A, as before, it enters only in the ratio of one sixth, or 16$\frac{2}{3}$ per cent. The case is of course purely ideal, since no machinery or other fixed capital lasts forever; but the more durable it is, the nearer it approaches this ideal case, and the more largely does profit enter into the return. If for instance, a machine worth £500 loses one fifth of its value by one year's use, £100 must be added to the return to make up this loss, and the price of the commodity will be £800. Profit, therefore, will enter into it in the ratio of £200 to £800, or one fourth, which is still a much higher proportion than one sixth, or £200 to £1200, as in case of A.

"From the unequal proportion in which in different employments profits enter into the advances of the capitalist, and therefore into the returns required by him, two consequences follow in regard to value. One is, that commodities do not exchange in the ratio simply of the quantities of labor required to produce them, not even if we allow for the unequal rates at which different kinds of labor are permanently remunerated. Suppose as before an article A made by £1000 worth of immediate labor. But instead of B made by £500 worth of immediate labor, and a machine worth £500, let us suppose C, made by £500 worth of immediate labor by the aid of a machine which has been produced by another £500 worth of immediate labor; the machine requiring a year for making, and worn out by a year's use; profits being as before twenty per cent. A and C are made by equal quantities of labor, paid at the same rate; A costs £1000 worth of direct labor; C only £500 worth, which however is made up to £1000 by the labor expended in the construction of the machine. If labor, or its remuneration, were the sole ingredient of cost of production, these two things would exchange for one another. But will they do so? Certainly not. The machine having been made in a year by an outlay of £500, and profits being at twenty per cent., the natural price of the machine is £600; making an additional £100, which must be advanced over and above his other expenses, by the manufacturer of C, and repaid to him with a profit of twenty per cent. While therefore the commodity A is sold for £1200, C cannot be permanently sold for less than £1320.

"A second consequence is that every rise or fall of general profits will have an effect on values. Not indeed by raising or lowering them generally, (which is a contradiction and impossibility,) but by altering the proportion in which the values of things are affected by the unequal lengths of time for which profit is due. When two things, though made by equal labor, are of unequal value because the one is called upon to yield profit for a greater number of years or months than the other, this difference of value will be greater when profits are greater, and less when they are less. The wine which has to yield five years' profit more than the cloth, will surpass it in value, and much more if profits are forty per cent., than if they were only twenty. The commodities A and C, which, though made by equal quantities of labor, were sold for £1200 and £1320, a difference of ten per cent., would, if profits had been only half as much, have been sold for £1100 and £1155, a difference of only five per cent. It follows from this that even a general rise of wages, when it involves a real increase in the cost of labor, does in some degree influence values. It does not affect them in the manner vulgarly supposed, by raising them universally. But an increase of the cost of labor lowers profits; and, therefore, lowers in natural value the things into which profits enter in a greater proportion than the average, and raises those into which they enter in a less proportion than the average.

All commodities in the production of which machinery bears a large part, especially if the machinery is very durable, are lowered in their relative value when profits fall; or, what is equivalent, other things are raised in value relatively to them."

In other words, the more, or the more durable the machinery in the production of a commodity, the larger the element of profit in the price now absolutely reduced; on a rise of the rate per cent. therefore, the value of the commodity made by more or more durable machinery will relatively rise.

Having traced completely the influence of machinery on profits, a few things must now be said on its influence upon wages. Formerly the prejudice was almost universal, and is still wide-spread in many parts of the world, that the general introduction of labor-saving appliances does an injury to the laborers by taking away their work. So strongly has this been felt by the laborers, that in England, and especially in Ireland, mobs and riots have usually accompanied the introduction of machinery into those departments of production in which hand-work had previously prevailed. If *work* were what laborers really wanted, the prejudice in question would cease to be such, and become a sound opinion; since the only object and result of introducing machinery is to lessen work, at least with reference to a given product; and the laborers, to be consistent, should not stop with opposing new inventions, but should destroy all forms of existing capital, that there might be work a plenty for simple human hands. What the laborers really want, however, is not work, but wages, or rather, those commodities for which their wages are expended; and the question is, whether labor-saving processes tend to lessen, not work, but work's remuneration. There is no form of proof that I know of, which amounts to a moral demonstration that the substitution of machinery for labor cannot lessen the laborer's wages; the opposite has perhaps sometimes happened, and is possibly liable to happen, especially in agriculture, in certain transitory states of society. But the general appeal can be made to experience with all safety. As a matter of fact and experience, it has not been found true that the introduction of improved processes, the substitution of Nature's forces for human muscle, has deteriorated the condition of laborers in those departments into which the inventions have been brought, or the condition of laborers generally. Exactly the reverse has usually taken place; and wages are apt to be highest rather than lowest in connection with the most and the most durable machinery, and higher rather than lower, after the introduction of more and better machinery. Operatives in manufactories, for instance, are, as a rule, better paid than farm laborers; and better paid in the first class than in the inferior establishments. Teamsters, in this country at least, and I suspect in all countries, are as well to do as before the construction of railroads. So of spinners, weavers, and artisans of every name. In explanation of these general facts, it may be noticed, (1) that labor is always required in the construction and repairs of all kinds of labor-saving appliances, and so far forth, a new market for labor is opened up in place of any loss of market possibly resulting from their introduction; (2) these forms of capital always tend to cheapen the products which they help to create, and such products because they are cheap find a wider circle of consumers, and more must be produced to supply a now broader market, and so far forth the demand for labor may be stronger than it was before; (3) These improvements cheapen also the commodities consumed by the laborers themselves, and therefore a given rate of wages now secures for them a higher grade of comforts. Combining these observations with the law of distribution already pointed out, and the conclusion is fairly established that the effect of machinery is, and will be, rather favorable than otherwise to the laboring classes.

Now, as a result of this entire discussion, attention must be called to a generalization, which has been more or less fully noticed by several writers, and with the presentation of which, this branch of the subject will be concluded. Since, by the aid of the different forms of capital, and such a division of labor as that every part of it is made most efficient, the cost of production of most kinds of manufactured articles tends to decline as compared with the cost of production of food and raw materials, in whose production these advantages are less perfectly attainable, there is a constant tendency towards approximation in the value, and, if money remain unchanged, in the price, of raw materials and of finished products; and in the degree of this approximation will be found a gauge of the success with which gratuitous natural forces and improved facilities of art have been made available in production. This single statement, clearly perceived in its grounds, grasps and holds the principal results of our discussions thus far. Examples of the principle offer themselves on every hand. Let us look at cotton cloth; an example somewhat marred at the present moment by the consequences of the existing war, and disguised by a depreciated currency; but which, allowance being made for these, is an excellent illustration. At the opening of this century, the average price of raw cotton was just about twenty cents a pound; at the middle of the century, and onwards, the average price was just about ten cents a pound. At the first period, although accurate tables are wanting, the average price of cotton cloth could not have been less than sixty cents a yard; at the second period, it could hardly have been more than ten cents a yard. The absolute price of raw cotton diminished in the interval in the ratio of 2 to 1; while the absolute price of cotton cloth diminished in the interval in the ratio of 6 to 1. Relatively to a yard of finished cloth, the raw material greatly rose in value, since at the first it took three pounds to buy a yard, and at the last but one pound. There was a marked approximation all the while of the price of the finished product towards the price of the raw material; in other words, less and less difference of price was due to the cost of manufacture, which lessening cost marks the ever-increasing efficiency in the production of commodities of the gratuitous powers of Nature applied through machinery. According to Dr. Ure, the introduction of machinery into the manufacture of lace, lessened the cost of that product in the ratio of 50 to 1; and thereby, and to that degree, approximated the price of a pound of such lace towards the price of a pound of the cotton from which it was made. Food, raw materials, and labor, and the last more than the other two, tend steadily to advance in their power to command, that is, to buy, most kinds of finished products; and therefore, the millions who labor with their hands, and the other millions who own the soil and till it, have already advanced, and will still more advance, in a scale of comforts, with the advancing centuries.

CHAPTER X.

ON MONEY.

THERE is no use in saying that money is such a mysterious and complicated agent that nobody can understand it. That is the language of indolence. Money is wholly a matter of man's device; it was invented, just as any other instrument is invented, to accomplish a certain purpose; and it would be strange if men cannot comprehend what men themselves have devised. In all departments of God's works, indeed, we constantly meet with what cannot be fully comprehended nor perfectly fathomed, because an infinite mind has been there at work upon an infinite plan. But there is no such profundity in the works of men; unfathomableness is not an attribute of human skill; and since money is an instrument devised by men to aid them in accomplishing a certain purpose, it is as unreasonable to pretend that it is incomprehensible, as it would be to pretend that the steam-engine is incomprehensible. I hold it for certain that whatever men have devised, men can comprehend.

The general purposes which money was designed to answer, and which it is found admirably to fulfil, are best perceived under the supposition that there were no money. Exchanges begun, and were profitable, long before money came into existence. Men first exchanged services directly for each other, without the intervention of any medium. This form of trade is called Barter. Hiram, king of Tyre, furnished to Solomon a certain quantity of cedars from Lebanon, and Solomon, in return, furnished the Tyrians a certain quantity of wheat and oil. This may serve as an instance of barter, although money had been in current use long previously to that transaction, as is seen in the purchase by Abraham of the cave and field of Machpelah, for which he weighed out four hundred shekels of silver, current money with the merchant. It is obvious, however, that while barter is a great deal better than no exchanges at all, there are inherent difficulties in that form of exchange. Under pure barter, exchanges are pretty much limited to those parties each of whom is in position to render to the other such services, and in such quantities, as the other stands in direct and immediate need of; it is not enough, under these conditions, that a man should have a service to sell, but also he must find a man who wants that specific service, and more than this, a man who not only wants that specific service, but also has a service to render in return, such as the first man wants. If A has wheat which he wishes to exchange for a coat, he must find a party who wants wheat, and who also is in position to render a coat in exchange for it, and moreover who wants just as much wheat as will pay for a coat, no more and no less; if he wants more, he may have nothing to render in exchange for the excess which A is willing to accept; if less, A may have nothing which the other wants, besides wheat with which to help pay for the coat. Even in the simpler states of society, the inconvenience, loss of time, and deterioration of commodities involved in direct barter, are very great, and in more advanced states of civilization would be intolerable, if it were possible, as it is not, for society to become advanced under those conditions. Exchanges are so limited in time, place, and variety, association is so hampered, and the development of all peculiar talents so impeded, under a system of simple barter, that one of the initial steps in the progress of all societies has been to hit upon some expedient to lessen these intrinsic difficulties; and so to facilitate exchanges. This expedient has been the invention of money, that is to say, the selection of some product, which, by general consent, instead of the particular purchasing-power of common commodities, should have a universal purchasing-power; so that, whenever anybody has anything to exchange, he may first exchange it for this product, whatever it be, and then with this product purchase at any time and place, whatever he may want. Money makes no alteration in any law of value, but merely substitutes for convenience' sake in every transaction in which it plays a part, a universal for a specific purchasing-power; a book, for example, has a specific purchasing-power; there is somebody who wants it, and is willing to give a sum of money for it; and the owner by the sale of it parts with a product which has only the power to purchase something from a few persons, and receives a product which has the power to purchase something from all persons; it is not true to say that the book is worth more than the money, or the money is worth more than the book, because they are just worth each other, as is demonstrated by the sale; but it is true to say that the seller of the book has substituted in the place of a limited purchasing-power, of which he was proprietor, a general purchasing-power, of which he has now become proprietor; and that the command of the money, which has no more value than the book had, does carry along with it a superior command over purchasable articles generally. In one word, value in the form of money is in a more available shape for general purchasing, than value in any other form. This is the exact expression for what truth there is in the common vague remark, that money is different from all other commodities; in point of value, it is different from other commodities in just one respect, namely, while they have the power of buying some sorts of things from some persons, it has the power, derived from the usages of society, to buy all sorts of things from all persons.

It might seem, at first sight, as if the introduction of money, instead of simplifying the operations of exchange, would only complicate them, since it necessitates two exchanges, where otherwise there would be but one; but reflection, as well as experience, is able to convince us that there is no machine which economizes labor like money; no instrument which plays so important a part in production; no invention, unless it be the invention of letters, which has contributed more to the civilization of mankind. While men still exchanged in kind, and knew no other mode, the purchasing-power of a service was very much confined in place, and would not be parted with except in view of the return service actually there present, the ultimate parties to an exchange must for the most part come together locally, in order to effect an exchange; under a money system, this is no longer necessary, for it is sufficient to constitute a market for any commodity that it is wanted anywhere on the globe, the middle man, paying the seller for it in money, transports it thither, and receives back his money with a profit from the ultimate consumer. Thus money brings conveniently buyers and sellers together commercially, no matter how far separated locally. So, also, money generalizes any purchasing-power in point of time. The fruit-dealer, for example, must dispose of his product quickly, or it perishes on his hands, but by transmuting his perishable product into money, he may keep its power of purchase locked in this form as long as he lists; the money, indeed, is only good to purchase with, but it puts an interval at the pleasure of the holder between selling and buying, and with this generalized power in his pocket he may buy when he will, and what he will, and where he will. Money, too, makes any purchasing-power portable, divisible, and loanable. A man may carry the value of his farm in his purse, and may divide it up for a thousand different purchases, and especially is able to loan it in this form, to receive it back again with interest at a future day. Value in any other form than money is not generally suitable for loaning, because there are comparatively few who are willing to borrow a merely specific purchasing-power, and guarantee its return in that form with the due increase; but money, as a generalized agent, will command all services at all times, will serve at any man's bidding, and work in all sorts of harness, and therefore it is rarely difficult for men to loan any sums of money they have not immediate use for, and to make every moment of their own abstinence pay tribute in interest, and the advantages to both lenders and borrowers secured through this form of value — money — are incalculable. Thus we see the reason why governments, corporations, and individuals, when they borrow, borrow money. This general view of the uses and advantages of money will show it to be one of the most potent of the social agents, and will serve also to introduce our first specific proposition.

1. *Money is a medium of exchange.*

The word medium in this proposition, is to be taken in its etymological and strict sense, as something that comes between two extremes, and serves also to relate them to each other. Money is only a medium of exchange, and not a real subject of exchange; it is a very great help in exchanging all other things, but is never exchanged for itself in an ultimate transaction. Small boys, indeed, swap cents, but men, the miser excepted, who is under a deplorable fallacy of the senses, use and estimate money only as the medium which facilitates the real exchanges of society. What is really exchanged is the wheat, the cloth, the lumber, the furniture, the service of every kind, and money is but the instrument making these exchanges easy, which might indeed go on without it, though with difficulty and loss. It is like a railroad ticket. What you want is to be carried to a certain place in the cars. That is what you really buy and pay for, but for convenience, merely, a ticket is given you, as evidence of the purchase. You care nothing about the ticket, except that it insures to you a seat. It is a mere bit of paper, but it stands you in good stead when the conductor comes along. It comes in as a medium between the railroad company and you, and while it facilitates the real exchange, at the same time it somewhat disguises it. It is exactly so with money, only money, instead of being a specific ticket for one purpose, is a general ticket for all purposes of purchase. We do not care anything about money, any more than we do about the ticket. We part with it freely and constantly for those things which we do care about. What we really care for is what the money will buy, is the command over all services and commodities which the possession of money insures. If we could give our own service or commodity, whatever it is, and receive directly in return the service or commodity which we want, whatever it is, there would be no need of money. This is generally inconvenient, and sometimes impossible. Therefore we introduce a middle term between the two extreme terms. Money is only a mean which helps exchange the two extremes. And the value of the money of any country is a very small fraction, probably not over one fortieth, of the value of that which it helps to exchange. By the last census the estimated value of real and personal property in the United States was, in round numbers, $16,000,000,000. The whole currency of the country in 1860 was certainly less than $400,000,000; so that the money of the country stood to its aggregate material wealth in the ratio

at least of one to forty. Besides all that portion
of this real and personal property which changed
hands in that year, the currency helped to exchange
all the simple services, as those of professional men,
teachers, servants, and so on, which were rendered
in that year, and which are not included in the census estimate, except partially and indirectly, so far
as the returns to such services had been transformed
into real and personal property. If we suppose that
transactions to the value of \$16,000,000,000, were
concluded in this country in the year 1860, and
that \$400,000,000 constituted the money in circulation, then it follows that each dollar of money circulated on the average forty dollars of value, or,
what is the same thing, each dollar of the circulation made on the average forty payments, in the
course of the year. It is, of course, impossible to
determine with exactness the aggregate value of
the money exchanges of any country for any given
period, but if this could be determined, and should
then be regarded as a dividend, for which the aggregate money of the country were a divisor, the quotient would express what has been called the rapidity
of circulation, that is, the number of times which
each dollar changes hands on the average in order to
effect the given amount of exchanges; and it would
also express how many more times the value of that
is which the money of a country helps to exchange,
than its own value is. That it should express this
last, however, accurately, we must suppose that the
same product is exchanged by the help of money
only once between the producer and the consumer.
Probably the ratio of one to forty is below rather

than above the true ratio of the aggregate money of the commercial nations to the money value of those products, reckoned only once, which this money helps to exchange. Therefore we see that the hub and spokes, and rim of the wheel of exchange consist of services and commodities of every description; while, to borrow the famous comparison of Hume, money is but the grease which makes the wheel turn easier. It is a vast mistake to suppose that the grease is the wheel itself.

Hume's comparison, though exact as far as it goes, and for the purposes for which he used it, is nevertheless capable of misleading the mind. It is true that money is the grease which facilitates the revolution of the wheel of exchange, but it is also true that the dimensions of the wheel itself are vastly greater than they would have been had it not been for money. Money indeed helped exchange the products that already existed at its first invention, but by far the largest part of products since have come into existence largely through the agency of money. We get quite too low a view of the function of this potent agent, if we think of it merely as an aid in circulating products that would have existed whether or no; some products would have existed whether or no, and money certainly is of great use and convenience in helping bring these to the ultimate consumers; but this is a partial and wholly inadequate view of the true function of money as a medium of exchange. The fact that such a medium is in universal circulation, and that the holders of it are ready to exchange it against any sort of services adapted to gratify their desires, exercises a kind of creative power, and brings a thousand products to the market which would otherwise never have come into existence. Since money will buy anything, men are on the alert to bring forward something which will buy money; and since money is divisible into small pieces, an incredible number and variety of small services are brought forward to be exchanged against these pieces, which services we have no reason to suppose would ever be brought forward at all, were it not for the strong attraction of the money. In this point of view, the true nature of money is best perceived, when it is considered, as it really is, as a very important portion of the capital of the world. Capital, as we have already learned, is any product reserved to be employed in further production. The circulating medium of any country is the most active, the most profitable, and the most essential of all those instruments reserved in aid of further production. The axe, the plough, the spindle, the loom, the wheel, the engine, are all instruments, are all capital, and they each aid respectively some part or parts of the processes of production; but money is a form of capital which stimulates and facilitates all the processes of production without exception. Just as we have seen that money is a form of value generalized, so is it also a generalized form of capital, that is to say, it is an instrument capable of aiding all production in every department, while every other instrument is capable of aiding but few processes in one department. Without money, there could be no thorough division of labor, because there would be no adequate means of estimating or rewarding each one's share in a complicated process. By means of money, all services, small or great, contributing toward a common product, are neatly measured and paid for by some one, who thereby becomes proprietor of the whole product; or, if the contributors chose, they may wait till the product itself is sold, and then the money received is divisible without loss to each contributor, according to the service rendered. Thus the influence of money, as capital, pervades the whole field of exchange, from centre to circumference, facilitating every transfer, and stimulating to new transfers.

Money, then, is a medium of exchange; and the question arises in this connection, how much of it is wanted? Clearly, only so much as will serve the purposes which such a medium is fitted to subserve; there should be enough fairly to mediate between the services actually ready to be exchanged then and there, and also enough fairly to call out other services, proper and profitable in the then circumstances of society, and whose only obstacle to a profitable exchange then and there, is the lack of a facilitating medium. All increase of money beyond this point, which the very nature of money itself marks out as the boundary, leads to an inevitable depreciation of the whole mass, to a consequent disturbance of all existing money contracts, to a universal rise of prices which are illusory and gainless, to unsteadiness and derangement in all legitimate business, and to a spirit of restless enterprise and speculation, which seeks to draw off the excess of money in untried and reckless experiments. These consequences from this cause have been again and again witnessed in every commercial country, and in the United States on a gigantic scale during the past three years. I cannot help thinking that Mr. Carey, who has thrown so much light on certain portions of the field of Political Economy, is decidedly in the wrong in the view he maintains that there cannot be too much money in any country. No writer has brought out more clearly than he has, the intimate relations of money with all industrial development; but he seems at times to forget that money, essential and potent as it is, is essential and potent only as a *medium*. The real subjects of exchange are mutual efforts, mutual services, and money is the instrument merely that comes in between the real services exchanged to facilitate the exchange; and therefore it seems to me to be perfectly conclusive on the point to remark, that the quantity of money needed in any country, or in the whole world, is limited by the number of the services ready to be exchanged, to facilitate the exchange of which is the only purpose and end of money. The physical and mental powers of men, which alone give birth to services, when considered, as they must be in this connection, as belonging to a given number of men at a given time and place, are strictly limited; and although the presence of money then and there is both a stimulus and an aid to their bringing forward services of all sorts to the market, there are obvious limitations both in their powers and in their circumstances; and the quantity of money needed among them is just that quantity which will fairly act as a medium in exchanging the services which they are able and willing to render to each other. All increase in the quantity of money beyond that point would have, and could have, the only effect of increasing the nominal prices of services, without making the services themselves any greater in number or better in quality. It is with money exactly as it is with any other form of capital, allowance being made for the fact that money is a kind of generalized capital. How many ships does a commercial nation need to employ? As many as will fairly take off its exports and bring in its imports. Ships are wanted for one definite purpose; and when enough are secured to answer that purpose, all additions to the number will lessen the value, that is, the purchasing-power of ships generally. So of all instruments whatever. Enough is as good as a feast. Enough is better than more. In regard to every form of capital, the point of sufficiency is determined by the quantity of work to be done. Now, money is a form of capital, an instrument, having this peculiarity only, that it is capable of aiding to a certain extent all branches of production; and the point of sufficiency in the quantity of money for a country, or for the world, is determined by the amount of products of all kinds, otherwise ready to be exchanged, and only waiting the facilitating agency of an exchange medium. The quantity of money being given, an increased aggregate of exchanges can be facilitated by it, by means of a greater rapidity of circulation of that given quantity. $400,000,000, changing hands forty times, will effect exchanges to an aggregate of $16,000,000,000 in a year; the same sum, by a circulation doubly rapid, will effect twice that aggregate of exchanges; so that, it follows, that an increased amount of business to be done, does not necessarily require an increased volume of money, but sometimes only a brisker use of that already in circulation. As in mechanics, so in money, the whole power is the product of the two factors, mass and velocity. Money is like any other tool, the more constant its use the more profitable its agency. If $16,000,000,000 of value are to be exchanged, it is very much cheaper that $400,000,000 of money should do the work, changing hands forty times, than that $800,000,000 should be employed, changing hands only twenty times. The quick movement of a small mass is better than the torpid movement of a big mass, both in what it saves of expense, and in what it presupposes of the general conditions of exchange. It only remains under this proposition to add, what will be more clearly perceived when we come to treat of foreign trade, that no enterprising commercial nation, so long as the natural right of exchange is left unimpeded, and so long as the money of the nations consists of gold and silver, or paper, the genuine representative of these, can ever lack, for any great length of time, a sufficient quantity of money to serve as its medium of exchange.

2. *Money is a measure of value.*

I hope it was made very plain, under the preceding proposition, what is meant when it is said that money is a medium of exchange. Closely commingled with its function as a medium, money has another very delicate function, as a measure of value. How important this second function is may be seen by supposing for a moment that there were no instrument in existence capable of performing it. Without a common measure of values of different sorts, it would be inconvenient, not to say impossible, to carry on traffic at all. For instance: A baker has only loaves of bread, and wishes to buy a hat, a horse, a house. How many loaves shall he give for each? Without some common denomination in which these differing values can be expressed, and by means of which they can be brought into numerical relations with each other, it would be an awkward piece of business to effect even the three exchanges; and every time he wished to purchase another article, there must be an independent calculation from different data, to decide the terms of the exchange. Introduce now some common denominations in which each of these values can express itself, and the difficulty disappears in an instant. " My loaves are worth ten cents each," says the baker. " My hat is worth ten dollars," says the hatter. The terms of exchange, then, are 100 for 1, and no parleying. So of the rest; so of everything that is ever bought or sold. Dollars and cents are the denominations in which values are reckoned, and by which they can be compared with each other numerically, just as feet and inches are the denominations by which different lengths are compared, and pints and quarts the denominations by which capacity is measured; and the builder and the surveyor would not be more at a loss in their work without the units of length, or the vintner without the units of capacity, than everybody would be at a loss without the units of value. Dollars and cents are, as it were, the language in which values express themselves; and, without some such language, the busiest marts of exchange would soon become not only a silent but a deserted scene.

The difference between money as a medium and money as a measure is one that should be clearly delineated and perfectly apprehended, because there is no such thing as adequately understanding the subject of money unless the two functions be kept distinct in the mind, as well in their single as in their commingled action. There is the same difference between money as a medium and money as a measure that there is between a bushel of wheat and that round vessel by which we determine that there is a bushel: dollars and cents perform their duties as a medium by virtue of their being commodities; they perform their duties as a measure by virtue of their being denominations. For example: A Berkshire woollen-manufacturer goes to market to buy wool, and calls on five dealers, each of whom demands a certain price, and in conversation with each of whom, consequently, our manufacturer uses money as a measure; that is to say, uses the denominations as a means of comparison; but with that one only with whom a bargain is consummated does he use money as a medium; that is to say, pay it out in exchange. The distinction between denominations and those things themselves which are reckoned by denominations seems a very obvious distinction, and one would suppose the two not likely to be confounded; but, the truth is, the two are perpetually confounded, even in some of the most recent and approved works on money. Indeed, the grand difficulty and source of error in discussions on money heretofore has been that this distinction has rarely, if ever, been consistently attended to; and I flatter myself that I am doing the science a service at this point by calling attention to this confusion, by explaining how it arises, and by clearing up, so far forth, a vexed portion of the subject.

How does it happen that money is constantly confounded with the denominations in which it is reckoned, while feet and inches are never confounded with lumber or lath, pints and quarts with milk or beer, acres and rods with meadows or pastures? The reason is this: all other tables of denominations have a basis independent of the things which they measure, and are not variable by the quality or quantity of those measurable things. A French metre, for example, is an invariable unit of length the world over; so is one of Troughton's inches; but this is not true of the denominations of money at all. Pounds, dollars, guilders, francs, and their subdivisions, are denominations of *value*, which is a variable relation, and as denominations they follow the fortunes of the coins whose names they are. When the current dollar, for instance, sinks to one half, or rises to twice, its previous purchasing-power, we call it a dollar all the while, the denomination perpetually shifting with every variation of the thing, and the illusions and mistakes are numberless which result from calling a thing which is no longer the same as before by the same name as before. Mr. Charles Moran, in his late interesting book on "Money," quotes approvingly from the "Edinburgh Review" the following sentence: — " Were an ounce of gold to fall to one tenth of its present cost of production, or to cost ten times as much labor as it does now, still, while the regulations of the mint are unaltered, it will be worth £3 17*s.* 10½*d.*"[1] Here is an instance of perfect confusion between the name pounds and the thing pounds. No doubt, under either of the conditions supposed, the result would be as stated so far as pounds, shillings, and pence are denominations; but so far as pounds, shillings, and pence are purchasing-powers, there would be a difference in their value under the two conditions, other things being equal, of 1 to 100. The denominations of value, then, are not an independent standard to which values themselves can be referred, as lengths are referred to the metre, but vary with the varying purchasing-power of the coins, so that money as a measure is only uniform when money as a medium is uniform. So indispensable, however, in all exchanges is some common measure of value, that the denominations of money, notwithstanding their variable character, are universally employed in estimating and exchanging commodities, even when no money as a medium is used.

Without reflection, it might be supposed, that, since the measure rises and falls with the medium, no practical error is liable to follow the confounding of the two functions; but it is the very sympathetic connection between the two that gives rise to the possibility of error. If the units of money were, like the linear units, inflexible, so that all variations of the medium could be instantly detected by a reference to the standard of measure, there would be no difficulty at all: I could loan a thousand dollars

[1] Money, by Charles Moran. New York. 1863. Page 66.

for one year, or ten years, and, however much the medium might vary in the interval, be sure that I should receive back just as much purchasing-power as I loaned, with the interest on the same; it might be more or fewer *dollars* than the number I loaned, which is a matter of indifference. As it is, no lender can have any such assurance. The borrower is bound to pay back with interest the same number of dollars as he received, although the dollar-medium, and hence the dollar-measure, may meanwhile have fallen or risen greatly. In the United States, for the past three years, the current money has exchanged against gold from 130 to 285 of the one for 100 of the other; and it is very obvious that all debts of old standing, paid in this period, have been only legally, and not actually, liquidated; and that debts contracted when the depreciation was more and paid when it was less were more than actually liquidated. This, of course, presupposes, what we are not yet in a position to assume, that gold remained a proper and uniform standard. The subtle error to be avoided alike in discussion and in practice is, to suppose that money, either as a medium or as a measure, remains unchanged, simply because the name remains unchanged by which we designate its denominations.

It may be asked, why cannot this source of error be obviated? I reply, that the error may be obviated, but the source of it cannot be obviated from the nature of the case. It was shown in our chapter on Value that to find an invariable measure of value is a natural impossibility. Money, as it is the medium of exchange, is also the best attainable measure of value, and is used throughout the civilized world to compare with each other all values except its own; but since value in general, and the value of money as well, is a thing of relation, and varies with every change affecting either of the things exchanged, as much by changes affecting the things it exchanges for as by changes affecting itself,— the value of a hat, for instance, as estimated in gloves, increasing by any cheapened process in glove-making, though no change at all take place in the cost of hat-making,— a perfect measure of value is impossible. Therefore the denominations of money, which is the best attainable measure, can never have a meaning absolutely fixed, but slide up and down the scale along which the purchasing-power of money as a medium is moving, and they are consequently useless as a standard to detect any changes in the medium itself, while, the medium remaining uniform, they instantly detect the changes in all other purchasing-powers. This will always be so. The same difficulty does not occur in having a perfect measure of length or of capacity,— a perfect inch or a perfect pint. The French have a perfect system of measures and weights. Their mathematicians measured an arc of the earth's circumference, and thus determined the absolute length of a degree of latitude. Three hundred and sixty times this length makes up the length of the earth's circumference,—an invariable measure recoverable again even if it should be once lost. This measure divided by 40,000,000 gave the French nation their *metre*, which is a perfect unit for the measure of length. A tenth part of the metre cubed gave them their *litre*, which is a perfect unit for the measure of capacity. The weight of a hundredth part of a metre cubed of distilled water at the temperature of maximum density is the *gramme*, an invariable unit of weight. A linear length of ten metres squared gives the *are*, the unit of surface. A perfect measure of anything demands for its starting-point something absolute and invariable: in value there is nothing absolute; we begin with a relation, and therefore an unchangeable measure is not to be looked for. Still, it is vastly important for the interest of exchange that the accepted measure of value be as little liable to fluctuations as possible, especially in all cases in which lapse of time is involved before the exchange is fully consummated. For precisely the same reason that the bushel-measure should be of the same capacity in sowing-time and in harvest, to sell by and buy by, always a bushel, no more and no less; and the yard-stick an inflexible measure of length, the same for buyer and seller, always thirty-six of Troughton's inches, no more and no less; so, as far as it is possible in the nature of things, ought the measure and the denominations of value to represent year in and year out a uniform degree of purchasing-power. All experience has shown that it is much easier to find something which will serve as a medium of exchange, and thus answer the first purpose of money, than to find anything which will serve permanently as a measure of value, and thus answer the second and more delicate purpose of money. The two functions of money are indeed often commingled, for while money helps to exchange values, it also at the same time in a manner measures them, but they are also quite as often separated, as when a hundred dollars' worth of goods is sold to be paid for six months hence; and we have just now seen the radical reasons why no money which is not tolerably uniform in its value as a medium can even tolerably perform its function as a measure. This consideration brings us naturally to our third specific proposition.

3. *Gold and silver constitute the best money.*

The purposes of money have been served in different countries and in different ages by a variety of products, according to the taste and circumstances of the people. Cattle have been employed as money among pastoral people in almost all periods of the world, and are still employed for this purpose in Africa. Slaves among the Anglo-Saxons; wampum among the American Indians; salt in Abyssinia; codfish in Newfoundland; tobacco in Virginia; wheat in Massachusetts; nails in Scotland; stamped leather among the Carthaginians, and others; bark stamped with the image of the sovereign in China; platina in Russia; copper, simple or compounded with other metals, among the ancient Romans, and most other nations; iron among the Spartans; gold and silver among all civilized nations sooner or later; have been or still are used as money. Of all these products, the two last have shown themselves to be best adapted for the purposes of money, and have come consequently into universal use in the commercial world. Experience has not only demonstrated the superiority of these metals over all other forms of money, as is shown by the fact of their universal adoption, but reason also is able to tell us why gold and silver are the best money.

(1.) *On account of their comparatively steady value.* This is the main reason, and it must be firmly grasped. There is no end to the confusion which has crept over discussions on money from the circumstance that the writers have not first of all determined for themselves with fixed clearness what value is. This must be done at the outset, if there is to be the least hope of sound results; and accordingly those writers have succeeded best in their treatment of money who have made its discussion a part of a general theory of value. Mr. Moran, who has treated money distinctively, and whose book is in many respects an excellent one, has failed at this point, and for this reason. He does not exactly know what value is, and consequently he does not exactly know what money is. He speaks of "intrinsic value," of circulating-coin "as losing for the time its intrinsic value," of "metallic money as identical with paper money in respect of being destitute of intrinsic value," and so on.[1] Now, value is value, and there is only one kind of it, and the epithet intrinsic is only used to help out a lame theory, and no such epithet is pertinent to the word value, and no one can show anything different in the value of money, either in respect to the way in which it arises, or in the laws which control it, from the value of any other commodity, excepting only the difference already pointed out, that money by the usages of society has a generalized instead of a specific purchasing-power. It is all false to speak of gold

[1] Page 26, note.

and silver money as the representative of value. It represents nothing but itself. It will buy other things certainly, and so will a bushel of wheat. Value is simple purchasing-power, and money has value because we can purchase with it, exactly as everything else has value for that very reason. Society is so constituted that a want is felt in it of some medium of purchase; this want cannot be supplied without an effort; whoever makes the effort will demand a corresponding effort made for him; when it comes to the exchange of the medium for the wheat, for example, there stand face to face, as in every other instance of exchange, two desires and two efforts; there is then, as always, a reciprocal estimation of the two services about to be exchanged, and the estimation agreed on is the *value* of the medium expressed in wheat. If the want of any medium of exchange is less felt in any community, or if the effort required to secure it be for any reason less, other things remaining the same, the value of the money will be less, that is to say, it will purchase less of other things. If the demand for money as an instrument of purchase be greater, or the obstacles in the way of its supply be increased, other things as before, the value of the money will be more. It is the old circuit over again of wants, efforts, estimations, satisfactions. The value of money arises under the same conditions as every other value, and is variable by any change in any one of the four elements which alone can vary the value of anything. Two desires and two efforts invariably precede every exchange. A change in any one of these, the rest unchanged, can vary value, and nothing else can vary it; and, as it seems to me, no person has ever shown or can show that the value of money is in any respect, save the superficial one already noticed, exceptional and peculiar. And it also seems to me that nothing more is needed in order to remove the last vestiges of the dark cloud which has so long overhung this subject, than to familiarize one's self first of all with the true doctrine of value in general, and then hold fast the truth, exemplified on every side, that the value of money is just like any other value.

Gold and silver, then, as money, have value in the same sense and for the same reason as any other productive instrument, and we must now attend to the reasons why their value is so steady.

(*a.*) On account of the comparatively steady demand for these metals. Gold and silver are wanted for two general purposes: first, to be used as money, and second, to be used in the arts; and it has been estimated that about two fifths of the aggregate quantity in the world is in the form of money, and the other three fifths in the form of plate, utensils, and ornaments. Now, so far as the element of desire controls value, the purpose for which any article is desired is a matter of indifference. The aggregate desire for it for all purposes, accompanied with the offer of something with which to buy it, constitutes the demand; and the more universal the desire, no matter for what purpose, the steadier the demand, and, so far forth, the steadier the value. It is worth noticing, in opposition to Moran and others, that it is not the demand for the precious metals as coin alone that determines their general value, nor the demand for them in the arts, but the combined demand for all purposes; just as the value of barley is regulated, partly by the demand for it for food, and partly by the demand for it for malting purposes. Hence an ounce of bullion of the standard fineness, destined for the smelting-pot of the artisan, is worth within a very trifle as much as an ounce of coined money. By the law of the Bank of England an ounce of standard gold is coined into £3 17s. 10½d., and the Bank is obliged to buy all bullion and foreign coins of the standard fineness offered to it at £3 17s. 9d. per ounce — a difference of three halfpennies. Now, gold and silver are so indispensable in the form of money, so beautiful in the form of ornaments, so well adapted to serve the purposes of luxury and love of distinction, so really useful in the arts, that the demand for them is constant and well-nigh universal; and if, in the progress of civilization, a less quantity should be desired for personal ornamentation and purposes of luxury, a greater will doubtless be required for the other uses; and so, as the demand in the past has been steady, and perhaps steadily increasing, there is every reason to expect the same for the time to come. And it contributes to the steadiness in value of the gold and silver coin, that there is at hand in the form of plate a reservoir from which a chance chasm in the coin may be replenished, or an extra demand for it answered.

(b.) On account of their tolerably uniform cost of production. Not desires alone, but efforts as well, regulate value. Supply is the correlative of demand; and when to a steady demand there answers a steady supply, realized under conditions of pretty uniform difficulty, there will be of course a pretty steady value. Nature herself has indicated, in a manner not to be mistaken, her intention that these metals should be the money of the nations. She has scattered them all over the earth, and so scattered them that the cost of their production has been wonderfully uniform ever since civilization and commerce begun. There have been but two marked changes in the value of gold and silver throughout the commercial world in the last thousand years; the first, in the sixteenth century, in consequence of the occupation of Mexico and South America by Europeans, when the value of the precious metals diminished, according to Chevalier, silver in the ratio of 1 to 3, and gold considerably less; the second, in consequence of the discovery of the gold-fields of California and Australia in the present century, which has still further diminished the value of gold perhaps twenty-five per cent. With these exceptions, and similar ones are not likely to recur, these metals have always maintained and are likely to maintain a remarkable uniformity of value, on account of a remarkably uniform cost of production. Even these changes became only gradually perceptible, and did but little injury to individuals, scarcely disturbing the justice of exchange or the measure of value, except in cases of long annuities and similar obligations. A universal rise of prices soon adjusted exchanges to the new state of things.

(c.) On account of their quantity. The amount of gold and silver in circulation in the commercial world, to say nothing of the quantity so easily brought into circulation from the reservoir of plate, is so vast, that it receives the annual contributions from the mines much as the ocean receives the waters of the rivers, without sensible increase of its volume, and parts with the annual loss by detrition and shipwreck, as the sea yields its waters to evaporation, without sensible diminution of volume. The yearly supply and the yearly waste are small in comparison with the accumulations of ages; and therefore the relation of the whole mass to the uses of the world, and the purchasing-power of any given portion, remain comparatively steady. It is probable that production at the mines might cease altogether for a considerable interval without very sensibly enhancing throughout the commercial world the value of gold; as it is certain, from experience, that a production very largely augmented only gradually, and after a considerable interval, diminishes its value. The mass of the precious metals has been aptly compared to the heavy balance-wheel in mechanics, which preserves an equable and working condition of the machinery under any sudden increase of the power, and even when the power is for a moment withdrawn. At this point a caution is needful. Because it is affirmed that the great amount of the precious metals is a ground of their firm value, it must not be supposed that we are going beyond our general doctrine, and introducing another element, namely, quantity, besides the four elements which, as we have so often alleged, can alone vary the value of any service; quantity, in itself, is not an element capable of varying the value of anything, but taken in connection with durability, it is an element of what might, perhaps, with propriety be called the *inertia* of value, and tends to keep the purchasing-power of gold and silver where it is. Value and steadiness of value are two distinct ideas. The present value of an ounce of gold expressed in any other commodity is decided by four things alone; but other elements besides these may help determine that that ounce of gold shall have ten years from now a purchasing-power approximately the same as now. It will depend, of course, in the last analysis, upon the relation of the then demand to the then supply; yet the vast quantity of the precious metals in existence, combined with their durability, prevent those fluctuations in the supply which are so destructive to a steady value. It is not as with the fruits and the grains, whose value varies perpetually with the seasons, and which are so perishable that they must be sold soon or never: gold and silver are almost indestructible, and except by wear and accident, the existing mass is not liable to be lessened, and in so far as the annual production from the mines exceeds the yearly waste there is a natural provision made for the natural increase of demand, to supply the wants of the world for currency and for the arts, without much disturbing the relation of the demand and supply. The quantity, in connection with the durability of the precious metals, helps preserve to them a tolerably steady value from generation to generation.

(*d.*) On account of their fluency. Gold and silver are in demand the world over. Having great value in comparatively small bulk, they are easily transported from continent to continent; and whenever, from any cause, they become relatively in excess in any country, and thus lose there a portion of their previous purchasing-power, there is an immediate motive to export them to other countries where their power in exchange is greater, and thus the equilibrium is restored. The value of gold and silver throughout the commercial world is thus kept pretty steady by the facility with which they are carried from points where they are relatively in excess to points where they are relatively in deficiency. There is a gain in carrying them to those countries where their power of purchase is the greatest, because more commodities can be obtained for them than at home; and private motives here coincide with public welfare, since what the traders do in transporting gold and silver, with an eye to their own interest, helps maintain at home and abroad the steady value of these commodities. This law of the distribution of the precious metals by commerce, and the equilibrium of value resulting therefrom, is as natural and beautiful as the law which preserves the level of the ocean, or that which balances the bodies of the planetary system. This has come at length to be recognized by the nations, and the laws which used to forbid by heavy penalties the exportation of gold and silver are all swept away, and these metals are now free to go, and do actually go, where they can obtain the most in exchange. It is absurd to suppose that their owners would carry them out of a country, unless they were worth more abroad than at home, and therefore the prejudice which exists still in this country against the exportation of gold is a senseless prejudice. The gold is not given away; it is sold, and sold for more than it will buy at home; otherwise it would not be carried abroad. There is the same kind of gain as in all other exchanges, and this great incidental advantage in addition, that, by means of free commerce in the precious metals, their general value is kept pretty uniform throughout the world, and a chance redundancy in one currency is drawn off to supply a corresponding deficiency in another. It may be laid down as an axiom, that no country will export, for the sake of getting other things, those things which are more needful for its own welfare; and there need not be the slightest fear that any nation which cultivates its own advantages under freedom will ever lack a sufficient quantum of the precious metals. Under freedom, and so long as human nature continues what it is, these metals will go, and go in just the right proportions, to and from those countries which produce and offer in exchange those desirable services which other countries want. The greater the enterprise and skill, the keener the development of all peculiar and presently available resources, the more honorable and free the commercial system, the surer is any nation, whether it be a gold-bearing country or not, of securing the gold and silver which it needs. This is so, because *there* will be a good market to buy in, and they who have gold will resort thither to buy. But such a nation will also want to buy other things besides gold and silver, and when enough of the latter are secured for the currency and for the arts, the residue will be exported, perhaps to the very countries from which it originally came, in payment for some products which those countries have an advantage in producing.

The United States is a gold-producing country, and exported in the years 1850–1860, both inclusive, $502,789,759, coin and bullion; and during the same period we imported from other countries $81,270,571, coin and bullion.[1] Now, there was a double advantage in that exportation. In the first place, more and better commodities were secured to the country than the gold could have bought in the country, for otherwise it would not have been carried abroad; and, in the second place, this large sum carried abroad to various countries in exchange, not only prevented the disturbing effect on our own currency of more than doubling in ten years' time our stock of gold, thus inevitably depreciating the whole mass, but also, by causing the new gold to impinge on the whole world's stock instead of on the currency of a single nation, the shock of the new production on the measure of value, though perceptible, was reduced and deadened. The world's mass of the precious metals is comparatively torpid beneath the action of an accretion which would break down by its weight the currency of a single nation. Therefore, the fluency of gold and silver, by which they pass easily in commerce to those places where their present value in exchange is greatest, and return as easily when the conditions are reversed, tends powerfully to make their general value uniform throughout the world, and consequently to make them the best medium of exchange and the best measure of value.

(*e.*) On account of this circumstance, that every general rise or fall in the value of gold and silver tends to check itself. This principle, indeed, is ap-

[1] Report on the Finances, 1863.

plicable to the value of all commodities, but owing to their quantity and durability preëminently applicable to the value of the precious metals. The check is double in either direction. First, let us suppose that the purchasing-power of an ounce of gold or silver be rising: then, production will be stimulated at all the mines, and the more stimulated as the rise is more, and the new and enlarged supply will tend to check a farther rise, and, unless the permanent demand has been intensified, to bring back the value to the old point; moreover, when there is a rise in the value of the coin, there is a less quantity required to do the same amount of business, and the demand for gold which causes the rise tends to be checked by the rise itself, because a less quantity is needed in the currency in consequence of the rise. This supposes, of course, that the exchanges mediated by money are no greater than before. Thus a rise of value in gold and silver checks itself by natural laws in two ways. Just so of a fall in their value. Production is thereby slackened at the mines, and the lessened supply tends to enhance value; and, if the same business is to be done as before, there is a stronger demand for currency while the fall continues, and this demand tends also to restore the value. All this is in the interest of a steady value.

(*f.*) On account, lastly, of this circumstance, that a stronger demand for currency is met either by increasing the stock of coin, or by an increased rapidity of circulation of that on hand. A brisker demand for money, especially if it be temporary, does not necessarily enlarge the supply, or alter the value, but only hurry round the existing circulation.

Oscillations in the demand are responded to by a slower or more rapid circulation. This tends most admirably to keep the value steady within certain limits. When enterprises are multiplying and exchanges are being permanently increased in number and variety, then there must be a larger amount of money, and this larger amount is secured in the ways already indicated, with perhaps slight disturbances of value; but the temporary ebbs and flows of business have no effect at all on the mass of money, but only on its movement, and its value consequently is not disturbed at all.

These six grounds appear to be satisfactory and sufficient to account for the superior steadiness of the value of gold and silver, so far as their value is determined by considerations relating to the metals themselves. We now proceed to the reasons additional to this why gold and silver constitute the best money.

(2.) *Because they are self-regulating.* These metals came to be, and continue to be, money, independent of the enactments of any government. Government indeed coins them for the use of the people; but coinage is nothing in the world but a public attest to the quantity and quality of the metal contained in the coin. For the trouble and expense of assaying, stamping, and thus attesting the quantity and quality of the metal in the coin, governments usually charge the depositors of bullion a small seigniorage; England, France, and the United States charging at present for gold coins, respectively, three half-pennies per ounce, which is coined into £3 17s. 10½d., ⅓ of 1 per cent., and ½ of 1 per cent.; so that a very insignificant part of the value of coins is due to the process of coining. The value of coined money regulates itself on just the same principles as the value of wheat regulates itself, and governments are as powerless to alter the one as the other. Indeed, the coining of either metal by itself is a matter of quantity and quality alone, and not a matter of value at all: the United States say by law that a gold dollar shall consist of 25⅜ grains troy, of which nine parts shall be pure and one part alloy, but of the value of this dollar thus coined the law says nothing. It can say nothing. The coin is publicly attested so heavy, so fine, and thereafter it takes its chance as to value. All governments have now learned, after oft-repeated and always vain trials to regulate the value of their coins, that all they can do is to regulate the amount and fineness of the metals contained in them. When, however, it is designed that both metals shall circulate in the same currency, then it becomes necessary that government shall determine, as well as it can, not the absolute value of either, but the relative value of each in each. And here too the value of each, estimated in the other, regulates itself independently of edicts or enactments. If the legislators can ascertain in what proportions they are exchanging for each other in a free market, they may mark that as the legal relative value of the two, but they must not suppose that their work will not require revision from time to time. In 1792, when the mint of the United States was established, the relative value of gold and silver was fixed by law at 1 to 15, which was the legal rate at that time in France and other European nations. It was soon noticed, however, that the gold coins issued from the mint did not come much into circulation, but were always sent abroad in preference to silver to liquidate balances in trade. The truth was, the ratio of 1 to 15 was an undervaluation of gold, that is, a legal valuation beneath the real valuation; and the gold coins would not circulate in a currency in which they were undervalued. It was beneath their dignity. They preferred to go, and went, where they had more consideration in exchange. The law of the mint had tried to find the true point of relative value as determined by the laws of Nature, but did not hit it, and the real value held right on in spite of mint and Congress. To remedy this state of things, the legal ratio of value was changed to 1 to 16, in 1834, being an increase on the former mint-valuation of gold, as compared with silver, of $6\frac{68}{100}$ per cent. But this was going too far. Thereafter the silver coins, being legally undervalued, were worth more in commerce than in the currency, and the foreign balances were preferentially liquidated in silver. This continued till 1853, when important changes were effected. By the preëxisting laws, gold and silver coins were each a legal tender for any amount; but at this time silver ceased to be a legal tender, except for amounts under five dollars; and the mint ceased coining silver for individuals, and, buying silver bullion at the market price, coined it only on government account, at the same time slightly debasing the coins, so that they should not be exported. Since 1853, therefore, gold has been the legal currency of the country, and silver has been entirely subsidiary to that, and yet the value of silver bullion has steadily maintained itself by natural laws, and from November, 1858, to January, 1862, it appreciated from $1.21 to 1.22\frac{1}{2}$ per ounce troy; from which is minted $1.25 in silver coins, making the seigniorage for coining, when the price is $1.21 per ounce, $3\frac{3}{10}$ per cent. In the first decade of the operation of this law, $48,513,037.50 of silver coins issued from the mint. In England silver is similarly treated; since 1817 it is legal tender only for forty shillings and under, the coins are slightly debased, to prevent their exportation as coins, and the issue department of the Bank of England is only allowed to hold silver as the basis of circulation to the extent of one fourth of the gold coin and bullion held at any one time; and yet silver maintains its own value in England in spite of these disadvantages, and is thought to comprise about one fifth of the whole metallic circulation.

These statements go to show that the value of gold and silver is self-regulating, and even their relative value in each other is a matter which governments endeavor to discover rather than arbitrarily to fix. The legal ratio has been repeatedly varied by the governments under which both metals were legal tender, according as the real relative value varied or was supposed to have varied. The general relative valuation now in Europe is 1 to 15$\frac{1}{2}$. The English overvalue legally their silver coins, in order to keep them at home, having made the ratio 1 to 14.287. For the same reason the United States overvalues the silver coins in something like the same proportion. It may be asked, why governments attempt to maintain a double standard, if the real relative value of the two metals be so independent of the action of law, and require so frequent revision? One answer is, that it is a convenience to have at least two metals in the currency, so that silver coins may serve for the lesser exchanges, for which gold-pieces would be inconveniently small; and gold coins for the greater exchanges, for which silver-pieces would be inconveniently large. Most currencies, our own included, have also a third metal or mixture of metals, to serve the purposes of the smallest exchanges, and the coins made of this are usually largely overvalued, — our nickel cents at present cost the government about half a cent, — and are not legal tender except to the amount of the smallest silver coins. Our copper cents have always been rather counters than coins, and our smaller silver coins, that is, the half-dollars and lesser pieces, in so far as they are at present debased, so far forth resemble counters; and there is no objection to this, so long as their overvaluation is well understood, and they are not made legal tender. Our gold coins are value-money purely, while a nominal dollar's worth of the smaller silver coins are intrinsically $7\frac{42}{100}$ per cent. less valuable than a silver dollar, and the cents are about 100 per cent. overvalued. This statement accounts for the fact that the silver dollar-piece does not come into the circulation at all, and that the smaller silver-pieces when sent abroad, as for instance to Canada of late, circulate at a large discount, or are rejected altogether. Another reason for the double standard, especially in those nations in which both metals are a legal tender, is the increased stability in value thereby secured to the whole currency. The relative value of the two requires careful watching and frequent readjustments, but then, the immense quantity in the world of both metals combined, and the opportunity which the double standard furnishes of replenishing a chance deficiency of one from the the stores of the other, give, in accordance with principles already explained, superior stability in value.

It is, then, a principal merit of metallic currencies, that the gold and silver comprised in them determine their own value by natural laws, both relatively to each other and to all other purchasable things; and hence the quantity required in each currency of the world to do the business of that country is a matter which natural laws are perfectly competent to regulate, without any direct action of government; and governments may be relieved from the difficult or rather impossible task of determining how much money their country shall have. The distribution of the precious metals over the earth by commerce, according to the wants and circumstances of each country, is not perfectly accomplished at present by the natural laws which are competent thus to distribute them, because some of the nations use still some form of credit-money as a part of their currency, and also because all the nations have not yet come to an agreement as to the degree of fineness of the metals used in their respective coinage. These obstacles impede somewhat at present the action of the comprehensive laws which will one day be allowed to control this matter perfectly. Nature herself has made the first grand provision for the self-regulation of the money of the world, by making pure gold and silver of exactly the same quality all over the wide earth. No matter where it is mined, or when, gold is gold and silver is silver. The gold mined to-day in California differs in no essential respect from the gold used by Solomon in the construction of the Temple. So that, if the commercial nations would come to a common agreement as to the amount of alloy they will put into their coins, and then bring these coins, as might easily be done, into decimal or other easy numerical relations with each other, it would be a matter of indifference to every nation whether the coins circulating therein were exclusively national coins or not. Foreign coins, to the extent to which commerce would naturally bring them there, would have just the same circulation and credit as their own: there would not be, as now, the trouble and expense of melting up and recoinage; the balances of trade could be paid indifferently in any coinage, and, as we shall soon see, every nation would secure without friction or legal enactment its due proportion of the money of the world. We are not now so far removed from this state of things as might at first sight be supposed. The gold napoleons of France, for example, circulate without difficulty all over the continent of Europe, and are largely current in Asia and Africa. In respect to the degree of fineness, I find by a reference to the Report of the Director of the United States Mint for 1862, that the standard of the United States for both metals, namely, $\frac{9}{10}$ fine, is also the standard of eight gold coins and eleven silver coins of different foreign countries, while the average of all the rest of the foreign coins would vary but little from that. France, the United States, Belgium, Switzerland, and some of the states of Germany, have already adopted this as the standard for their new coins; it is decimal and convenient, and the tendency seems to be decidedly towards its general adoption. England, however, adheres to her old standard of 1½. If a commercial congress, like those which have been held of late years in Europe, should agree to recommend to the governments the adoption of this standard, giving the cogent commercial reasons therefor, the recommendation would doubtless be adopted, and one obstacle to the perfect self-regulation of the world's money would be removed.

In respect to the decimal or other easy numerical relation of the different coins to one another, that would not be a matter of very great difficulty. From the report just referred to it appears, that, with a very slight change in the quantity of gold and silver put into their coins, the money of all the leading nations might circulate in common, without the least perplexity. The difference in value at present is very trifling between five American dollars, one English sovereign, twenty-five French francs, five German rixthalers, one hundred Spanish reals, five Brazilian milreis, and five dollars of the Central and South American States. If by a commercial congress, or otherwise, the money denominations of the few remaining commercial states could be brought into relation with these, so that all should be divisible by five, then each nation might keep its own names of coins with which it is familiar, and yet the money of all circulate everywhere without discount or difficulty.

Now, although the Bank of England circulates a paper money partly based on government credit, and though the United States has under the national banking law a similar paper money; yet every pound or dollar of this paper money is or is to be redeemable in gold and silver; and, as more than half the aggregate circulation of Great Britain is in metallic money, and as a similar proportion is perhaps likely to prevail in the United States, the maintenance of a paper money based on credit for the home circulation alone may or may not be sound financial policy; but it is evident that it cannot, under these circumstances, substantially interfere with the self-regulation of the metallic money of the world. Nevertheless, that we may see with distinctness the scope and efficiency of the magnificent natural law which distributes the precious metals over the earth in accordance with the business-wants of each nation, let us suppose that there were no paper money; that all the nations minted their metals with a common proportion of alloy; and that the real relative value of the two were ascertained by law in the countries where both are legal tender, and were well understood also in the other countries. In this case there would be no motive to debase any part of the coinage to prevent its exportation, and all the money of all the nations would be value-money purely. Now then, money is the medium of exchange, and is wanted where the exchanges are, and not elsewhere, and goes of necessity under freedom whither it is relatively most wanted, that is to say, whither the most can be obtained for it in exchange. If the country be gold-bearing, and its people at the same time be enterprising in the production of all sorts of services for exchange among themselves, they will retain enough of their own gold to mediate their own exchanges, for the simple reason that they want it, and have services to offer in exchange for it; and if they have been allowed in freedom to develop their own peculiar advantages, no foreign nation can outbid them in the offers they are able to make for a sufficient quantity of this gold. If foreigners draw away the gold from them, it shows that the home people have less industry and less skill to produce those things which the gold-producers want. The home people have the advantage in one respect. They are on the spot. There is less expense to them than to foreigners in transporting the services offered in exchange for the gold, and also the gold received in return. If, with this advantage, foreigners can still outbid them in offers for the gold, it shows that they need it most and deserve it most, since they have had the industry and the skill to produce that which is preferred by the miners to the home services offered, and have also overcome an additional obstacle. The gold-producer, like every other producer, has the right to get the most he can for his service. Whoever can offer him that most has the best right to the gold. Therefore the gold goes in the first instance into their hands, whether natives or foreigners, who offer the most for it in exchange. If the people of the gold-bearing country have equal natural advantages with others to produce those things which are wanted in exchange for their gold by those who practically work the mines, and then fail to get the gold they need, the blame lies nowhere except on their lack of industry and skill. Let not such people think to find any shelter behind natural laws. Natural laws are justly and eternally against them. If, however, they are naturally placed at a disadvantage in respect to those specific products in demand by the first owners of the gold, they are then brought into the same category with non-gold-bearing countries. They will then get their gold at second hand, and if they deserve it, will be just as sure to get it as if they retained it in the first instance. Every nation has natural advantages in some sorts of products. Just so soon as these are properly developed, it has some things to offer to the world at a better rate than anybody else can offer them. Thither, and to buy those things, will gold flow, if not directly from the gold-producing lands, then indirectly but inevitably, from those lands where the gold at present is. Under our supposition, it makes no difference where the gold came from, or what nation minted it, it is drawn by a natural force not to be resisted to that people, which, by offering services in general demand, requires gold to mediate the exchange of those services. Thus, by a law as unerring as gravitation, the precious metals make the circuit of the earth, abiding certainly in large masses within all the commercial nations, because there is where they are constantly wanted and cannot be spared, but passing off also perpetually in smaller masses from all the great centres of business towards those points where their purchasing-power for the time being is greater than at home. The one only impulse that can stir the precious metals from their usual haunts, is the belief that elsewhere they are worth more in exchanges; and hence, just as soon as the demand for a currency is fairly met in any country by the presence of gold and silver, coin ceases to flow thither as a permanent thing, but rather ebbs and flows in obedience to the ever-shifting exigencies of trade. The nation that does a large business will require a large stock of coin, will be able to pay for it, and will inevitably secure it; a nation with fewer exchanges to make will less need the instrument with which exchanges are made, will buy and keep a less quantity; and if, in the chances of trade, more comes than is needed, it flows off at once to the places where the demand for it is stronger; and thus the proportionate amount due to the commercial interests of every nation goes thither under a natural law, and abides there under a natural law. Hence the general purchasing-power of gold and silver tends steadily to an equality the world over. If it be appreciably higher in one nation than in the others, the metals are drawn toward that nation by an irresistible attraction till the equilibrium is restored. Add to this, that there is at all times a vast reservoir of plate from which any sudden or steady demand for currency can easily be supplied, and into which any fortuitous or steady superfluity can as readily be drained, and the reasons are apparent why gold and silver currencies are self-regulating in value and amount. If, on the other hand, a currency is to be of paper, independent of gold and silver, there is no self-regulation about it: we pass at once from the region of natural laws into the region of statute and enactment; somebody must take upon themselves to decide how much of this paper there shall be, — a power which could not be lodged in more dangerous hands than in those which thought themselves competent to exercise it.

(3.) *Because they are conveniently portable, divisible, and impressible.* Our proposition is, that gold and silver constitute the best money; and in proof of this we have already demonstrated the steadiness of their value, and their self-regulating power; incidental to these great advantages are the material qualities of these metals, by which they are admirably fitted to be the money of the nations. Their weight is little relatively to their value. A thousand dollars in gold are not indeed carried so easily as a bill of exchange or a bank-note; and expedients are easily adopted, and always have been used, by which the transfer in place of large masses of coin is for the most part obviated; and our proposition does not deprecate at all the use of the economizing expedients of commerce; but for the money of the people, for the currency that passes from hand to hand in ordinary exchanges, we maintain that gold and silver are sufficiently portable. A pound weight of English sovereigns, which one can put in a glove-finger and carry in his vest-pocket, almost without knowing it, is worth about $230; and the experience of those countries, like France and Germany at present, where the money is mostly metallic, has not pronounced it onerous on account of its weight. At any rate, it is better to accept all the other immense advantages of gold and silver money, together with a little inconvenience as to weight, if one chooses to insist on that, than to adopt substitutes every way inferior as money, except that they are lighter in our purses.

Moreover, gold and silver differ from jewels, and most other precious things, in that masses of them are divisible, without any loss of value, into pieces of any required size. The aggregate of pieces is worth as much as the mass, and the mass as much as the pieces. For currency purposes this is a great advantage. For its utmost convenience, business requires a considerable variety of coins, and if any of these kinds be minted in quantity in excess of the demand, nothing more is required than to remint them in other denominations, and their whole value is saved to the currency in the most convenient form. It is this quality which enables coins to flow into plate whenever the metal in them becomes more valuable in the form of plate, and plate again to flow back into coins whenever the metal in it is more in demand as coin.

Lastly, these metals are capable of receiving and retaining any stamp which government chooses to impress upon them. A certain proportion of alloy, say $\frac{1}{10}$, hardens them to such a degree that they exhibit with sharp distinctness the cut of the die, and permanently retain its impress. This quality of the metals, when they are skilfully coined by the improved machinery of modern times, makes the pieces of money objects of beauty, and practically indestructible also, since the perfect circular form, the device covering the whole piece, the milled and fluted edges, make clipping without detection impossible, while the hardness of the pieces makes the annual loss of weight by abrasion scarcely appreciable. The Director of the United States Mint, in his Report for 1862, gives the results of some careful and comprehensive experiments made at the mint to ascertain the yearly loss of coins by the ordinary wear and tear of circulation. These results are exceedingly interesting and important, and throw to the winds the haphazard conjectures of a host of writers on either side of the Atlantic. On our silver coins, taken promiscuously, the average annual loss from abrasion was ascertained to be one part in 630; while the gold coins were tested separately, with this satisfactory conclusion, that the half-eagle averages a loss per annum of one part in 3550, the double-eagle one in 9000; and a cautious estimate as to the proportions of the various sizes of coin actually in circulation in the United States, made of the two metals, leads consequently to the conviction that the average yearly waste by wear on all the coins does not exceed one part in 2400. The cost, therefore, of maintaining a metallic circulation is by no means so great as it has been usually represented. An instrument in constant use that requires only $\frac{1}{2400}$ of its value for its yearly repair, and performs exceeding well the most delicate and important functions, is a cheap and durable instrument.

From these three main reasons, we conclude that gold and silver are the best money.

4. *An inferior money, so long as it circulates at all, invariably drives a superior money out of the circulation.*

This is a fundamental law of finance, and has been illustrated over and over again in every age and nation. It is as solid as the substance of truth can make it, though it looks at first sight like a paradox. We naturally think that what is excellent tends rather to displace what is inferior, but with money the exact reverse is the law, and the perfect coin of full weight, instead of driving out the light and the debased pieces, is always itself driven out of the circulation by them. The reason is obvious from the nature of money. Money is merely an instrument of exchange, and nobody wants it except to buy with, and so long as the government and the community treat light coin and full coin as of equal value, receiving them indifferently in payment of debts and of taxes, it is clear that nobody will give in payment of debts and of taxes that which is really worth more so long as that which is really worth less will go just as far. The inferior pieces will abide in a market where they will fetch just as much as the superior pieces, while the superior pieces will take on a form or migrate to a place in which some advantage can be gained from their superiority. Thrown into the crucible, or exported in commerce, this superiority immediately manifests itself; and therefore into the crucible or into the channels of foreign trade it might be confidently predicted beforehand that such money would be thrown, and all experience testifies with one voice that exactly those are the destinations of such money. Mr. Macaulay, in the twenty-first chapter of his history, mentions that Aristophanes, the Greek comic poet, in the fifth century before Christ, was the first writer who has noticed the fact that where good money and bad money are thrown in together the bad money drives out the good. The verses of the poet allude to the tendency as well known, and refer it to the naturally depraved taste of his fellow-citizens, like that which led them to entrust state affairs to such men as Cleon, whom he was satirizing; but, in truth, as we have seen, the tendency results from the common sense of men, which revolts at the idea of using a dearer instrument when a cheaper one will answer just the same purpose.

Out of a crowd of good illustrations of this law, I shall first select two which occurred in purely metallic currencies. The Dutch city of Amsterdam became in the seventeenth century a centre of trade for all Europe. The mercantile honor and solid financial ability of its merchants was proverbial all over the world; and yet it was noticed, about the year 1609, that bills of exchange on Amsterdam were always below par in other countries. The merchants had never failed to meet all the paper drawn on them with the utmost promptness, and the discount on this paper in other markets was a wonder to everybody. On search, however, it was found that the cause of all this was in the currency of the city. The extensive trade of Amsterdam brought into it large quantities of clipt and worn foreign coin, which circulated in the currency of the city, and reduced its value about nine per cent. below that of good money fresh from the mint. It was noticed, that the good money of full weight which the mint of Amsterdam poured into the circulation by wagonloads, did not stay in the circulation; that very few of such pieces were told out in the daily exchanges; it was ascertained that they were melted up, or carried away to other countries, in either of which cases their value corresponded to the value due to their weight and fineness, while at home in the currency their value only corresponded to the average value of the depreciated coins which constituted the bulk of the circulation. Bills of exchange, consequently, drawn on Amsterdam were liable to be paid in this depreciated coin, and the exchange was against the city even more than the coin was depreciated; because, the currency in such an uncertain state was naturally valued abroad even below what it was really worth. To meet this state of things, and bring up its exchanges to par, the city of Amsterdam, in 1609, established its celebrated bank. The bank received the clipt and worn coin which was circulating in the city, at its true value according to present weight and fineness, and after deducting a small charge for expense of recoining, and another small charge for management, gave a credit on its books for the remainder. This credit was called bank-money; it represented, guilder for guilder, money actually in deposit, and money too exactly according to the standard of the mint. The city ordered that all bills drawn on Amsterdam of more than six hundred guilders' value, should be paid in bank-money; thus every considerable merchant was obliged to open an account with the bank, and make his deposit. This instantly took away all uncertainty from bills of exchange drawn on Amsterdam. They went up to par at once in every market in Europe. This was the basis of the simple and beneficent operations of the Bank of Amsterdam, an institution which enjoyed unlimited credit in the commercial world for nearly two hundred years. The convenience of this bank-money; its unvarying character; its security from fire, robbery, and other accidents; the fact that the city was bound for it; and the demand for it occasioned by the fact that every merchant must have some of it, that is, must keep an account with the bank, in order to pay his foreign bills of exchange, gave the certificate of deposit, or the bank-money, a constant premium of about five per cent. over the good coin of full weight which came into circulation without difficulty as soon as the poorer coins were drawn into the bank for recoinage.

At the close of the same century, a similar series of events occurred on a much larger scale in England.[1] The old silver coinage of England was by a rude process introduced into that country by artists from Florence as early as the thirteenth century. The pieces were shaped and stamped by the hammer. They contained some a little less and some a little more than the due amount of silver; few of them were perfectly circular; the edges were neither milled nor fluted; the image of the sovereign occupied the centre of the pieces, and the superscription ran around the edge, but not so near it as that the letters were necessarily impaired by a little clipping. Consequently it was easy to pare off a pennyworth or two of silver from the crowns, half-crowns, and shillings, and then pass them along. It became a profitable branch of industry. It was in vain that Elizabeth enacted that the clipper should be henceforth liable to the penalties of high treason. About the time of the Restoration, that is, about 1660, it was noticed

[1] Macaulay's History, Chap. 21.

that a large proportion of the silver coin of the realm had undergone some degree of mutilation. At that time a new process of coinage was brought in. A mill worked by horses fabricated the new coins on better principles. They were exactly round, and the edges were inscribed with a legend, and they were all of just and equal weight. They were thrown out into the circulation to pass current with the hammered money, and it seems to have been expected that they would soon come to displace it. But they did not. Both were received at first without distinction by the individual traders and by the public tax-gatherers. But it was not long before the milled money was noticed to be scarce. One hardly saw a piece of it in a fortnight. The horses at the mint were all the time tugging away, and the bags of fresh money were carried continually from London Tower to London town, but the new money nevertheless became scarcer every day. In the payments made at the Treasury not one piece in two hundred was milled silver, and a merchant complained that, being paid a debt of thirty-five pounds, he only got one half-crown of good money. Indeed, the money was getting perpetually worse. False coiners multiplied, and clippers abounded more and more. The penalties of an extreme law were utterly powerless to restrain the mutilation of the coins; until, at length, public opinion decidedly turned against the promiscuous hanging of clippers; officers were reluctant to arrest, and juries reluctant to convict, and the people sympathized with the sufferers as only guilty of a moderate fault. Thus things went on till 1695. The lighter the old coins became, the scarcer became the new ones; for who would pay two ounces of silver when one ounce was legal tender? The new money was melted, was exported, was hoarded, but circulate it would not. At length the lightest pieces began to be refused by some people, and other people demanded that their silver should be paid to them by weight and not by tale, and there was wrangling over every counter, and a dispute at every settlement, and the coin was really so diverse in its value that there was no longer any measure of value in the kingdom; business was in utmost confusion, society was by the ears, poor people were unmercifully fleeced, and shrewd ones grew enormously rich; and the Jacobites secretly exulted in the hope of being able to avail themselves of the prevailing discontent to overthrow the scarcely established revolutionary government of William and Mary; when, by the joint counsels of two such philosophers as Locke and Newton, and two such statesmen as Somers and Montague, the government took the bold resolution of recoining all the silver of the kingdom. An early day was fixed by Parliament, after which no clipped money could pass except in payments to government, and a later day after which it could not pass at all. It was wisely determined that the loss on the clipped money should be borne by the whole public, and not by the present holders of it; and it was estimated that £1,200,000 would be required to make up the currency to the old standard of weight and fineness; and this sum the Bank of England, just established, was willing to advance on the security of some new and good tax; and the window-tax was passed to raise the money; the old coins were rapidly drawn in, melted up, and recoined, and thereafter there was no difficulty in keeping the circulation full of milled pieces of full weight.

In mixed currencies, the financial law we are now treating has a similar, but if possible a more disastrous operation. If the paper in circulation be not nominally redeemable in gold and silver, then as soon as it depreciates below the value of gold and silver, as such paper has never yet failed to depreciate in a short time, it drives the metals completely out of the circulation, and keeps them out just so long as itself circulates, or until the quantity of such paper is so reduced and its character so improved that it rises again to a par value with the metals, in which case, though it has never to my knowledge actually occurred, the metals would come back into the currency alongside of the paper. The suddenness and the thoroughness with which the gold and silver will abandon a currency of which a depreciated, irredeemable paper forms a part, was illustrated on a large scale in this country in 1862. A gigantic civil war had been in progress in the nation for a year; difficulties and disasters had thickened around the path of the government; its financial embarrassments were of the most formidable kind; and yet, until April of that year, 1862, the paper money of the loyal States, which consisted of about $140,000,000 of bills of the various State banks, had not much depreciated as compared with coin. In January, indeed, when the national government had added to this mass of paper about $30,000,000 of demand-notes, gold was at a premium of five per cent.; but as soon as the law authorizing the issue of national legal-tender notes was passed, the government drew in the demand-notes, and for a little interval the paper currency was reduced to about $140,000,000, and on the first day of April, when the legal-tenders were ready for circulation but not yet issued, the coin bore a premium of only one per cent. It had not yet in any sense abandoned the circulation. The State banks had all suspended specie payments on the last day of the preceding year, but had not yet much expanded their usual circulation. And now it is to be noticed that the steady depreciation of the paper currency of the country, both state and national, commenced at the very time when the national legal-tender notes were thrown into the circulation. All the paper was now irredeemable, and its volume was now expanded, and the depreciation begun; it was liable to still further expansion, both from the absence of restraint on the circulation of the State banks and from the urgent necessities of government leading to the issue of more legal-tenders, and the depreciation continued. In May it was three per cent., June nine per cent., July fifteen per cent., September twenty-one per cent., October twenty-nine per cent., and December thirty-two per cent. Step by step, as the volume of the currency increased, did its value decrease as compared with gold; and what is more to the present purpose, no sooner did the depreciation become sensible, than the scarcity of coin became sensible also, and in a very few weeks' time the currency was swept utterly bare of metallic money. The silver went first, and then the gold; and a little later even the copper cents followed the example;

and the government was obliged to authorize the use of its postage and revenue stamps for small change; and, until it was prohibited by law, cities, corporations, and individuals issued shinplasters and metal tokens of various kinds to take the place of the small coins. This present writing is at the summer solstice of 1865, but with the exception of a few of the cents, the coins have not yet returned to the circulation, for the sufficient reason that the paper-money is still depreciated as compared with them. The war is over, peace has returned, business is reviving, and a career of unprecedented prosperity is opening up before the country, but the coins have not come back, and, under the commonest principles of human nature, cannot come back, until the paper dollar of the country is equal in purchasing-power to the gold dollar, and is redeemable in that. Since April 1st, 1862, the paper money has varied from par to one hundred and eighty-five below par, and is to-day about forty per cent. below par. The whole body of the paper money now in the country at large cannot fall much short of $1,000,000,000, of which about $700,000,000 are in national legal-tender and fractional money, and the rest about equally divided between the bills of the new national banks and the bills, now being retired, of the old State banks.

So long as the paper money of a country is nominally redeemable in gold and silver, the operation of the law we have in hand is somewhat peculiar. In times of ordinary confidence and prosperity the paper and the coin circulate indifferently together, and an undue increase of the paper beyond the just demands of business does not indicate itself in a premium on the coin, but the whole circulation, gold and paper, goes down together, and the depreciation is of course indicated in a general rise of prices. There is nothing anomalous in this, for increase of supply, other things as before, always lowers the value of anything; and the direct interest of the parties who furnish the paper leads them to increase their circulation as much as they fairly, and sometimes as much as they unfairly, can. But a market in which prices are high and gold is still circulating is a good market to sell in, and increased importations never fail to accompany a rise of prices caused by the depreciation of a mixed currency. In the home market the paper is still as good as gold, but to pay the balances in a foreign trade it is good for nothing. The natural superiority of the gold to paper appears as soon as a payment is to be made abroad. In obedience to this impulse gold naturally and inevitably goes abroad; and it has repeatedly gone abroad under these circumstances from the United States to such an extent that the parties who furnished the paper, that is to say, the banks, could no longer redeem their paper in coin, but were obliged to suspend specie payments, which is a euphonious circumlocution to express going into temporary or permanent bankruptcy. In this case also, though less directly, the inferior money pushes the superior out of circulation. I have no hesitation in calling the paper the inferior money, both for other potent reasons soon to be specified, and because at any rate it is powerless in international exchanges. There is believed to be nothing in the monetary history of the United States, as there is certainly nothing in the known principles of human nature, which does not abundantly confirm as a universal truth the proposition in hand, namely, that worse and better money being in the currency together, the worse will expel the better sooner or later; sometimes into hoards, sometimes into the melting-pot, and sometimes out of the country.

5. *A paper money is only tolerable when it is actually and instantly convertible on demand into gold and silver.*

I lay down this proposition, and shall attempt to prove it, well aware that it is directly opposed to the views of the late and able writers on money, Mr. Carey and Mr. Moran. I differ with such a man as Mr. Carey, to whom I have already acknowledged my obligations, with regret; but I cannot help opposing, to the extent of my ability, his doctrines on money and on foreign trade, because, after thoroughly canvassing them, I am persuaded that they are fundamentally and perniciously erroneous. Both these writers, Mr. Moran more distinctly, advocate a paper money based simply on the credit of the issuers; they advocate the principle that the manufacture of money should be as free as the manufacture of coats; that every man, or association of men, so choosing, should open what they call a money-shop to supply the community with money; and that no public regulation of the quantity or quality of such money should be attempted or desired. In developing the present proposition some reasons will appear for dissenting totally from these views.

It is here necessary to anticipate the discussions of a subsequent chapter so far as to define Credit *as the sale of a service for which the return is not yet received, but only promised.* In an exchange proper, two services are reciprocally rendered by two persons, and the transaction is then and there terminated; but in simple credit, one service is rendered, and the return service is delayed, and usually some paper evidence that such service is due springs up in connection with the transaction. It is an exchange begun, but not yet consummated, and no matter through how many hands the paper evidence may pass, it is nothing but an obligation resting on somebody to pay to somebody the return for a service which has been actually rendered. Now the grand distinction, and one of the utmost importance, between gold and silver money and paper money is, that paper money always has in it the element of credit, while the other has in it no element of credit at all. A gold eagle is not a sign of anything, it is not the representative of anything; it stands in its own right, just as a bushel of wheat does; it is true that its only use as money is to purchase other things, but its purchasing-power is within a trifle as great whether it be in the form of money or bullion; and therefore a service that is paid for in specie closes up the transaction completely, the exchange is consummated, there is no element of delay, of promise, of credit in such an exchange. It is just as when the miller renders a bushel of corn to his neighbor, and that neighbor renders him a day's labor in return. In both cases, there is an end. But paper money is credit-money. It may be more convenient than real money; its value, that is to say, its purchasing-power, may be equal to that of real money;

it may even in some circumstances bear a premium over real money; but all this does not alter the fact that there is in it an unlucky element, an unstable element, an element which, as men are, is liable to some suspicion, the element, namely, of a present promise to be fulfilled in future. Paper money walks by faith, and not by sight. It is the sign, and not the thing signified. It is the representative of something, and not that something itself. It is a promise to pay, and not the pay itself. It is a credit, and not a service. And what makes this very certain is, that all paper money knows it to be true about itself. It bears this truth stamped on its very face. It does not even profess to stand on its own bottom, but leans consciously and conspicuously on some solid support. The French assignats promised to redeem themselves in land; the continental bills of the old American Congress were all to be paid in Spanish milled dollars; an $100 note of the late so-called " Confederate States of America," now lying before me, speaks complacently of a redemption to take place "two years after the ratification of a treaty of peace with the United States of America"; the bills of the Bank of England profess to be, and are, redeemable in gold and silver; the present irredeemable legal-tender notes of the United States are all fundable in a six per cent. government stock, of which the interest and principal are payable in coin; and the bank bills of the country, both state and national, are nominally or actually convertible into specie.

Since, then, the various forms of paper money, even the best of them, are mere promises to pay on demand, it must be conceded that they are credit-money; and the question is narrowed down to this, whether the functions of money can be well performed by the evidences of an obligation to pay for services already received. It is not denied that such evidences frequently have value, that their value is sometimes equal and sometimes superior to an equivalent sum in gold; the question is whether in their nature they can constitute a good money. In resolving this question, it must be noticed, that the fact of indebtedness is not of itself an evidence of an ability to pay: individuals, corporations, and governments have often become bankrupt through the disproportion of indebtedness to ability. It must be noticed, also, that, in the light of human nature and experience, men in all capacities are more or less willing to accept the services of others without rendering the equivalent return, even when their obligation to render it be certified on paper; also that the willingness of people to accept, in return for actual services rendered, mere promises to pay in future, by whomsoever issued, is quite different at different times — in times of confidence and prosperity they may be readily accepted, in times of disaster and peril all men prefer payment to promise. The functions of money are two: to serve as a medium of exchange, and to serve as a measure of value. To fulfil the first office well, money should be a commodity at all times acceptable to all men in return for services rendered; to perform the second function well, money should be as uniform as possible in quality, and vary in quantity according to the shifting demands of exchange, and not otherwise; in short, vary in quantity just as a good metallic currency does vary under natural laws alone. But credit-money is unfitted by its very nature to do well these two things; first, because it never has been, and in the nature of things never can be, acceptable to all men at all times in exchange for services even within the country itself, and in international exchanges it is not acceptable at all; and second, because, as has been already shown, a steady measure of value necessitates a steady value of the money, and the value of credit must certainly be as variable as the character of the issuers for integrity and solvency. Add to this, that the value of credit-money, like the value of everything else, depends in part on the supply, and the supply will vary with the varying disposition of the people to accept it, and thus the measure of value will be varied. It is in vain to talk, as Mr. Moran does in this connection, of the self-interest of the issuers, and of their honor, and so on; self-interest should keep men from becoming bankrupts, yet men do become bankrupt; honor forbids indeed the escaping from a debt, yet debts are escaped from. On principles merely, it would be as certain beforehand as any such truth can be, that credit-money, from the nature of credit, could not properly perform the two delicate and important functions of money.

But we are not left to principles alone. Experience throws a flood of light on this whole subject. At the beginning of the last century, under the auspices of John Law, France issued a paper money guaranteed by the State, resting back for its value on the national faith and on the whole national property. The notes were made receivable in taxes, were redeemable in coin, were made a legal tender, were nursed up by the government in every way; but in less than four years, owing mainly to their over-issue, to which credit-money, unless under the most stringent regulations, is always liable, they fell, as compared with specie, first to ninety, then to sixty and fifty, and shortly after, although they were made fundable in annuities, to twenty, and then to four per cent., and then their value vanished entirely. The notes depreciated at first because the people began to lose faith in the ability of the royal bank to redeem them in coin; and the subsequent action of the government confirmed their suspicions; and however good the public faith may have been, and it was sufficient to rescue most of the notes by funding them in annuities, it was a poor element in the people's money, because the functions of money are such as to be incompatible with any degree of distrust. It is well, in most cases, for a people to trust their government; it is safe for them usually to loan their money to it and take a government bond as security for payment; but money is very different in its nature from government stocks; and the public faith, which is an ample basis for the latter, is no suitable basis at all for the former. Again at the close of the century France tested the merits of paper money on a broad scale. As the great revolution went forward, and a scarcity of money was experienced, the government issued, under the name of "assignats," a paper money entitling the bearer to a certain value of the property of the royalist clergy and nobility, who had mostly left the country, and which the government had confiscated and now intended to sell. The assignats were receivable in payment for these landed estates at any public sale of the same. For about two years their value kept up above ninety per cent., and then began to droop. The government, in alarm, while issuing on the one hand enormous quantities of the paper to meet the vast expenses of the Revolution, which quantities were swelled by skilful counterfeiters in the prisons and elsewhere, took strong measures on the other to prop up their market-value: the use of coin was prohibited; a maximum price in assignats for everything was established by law; heavy penalties and at last death were decreed against those who refused to receive them at par; but it was all in vain. Down they went, says Carlyle, "with an alacrity beyond parallel." The discount increased with the issues, but in a greater ratio; by means of a forced loan, exacted in 1793, the Convention were enabled to draw in eight hundred and forty millions francs of the paper, and the depreciation was stopped for a little by this expedient; but in the next year the amount was as great as ever, and the discount greater. In 1795 they could be had for eighteen per cent., and in the beginning of 1796 they became utterly worthless as money. The government then offered to redeem them at thirty for one in "mandats," which entitled the bearer to take immediate possession, at their estimated value, of any of the lands pledged by the assignats. The mandats depreciated instantly, and in the course of a few months were all called in, and business, which had practically ceased under the paper money, began to revive again at the sight of the coin, which, of course, had been out of the circulation for years. The distress and consternation into which a country falls when its measure of value is disturbed and destroyed, as it was by the issue of the assignats, is past all powers of description. There can be no doubt that the depreciation and final worthlessness of the assignats caused more suffering in the French Revolution, a hundredfold, than the prisons and the guillotine. It may be said that the government ought not to have issued them in such excess — over fifty thousand millions of francs were put out in all. Perhaps it ought not. But there never has been a government yet, of the many which have issued irredeemable paper, which had the wisdom and firmness to resist for any great length of time the strong temptation to over-issue. There is no stopping when once the issue is begun. The first batch of such paper usually banishes the coin from the currency. There is no way to entice it back except to call in and burn up the paper. Revolutionary governments are not generally in position to be able to do this. Ordinary national expedients are denied them. They cannot borrow. Therefore they have recourse to credit-money, which is really borrowing without interest, and when once the press is set at work it must work on with livelier speed, because just in the ratio of the depreciation is a greater amount required to meet the ordinary payments. This example is significant, because it shows the powerlessness of even the strongest and most unscrupulous governments to regulate the value of anything. The assignats were depreciating during the very months in which Robespierre and the Committee of Public Safety were wielding the power of life and death in France with terrific energy. They did their utmost to stop the sinking of the revolutionary paper. But value knows its own laws, and follows them, in spite of decrees and penalties This example also exhibits well the fundamental vice of all credit-money, whose value arises just as all other value arises, and is amenable to the same law of supply and demand as other values, and the vice of which is that there is no natural limitation of its supply. There is relatively no obstacle to its indefinite increase; and therefore the value dependent on such conditions of supply has no sufficient stability; and therefore credit-money is necessarily, and by demonstration, inferior to gold and silver money in the cardinal point of a steady value.

The financial experience of the United States is so varied and so instructive that we shall devote the next chapter to a consideration of its history; but it is here in order to call attention to the fact that the bills of credit emitted by the individual colonies before the Revolution, and the continental money issued by the old Congress had a course and issue almost precisely similar to that of the assignats. The continental bills were at first willingly received at par. As their volume increased their value diminished, as was shown, as usual, by a universal rise of prices. The laws of the States continued to make these bills a legal tender when they had fallen to a tenth, a twentieth, and even a fortieth of their nominal value, thus sanctioning virtual frauds in private business, and making the burden of the money fall heaviest on the ignorant and helpless. At length, after $200,000,000 had been issued, from which the government had realized perhaps about $70,000,000 of specie value, $88,000,000 of the bills were received back by the government and replaced at the rate of forty for one in bills of the "new tenor" which bore interest at six per cent.; $40,000,000 were in the national treasury, having been received in the form of taxes, but could not be paid out again because the money was now universally rejected; $70,000,000, or more, were still outstanding, a part of it in the State treasuries, and a part in the hands of individuals. These were never redeemed in any sense. The bills of the new tenor also depreciated greatly, notwithstanding they bore interest; so that the whole loss to the people from the continental money was just about $70,000,000 specie, which may be considered in the light of a forced loan to government, and as the government used it to further the interests of the people, it would not seem so bad, except under the view that, in running this career of depreciation and repudiation, many times that amount of damage was done to individuals, since the same depreciated dollar so long as it was legal tender paid debts over and over again. It would have caused less loss and disturbance of contracts if Congress had just taken by force $70,000,000 of specie value from the pockets of the people. This example shows also in a clear light how unfit for the uses of currency is a national inconvertible paper.

The United States legal-tender notes, which began to be issued April 1st, 1862, and of which over $650,000,000 are now in circulation, have been more or less depreciated from the first, and at times very much depreciated; and this, not because there has been doubt about their ultimate redemption, not because of a lack of confidence in the stability of the government, for thousands of millions have been freely loaned by the people to the government on the public faith in the interval, but partly on account of their excessive quantity, and partly on account of the nature of credit-money unfitting it to maintain a high and steady value. It has been sometimes supposed that when two kinds of money are both made a legal tender, they will both circulate indifferently in the currency, and that their value will be equal. It is an utter mistake. Gold has been legal tender in this country all the while, and yet has borne a premium over the other legal-tender money of nearly one hundred per cent. on the average of the past three years. It may be questioned whether the making these notes a legal tender has tended to appreciate their value at all; so far as the demand for them was thereby increased it had such a tendency, but so far as the making them legal tender indicated the conviction of the government that they were not in themselves equal to gold in value, the tendency was the reverse. The faith of the people in their money is very properly more sensitive and more easily shaken than their faith in anything else; and this is one of several weighty reasons why the element of credit should not enter into the money at all. Credit is good in its place, but in the people's current money it is out of place. The fact that in the Eastern and Middle States the national legal tenders have had no more acceptance in the circulation than the bills of their State banks, which have been irredeemable since the beginning of 1862, and not like the others fundable in a gold-bearing government bond, is also an indication that the fact of their being a legal tender has not substantially enhanced their value.

Our proposition, however, if correct, condemns the money of these State banks also, and, in a general way, all the paper money which has had currency in this country from the beginning. This paper, although nominally redeemable in coin, has never as a whole been actually so redeemable. Some of it has been better than the rest, but none of it has deserved the praise of being a satisfactory and sufficient money. (1.) It has been liable to great and sudden contractions and expansions of volume. For example, in 1857 the bank circulation of the country was $214,778,822, and in 1858 $155,208,344, a contraction of $59,570,474 in one year. In 1862 the paper money of the banks was $183,762,079, and in 1863 $238,677,218, an expansion of $54,885,139 in one year. (2.) The ratio of paper to the specie reserved for redeeming it has been a high ratio. According to the Finance Report of 1863, from which the figures in this paragraph are all taken, that ratio for the whole country taken together on the first of January, 1863, was 4 to 1; while in particular States the ratio was remarkable; in Rhode Island, for instance, more than 12 to 1, and in Vermont more than 28 to 1. It is evident that such paper can only be called redeemable by stretch of courtesy. (3.) Consequently nothing could prevent a distrust of such paper, so soon as there began to be commercial stress and pressure; especially whenever the exigencies of commerce withdrew gold for foreign trade from reserves already so small. Four or five times have panics resulting from these natural causes attacked the paper currency of the country, and compelled all the banks to confess, what everybody knew before, that they were unable to redeem their promises. These repeated suspensions of specie payments proclaim the whole system to be unsound. They show that credit is no proper basis on which to build a currency. The banks, each under its own board of control, and under various and often conflicting State laws, have not acted in unison, have contracted and expanded their circulation according to a view of their own interest, have contributed powerfully in times of quiet by a system of generous loaning, on which their profits depended, to induce a spirit of speculation and a willingness to contract debts, and have experienced when the reaction came how much easier it is to loan paper promises than to fulfil them. Their inability to continue in troublous times the free loans which helped to bring them on, and their repeated failures to make good the obligation to redeem their own notes, have caused in the last fifty years innumerable failures of business men, and incalculable losses of property. There can be no hesitation in affirming that the expense of maintaining a gold and silver currency for all the wants of the whole country might have been met many times over from the losses resulting from the bank-paper system. The instability of the system has tended towards a reckless way of doing business among us, which has been a just reproach to us in foreign countries. Besides these considerations, which go to show the inadequacy of bank-paper money to answer the purposes of a good currency, the system is based on essential injustice. It allows certain corporations to borrow money of the people without paying interest, while other corporations and individuals, just as solvent, must pay interest. Bank-bills are nothing but promissory-notes which the people take of the issuers without interest, giving them as security for their return notes which are on interest. The greater currency of the bank-notes is supposed to be an equivalent for the difference of interest, and by this difference of interest the bank lives, but it has been found in the long run that the paper credit of banks as a whole, and as they have been administered, is scarcely better than the credit-paper of other corporations and individuals. Their money has never been actually and instantly redeemable in coin; and it is fortunate that the people have come to the practical conclusion no longer to allow joint-stock companies under State regulations to manufacture and issue their money for them.

But will the National-banking system, just now coming into full operation, furnish the people with a good currency? To this question I answer, that the National-banking system is every way preferable to the old State-bank system. The banks under it are all amenable to a central authority and to common regulations. Their circulation is all secured by an actual deposit with the national Comptroller of the Currency, of gold-bearing government stocks to an amount at least one tenth greater than such circulation, so that the redemption of the circulation is perfectly provided for, in case the bank itself refuses to redeem. The bills of all the banks are current everywhere within the country, and provision is made for the immediate redemption of them in each of the great central cities, as well as at the counters of the banks which issue them. The bills are so expensively engraved by the national government that the counterfeiting them will be more difficult than it has been to counterfeit the State-bank bills. If any form of credit-money can be regarded with favor, certainly this money can be so regarded, for the capital stock of these banks is all invested in the national debt, which is as secure a form of credit as any credit can be, and the bills are based also on the good faith of the individual banks which enlist the self-interest and the sense of honor of the stockholders and directors. As a form of credit nothing can be alleged against it; it has all the securities and guaranties that could be desired; when specie payments are resumed, as it is expected they will be in a year or two, no doubt the bills will be practically convertible into gold and silver, and so will be, in accordance with the words of the proposition, a tolerable money. Nevertheless, they will not be the most economical nor the best attainable money. If we could be assured that the $300,000,000 of this money already authorized would not be increased, then a good degree of confidence in it would be natural and reasonable; then the larger half of our whole currency would be gold and silver; the paper, like the bills of the Bank of England, would undoubtedly be at par all the while, and we should gain something by the superior convenience of the paper, and not lose much by its inferior steadiness. But the mischief of it is, this money cannot regulate its own quantity; it is not guarded, as gold and silver are, by a natural limitation of supply; a simple vote of Congress would be sufficient to double or treble its quantity, and thus derange its value, and postpone indefinitely its par with gold. After all that can be said in favor of it, it is credit-money still, and exposed to the dangers inseparable from credit-money, namely, the distrust of the people, the undue enlargement and sudden diminution of its volume, a consequent unsteadiness of value, and inconvertibility. I have but little doubt that Congress will be urged to enlarge the sum already authorized, and hardly less that they will lack the wisdom and firmness to refuse, and if we are to have a national paper currency expanding and contracting under the successive tinkerings of Congress, we shall yet experience more of those evils of credit-money, from which we have suffered in the past so extensively in property and reputation, and which nothing but our exuberant and exulting strength has enabled us to outlive and to forget.

The Bank of England stands in most men's minds as a synonym of security, and its bills as the perfection of paper money; but, like all other human institutions, it has had its ups and downs, and there have been repeated and persistent "runs" upon it for payment, and its paper has been at times discredited as much as twenty-five per cent. A child of the English Revolution, it was incorporated by Parliament in 1694, on condition that its stockholders should loan to government, then pressed for funds, the sum of £1,200,000, on which they were promised to receive eight per cent. as interest, and £4000 a year for management. It was supposed that subscriptions to the loan would come in slowly; but, to the surprise of everybody, £300,000 were subscribed the first day; £300,000 more in the next two days; and in ten days it was announced that the specified sum was raised. Thus the moneyed men rallied to the support of government; and the government was strengthened in one sense by its own very indebtedness; for it was felt that if James II. should regain the throne, no pound of the loan would ever be paid. "So closely," says Macaulay, "was the interest of the bank bound up with the interest of the government, that the greater the public danger the more ready was the bank to come to the rescue." Thus the whole capital stock of the bank, just like the capital of our new national banks, was invested in the national debt; the interest was to be paid from the proceeds of the taxes, and the original loan, if ever repaid at all, was also to come from the same source. At different times down to 1833, the bank advanced to the government various sums on various conditions, until, when the charter was renewed for the ninth time in that year, the public owed to the bank £11,015,000, and the debt has remained at that figure ever since. Instead of eight per cent. which was paid on the original loan, the rate has been gradually lessened, and the bank now receives but three per cent. on the whole debt. The entire capital of the bank is at the present time about £14,500,000, of which, as we have just seen, a trifle over £11,000,000 is in the permanent public debt of England. In 1844, when the charter was renewed for the tenth time, Sir Robert Peel caused a law to pass Parliament the object of which was to lessen the fluctuations in the quantity and value of the money. To make the notes in circulation vary in amount and value, under the exigencies of trade, just as a metalic money would do, was the praiseworthy purpose of the prime minister in the new constitution he gave to the bank in 1844. The bank is thereby divided into two separate departments, the issue department and the loaning department. The latter conducts its business like any other institution of loan, raising and lowering its rate of interest according to the state of the market, but usually keeping its rate a trifle higher than the market-rate, so as to be able to act as a support to private bankers and others in case of pressure. The issue department is subjected to a well-considered scheme of restraint. It is allowed to issue £11,000,000 in notes on the basis of the permanent debt which the government owes the bank, and £3,000,000 on the other public securities which are a part of the capital stock; but beyond this £14,000,000, secured by its permanent capital, it must have for every pound in notes issued, pound for pound of gold and silver in its coffers. The average circulation of notes is about £28,000,000, one half based on specie actually in reserve, and the other on the public debt. The bills of the bank are legal tender everywhere except at the bank itself, where coin must be paid on every bill presented for that purpose; and the bank is also obliged to buy, and pay for in notes, all gold bullion and foreign coins offered to it, at the rate of £3 17s. 9d. per ounce standard fine; so that, if the notes depreciate as compared with coin, they can at once be changed into coin, or if coin depreciates as compared with notes, it can be changed into notes. The bills of the Bank of England, consequently, are a better money than the bills of our national banks, which are only required to keep on hand in lawful money of the United States twenty-five per cent. of their liabilities in notes and deposits, because they are more certain to be instantly convertible into coin on demand, the provision for instant redemption is more liberal, and the constant presence in that currency of a larger body of coin than of paper makes everything firmer and redemption easier. A stoppage of specie payments is possible, but not probable, at the Bank of England, under the present constitution of the bank. It did however suspend in 1797, and did not resume till 1821, during which interval the notes, cautiously issued at first, continued at par for nearly three years, and then declined gradually down to twenty-five and even to forty per cent. discount, from which point they gradually rose as the prospect of resumption increased, until they came to par, and have remained so. The earlier period of the suspension proves this important point, that when a government possesses the monopoly of issuing paper money, and carefully limits the quantity issued, and both receives it and pays it out as legal tender, it may keep an inconvertible paper at par, and even, by sufficiently limiting its quantity, carry it above par. But this truth does not make an inconvertible paper a good money, because it does not make it a self-regulating money, and because no government is wise enough, or ever will be, to issue just enough and no more of such money. It is certain too that the present convertible money of Great Britain does not in fact vary so perfectly in volume and value as a metallic money would do under the impulses of trade; and twice since 1844 the government has allowed the bank to violate its charter, and to issue more than £14,000,000 on securities temporarily; once in 1847 and again in 1857. The opportune loan of a million to our generous countryman, George Peabody, made by consent of the government in violation of the charter in the latter year, saved him from otherwise inevitable failure. It shows that there is something factitious and unnatural about paper money, when so rigid a system of restraint is considered needful to prevent disastrous fluctuations in volume and value.

In my judgment, the most economical, and, taking all things into consideration, every way the best money, is the gold and silver which God has evidently designed for that purpose. This position does not exclude the freest use of those convenient economizing commercial expedients, such as bills of exchange, drafts, checks, money-orders through the post-office, and so on, which are sufficient to prevent for the most part all burdensome transfers of coin. The public has not yet reflected sufficiently on the peculiar functions of money, nor discriminated as it should the proper sphere of credit from the proper sphere of currency. Let the currency stand securely in its own right as value-money, and then the various forms of paper credit will safely come in to remove all the inconveniences and secure all the advantages of a perfectly sound, and everywhere acceptable, and a naturally self-regulating money. The great objection to this has been the expense of maintaining such a currency. If we may trust the competent director of our national mint, the expense would be $\frac{1}{2400}$ of the value of the currency per annum; that is to say, if the currency of the country consisted of $720,000,000, which would certainly be enough for the present, it would cost $300,000 per annum to keep it good. Considering the inevitable losses which always accompany the derangements of the standard of value, and the expenses of engraving, and of detecting, arraigning, and punishing counterfeiters of the paper, and the losses from successful counterfeits, and other similar items, it is believed that $720,000,000 of paper money, inferior as it is for the purpose designed, would cost at least as much to keep it good. The best money will certainly be found to be the most economical.

6. *Government ought to leave freely to the parties concerned the rate of interest to be paid on money loaned.*

The law of Moses forbade to the Israelites the taking from one another any interest on money loaned, but at the same time it allowed them to take such interest freely of strangers; the permission in the one case going to show that there is nothing in the taking of interest in itself unjust or sinful, and the prohibition in the other being readily explainable from the general purpose of the municipal regulations of Moses, which was to found an agricultural and not a trading commonwealth, in which every family was to possess land that could not be permanently alienated or sold, in which it was a great object to maintain the personal independence and equality of these families, in which the law for the recovery of debts was very summary and effective, lessening the risk of losing the principal, and which was to be and was sedulously separated in its usages from the surrounding nations. It has been well understood for a long time that the municipal code of Moses was local and peculiar, not necessarily applicable at all to the circumstances of other States, and in no sense binding on the conscience of legislators; and yet there doubtless sprung from the prohibition referred to a prejudice against interest, and this prejudice was perhaps deepened in the Middle Ages and onwards by the conduct of the Jews themselves, who, in addition to their sin of persistently growing rich in spite of the endless disabilities laid on them by the people of Europe, always demanded, in accordance with the permission of their great lawgiver, a per cent. of interest from those strangers to whom they became money-lenders. The Jews were everywhere hated, and consequently the usury which they practised was hated also. The fundamental absurdity of forbidding in trading communities the taking of interest on sums loaned to a borrower which he was at liberty to use for his own profit, deterred the nations from going to the length of prohibition, unless it might be in the case of the hated Jews. There is a clause of Magna Charta, interesting as showing how early the children of Abraham became the money-lenders of Europe, to the effect that, during the minority of any baron, while his lands are in wardship, no debt which he owes to the Jews shall bear any interest. The prejudice against interest embodied itself in what are called usury laws. These, without prohibiting the taking of interest, prescribe a maximum rate per cent., which lenders may receive, and announce a penalty in case they take more. The penalty is sometimes the forfeiture of the entire interest, and sometimes of the entire debt.

Usury laws, however, have not sprung wholly from the old prejudice that to take interest was a great moral wrong, and the greater the more was taken; they sprung also from a false notion which used to be pretty general, but which is now at length thoroughly exploded, that governments were competent to determine the value of their own money; and there has been, and is still, a curious and harmful confusion in respect to this term, the value of money. In the only proper sense of the term, the value of money means its power of purchasing services in general, and the value of money is high when a given sum of it will purchase much of general services, and low in the contrary case; but, unfortunately, the terms "high and low value of money" have also been used to denote a high or low rate of interest on money loaned, which is a very different signification, and a high or low rate of interest depend on a very distinct set of causes from those which determine a high or low value of money; nevertheless, so long as governments supposed that they could regulate the latter, it is perfectly natural that they should also suppose that they could regulate the former; and although all intelligent governments have given over the idea of being able to regulate the value of money, many of them still adhere to the idea, equally false as the other, that they are able to regulate the loanable value, or the rate of interest, at least to prevent any more than their prescribed maximum rate from being taken. Even the national banking law of the United States, lately passed at the instance of the excellent Committee of the Ways and Means, adopts the usury laws of the several States, and allows the banks to take the rates of interest current and legal in those States, although this rate varies between the extremes of 5 and 10 per cent., and denounces the penalty of forfeiture of the whole debt in case they take more. Are such laws needful? Are they beneficial? Are they in accordance with sound principles, or do they violate them? Has a government any right, after it has stamped or engraved its money, and parted with it to the people in return for value received, to say that they into whose hands it has rightfully come shall only have so much under any circumstances as a reward for foregoing the use of it themselves that somebody else may have the use of it?

Let us see precisely the nature of the transaction when one man loans money to another. It is a clear case of value. The lender does a service to the borrower, and for this service justly demands a compensation. The service is this: The lender might himself use the money to gratify his own desires. It is his money; he may use it, as he pleases, for his own gratification. Or, he may himself employ it productively, and, at the end of the period, receive back his principal with the customary rate of profit. If he surrenders this advantage to the borrower, if he passes over to him the right to use this money, say, for a year, he practises what we call in Political Economy *abstinence*. For this abstinence he has a right to claim a reward, precisely as the man has a right to claim a reward who foregoes working for himself in order to work for me. This reward of abstinence is *interest*. The money-lender foregoes an advantage. He performs a service for the borrower; and, therefore, the right to interest stands on just as unassailable ground as the right to wages.

The money-lender comes to society exactly as we all come, having a valuable service to offer in exchange; and he is anxious, as we all are, to make the best terms he can. So far as I can see, his case does not differ, in any respect whatever, from the case of all the rest of us. It is a case of pure exchange. Mr. Retired Merchant has money to loan, and Mr. Active Manufacturer would like to borrow it. The first is too old to work, but he can still practise abstinence and get gain. The second knows how to turn a nimble penny and make two of it, and is willing to give a part of the second penny to the man who will lend him the first. These two men, then, are in position to render each other a mutual service. They want to exchange. Why shouldn't they strike their own bargain? Every other two men when they exchange services strike their own bargain, and nobody thinks of prescribing to them the terms. It would be considered a vast impertinence if government should prescribe the terms of exchange in other cases, — why is it less impertinent in this case? The lender has as good a right to make the most of his money as the farmer to make the most of his wheat. But the farmer is allowed to exchange on the best terms he can make: can any good reason be given why the lender should not be allowed to exchange with the borrower on the best terms he can make?

I am perfectly aware that the national banking law does not prescribe terms to private lenders and borrowers; but the States themselves do this, and it is with the principle alone that I am now concerned. The principle is everywhere the same, and is nowhere soundly based. All values are variable. The loanable value of money varies under exactly the same conditions as every other value varies. It is determined, as every other value is, by the actual exchanges between lenders and borrowers; or, rather, by what would be the actual exchanges, if they were left free. Now for any government to compel a borrower to pay six per cent. when he might otherwise borrow for five, or a lender to take only seven per cent. when his money is worth eight, is a direct violation of the rights of property. It is a forcible and pernicious interference with the freedom of contracts. It is based on the false premise that the loanable value of money is uniform, and that government is competent to determine what it is. No value is uniform. And no government is less to be trusted with such a power than one which thinks itself competent to exercise it.

On principle, then, these are the two considerations which condemn usury laws. First, it is invidious to allow other men, in every department of business, to exchange their services on the best terms they can make, without any interference or control, and then, without rendering any solid reason for it, to deny this privilege to money-lenders, who offer just as honorable and useful services to society as any other class of men. Second, it is a false notion altogether, that the loanable value of money is, or can be made, uniform; and, therefore, a rate per cent. fixed by the government constantly infringes on the rights of property, — on the rights of the borrowers, if the rate is too high, on the rights of the lender, if the rate is too low. But there are two other considerations, each, if possible, better than these, which condemn all legal rates of interest. The first is, that such laws are rarely obeyed, and can scarcely be enforced. It is notorious that they are a dead letter on the statute-book, unless some mean-souled wretch pleads usury, out of spite, or to avoid an honest debt. Common sense is outraged by a law which requires a man to part with his property at less than the actual value; and when common sense is against a law, it stands a slim chance of observance. If the legal rate be six, and the actual worth be eight, who lends at six? Not the banks. They require deposits of their customers, the use of whose money shall make up to them the difference between the legal and the actual rate. The modes of evasion are various, but they are adequate. Conscience scarcely speaks at all, for self-interest and common sense both pronounce the law unjust. Is it possible that the honorable gentlemen of the Ways and Means Committee really suppose that their banks will loan money at seven per cent. at any time, when its actual worth shall be nine per cent? Doubtless they might loan at that nominal rate, but there will be deposits, or a consideration, or an "understanding" in the premises. Why then have a law that is sure to be disregarded?

But usury laws, if they were not disregarded, would be even worse in their tendency than they are now. They aim, I suppose, to aid borrowers, and make it easier for them to contract loans. But are borrowers, as a class, any more deserving of the fostering care of government than are lenders? Even if it could make its interference effective, as it can not, is there any reason why government, leaving these borrowers to make all other bargains, sales, and transfers according to their best skill and judgment, should rush to their rescue only when they propose to borrow money? If they are competent to do their other business for themselves, government pays their capacity a poor compliment in undertaking to help them in the single matter of making loans; and the borrowers in turn have reason to pray to be delivered from their friends, since they, of all others, would be the men especially injured, if all the lenders obeyed the usury laws. Suppose that a borrower is in great need of a loan, and that for some reason his credit is now a little weak. Many men would be willing to loan him at nine per cent., which affords a margin for the extra risk, but at seven, which we will suppose the maximum allowed by the law, he cannot borrow a dollar, because his credit is not quite equal to the best. If, therefore, the lenders obey the law, he, and such as he, must fail. And because it is unlawful to take over seven per cent., he will be obliged to pay those who are willing to violate the law ten or twelve, to compensate them for the risk and odium of such violation, while, under freedom, he could borrow at nine. Moreover, if the loanable value of money at the time be actually nine, while the law only allows seven, many men will attempt to use their own capital productively, who would otherwise loan it, in order to realize the high rate; and this action of theirs still further restricts the loan-market and makes it more difficult to borrow. If, then, the purpose of government be to aid borrowers, no means could be more unskilfully chosen for that end than to pass usury laws, since such laws, so far as they are obeyed, have necessarily the opposite tendency; and even when violated redound to the disadvantage of borrowers, so long as the laws themselves are popularly regarded as of any legal or moral force.

Governments have shown a noteworthy inconsistency in this matter, which incidentally proves the unsoundness of their whole action. While announcing pains and penalties to those who take or pay more than a given rate, they are careful never to bind themselves down to any given rate. Governments are always more or less borrowers, and if usury laws are necessary in order to help borrowers in a pinch, there ought to be a clause in the organic law of every country, forbidding the government to pay and its lenders to take any more than a certain rate per cent. There is no such clause in any organic law. Governments wisely follow the natural market, and borrow low when they can, and pay high when they must. In the last months of Mr. Buchanan's administration, the United States paid twelve per cent. on a public loan, and could get but little at that. Sauce for the goose is sauce for the gander, and if usury laws are good for the citizens, some solid reason ought to be rendered why they are not good for the government. The truth is, they are not good for either, since natural laws are perfectly competent to regulate the rate of interest, and do regulate it substantially in spite of a factitious, impertinent, and mischief-making interference. The rate of interest has little to do with the value of money, properly so called. It depends on the proportion between the sums of money ready to be loaned in any market, and the amount wanted at that time by good borrowers in that market. There is no value more constantly variable from day to day, and from month to month, than the loanable value of money. The natural law that holds the rate of interest in its grasp is most efficient. Every rise in the rate tends to lessen the demand of borrowers, and every fall to enhance that demand, and thus every rise and fall of interest tends to check itself, and while the daily and monthly variations of the rate for first-class borrowers are very considerable, the general average of the rate by years, especially in England, where every vestige of usury laws has been swept away, is remarkably uniform. The experience of England completely confirms our reasoning, and makes us sure that we are right. Indeed the law might just as reasonably say that every lender shall receive six per cent., as that no borrower shall pay over seven. To say either is to defy common sense, and expose law to contempt. Adam Smith left the "Wealth of Nations" disfigured by the concession that governments might properly enough pass usury laws; but it is gratifying to be able to add, that he was convinced of his error in that by Bentham's book on usury, and fully acknowledged his conviction in the spirit of a genuine lover of truth. We conclude, then, that usury laws are needless, since interest, like all other prices, will perfectly adjust itself. They are disregarded, since lenders will loan or withhold their money according to their own keen sense of interest. They are pernicious, since they infringe the rights of property, and tend to prevent weak borrowers from having a fair chance in the market.

CHAPTER XI.

ON CURRENCY IN THE UNITED STATES.

It is not so much a revolution through which we have been passing for the past few years, as it is a series of revolutions. There has been a political revolution, a military revolution, a social revolution at the South; and a monetary revolution the country over. It is difficult for us, who have all been in the current, to realize the rapidity with which as a people we have been borne onwards by all the movements, and the actual distance from our point of departure which we have already reached. The best place to watch the river is on the shore. If, for the sake of the view, we throw ourselves out in fancy from the rush of the stream, and take a fixed position to see how fast we have been moving and how far we have come in the matter of national money, we shall be struck with a marvelous transformation which has been silently and now almost completely effected. Unless every providential and political sign shall fail, we are to be hereafter one homogeneous people, distinct indeed in our States as the billows, but one in our Union as the sea; having one set of national rights for all the inhabitants within our borders, and having also, and this is the point of present consideration, one national money, current and good everywhere, a sign and seal of national unity and of consolidated strength.

I venture to offer to guide my readers in an attempt to trace the steps, State and national, as well the earlier as the more recent, which have been made in this country to find the way to a healthy, safe, and uniform currency. Paper money of almost every conceivable variety has been tried at one time and another; and the national government for itself, between 1836 and 1862, discarded in its own transactions every kind of paper, both paying out and demanding to receive gold and silver money only, minting indeed at a small seignorage for all parties and in all quantities gold and silver that was brought to it, but otherwise leaving the States and the people to fabricate and circulate whatever kinds of money they might choose.

From the first establishment of the English colonies in America, the matter of a suitable exchange-medium attracted public attention, and was found to be attended with difficulties. The colonists drew all their supplies from the mother country, and for a long time had but few native products to export in return, and consequently there was a constant tendency in the coin which reached them to flow off again to England in payment of these debts. But something must be used for the purposes of domestic exchange. Tobacco in the southern colonies, and corn and cattle in the northern, were employed for a long time as a local and legalized currency.

In 1690 Massachusetts set the first example, which was soon imitated all over the country, of issuing bills of credit, a government paper made receivable in taxes, and afterwards made legal tender in payment of ordinary debts. At first these bills, or treasury-notes, were issued, not to furnish a currency, but merely as a convenient way of anticipating the taxes, that is, to realize them at the beginning of the year, while they would be gradually paid in in the course of the year. They were, in short, an imitation in all respects of the English exchequer-bills. Afterwards, a scheme originating in South Carolina came into general favor, namely, to open loan-offices for the issue of colony-bills, which should furnish at once capital for borrowers, and a currency for the people, and the interest was to be a source of revenue to the colony.

But in whatever way issued, whether in the way of loan to borrowers, or in anticipation of the taxes, the essential and inherent vice of such irredeemable paper was soon everywhere apparent. There was a constant tendency to over-issue, and consequently a necessary depreciation. There never was a government yet, of all those which have attempted the issue of inconvertible paper, which had prudence and firmness enough to resist for any great length of time the temptation to issue such paper in excess. It always has depreciated from that cause, and it probably always will. So it was, at any rate, in these colonies thus early in our history. The bills of credit were issued profusely, and depreciated indefinitely. In 1748 Massachusetts had found paper money so utterly wanting as a measure of value, that she determined to abandon it altogether. She redeemed all her outstanding bills in cash at the current rate of twelve for one.

The demands of the old French war, and the various attempts to conquer Canada, led, on the part of all the colonies except Massachusetts, to new and large issues of bills of credit, which depreciated of course. Soon after the conquest of Canada the British Parliament passed an act prohibiting to all the colonies the issue of bills of credit; but from this restraint the Revolution set them free; and, to provide means for the desperate struggle with the mother-country, there was no resource but in paper money.

In April, 1775, Massachusetts, which had disused paper money for more than a quarter of a century, revived its use by authorizing the issue of colonial bills to the amount of £100,000, in sums small enough to circulate as a currency; and on the 23d of June following the Continental Congress began its fiscal operations by voting to emit two millions of dollars in continental bills of credit. In July another million was authorized to be issued, and the liability for the three millions was distributed among the colonies in the ratio of their supposed number of inhabitants; the bills to be redeemed in four annual instalments, to commence at the end of four years. In November an additional three millions was ordered, to be apportioned and redeemed like the former, only the redemption was to begin at the end of eight years. In the following February came four millions more, one million of which was in bills of a less denomination than one dollar. Eighteen months had elapsed, and twenty millions of continental paper had been authorized, besides large local issues, especially in New England, before any very considerable signs of depreciation made their appearance. It soon, however, became evident that the only way to stop the depreciation would be to stop the issues; and Congress made very persistent but ineffectual attempts to substitute for further issues a system of loans on paper bearing interest. At the same time they sought to sustain their failing credit by a resolution that their bills "ought to pass current in all payments, trade, and dealings, and be deemed equal in value to the same nominal sums in Spanish dollars"; and that all persons refusing to take them ought to be considered "enemies of the United States," upon whom it was recommended to the local authorities to inflict "forfeitures and other penalties." The States were also advised to make these bills a legal tender, to make provision for the redemption of the first six millions, to avoid the further emission of their own local bills, and to take measures to draw in those already out.[1] The loan system failing, Congress reluctantly had recourse to the press which printed the paper money, and the next ten millions increased the depreciation decidedly. This issue was authorized in February, 1777, and in August came two millions more, in November a million, and another million in December, making thirty-four millions in all. At the beginning of the year the bills were nearly at par, and at its close they passed at three or four for one. During the first half of the next year twenty-three millions and a half were added to the already superabundant mass, and the depreciation became alarming. Forty millions more were added in the last half of the year, and the depreciation at the beginning of 1779

---

[1] Hildreth's United States, Chap. 35.

amounted in the North to six, in the South to eight for one. Before that year was half gone, under the influence of large additions, the depreciation reached twenty for one. The paper was still lawful tender in payment of debts; and notwithstanding the confusion of contracts, the universal high prices, the sufferings of the poor, and the gains of the artful and unscrupulous, Congress felt obliged to give currency to the most wretched sophistries, to refer the existing depreciation mainly to "want of confidence," and to laud the paper as the only kind of money "which cannot make to itself wings and fly away! It remains with us, it will not forsake us, it is always ready at hand for the purposes of commerce, and every industrious man can find it!" The rest of the story is soon told. Before the end of the year, the remainder of the two hundred millions, which, in the vain hopes of stopping the depreciation, Congress had beforehand announced as the limit of the issues, was put out, and the press was allowed to rest. The value of the money was then about thirty for one. The States were now advised to repeal all laws making the bills a legal tender, and the scheme of the "new tenor" was devised, by which the old bills were to be drawn in at the rate of forty for one, and funded in government bonds bearing interest. This was the finishing blow, and the paper soon dropped out of circulation altogether. Just before the Revolutionary army in camp at Newburgh had combined to refuse it, and its circulation was wholly stopped, it exchanged for cash at the rate of one thousand for one. The whole country experienced in money matters just exactly what rebeldom has lately experienced, money going down and prices going up, till at last they would n't touch anyhow! A man in New England or New York would pay five hundred dollars for his dinner, and never ask the landlord to reduce the bill. I heard the story in my childhood of a certain gentleman well known in those parts, who stuffed his sulky-box with continental bills and then sallied forth to purchase a cow!

At this juncture the rudiments of a better system appeared. For nearly a hundred years the Bank of England had been issuing paper payable on demand in gold and silver. Alexander Hamilton had been a close student of English history and of English finance, and he conceived that the same thing might be done with advantage in America. In 1780, when he was only twenty-three years old, he wrote a letter to Robert Morris, a wealthy and influential member of the Continental Congress, and afterwards the Continental financier, in which, after showing the causes of the depreciation of the currency, and the necessity of a foreign loan, he furnished a matured plan of a bank, by means of which the loan might be so applied as to reëstablish the public credit and become the basis of a redeemable currency. This was, as I believe, the first suggestion of a banking institution for America. Hamilton's idea was briefly this: Public credit there was none; an established government there was none; the Continental Congress was exercising the unlimited functions of a revolutionary government; under these circumstances the only way to create public credit was to unite with it the private interests of moneyed men. Establish then a bank which shall be the fiscal agent of the government; obtain, if possible, a foreign loan, and deposit it in cash in the bank; let half the stock of the bank be subscribed by wealthy men, who can reasonably look for a fair profit on their investment; let government hold the other half and have half the profits; then let the bank issue bills on its cash basis, consisting of the loan, the private subscriptions, and the product of the Continental taxes as they are gradually paid in. Thus the bank, and all subscribers to its stock, and all holders of its bills would be directly interested to uphold the government and its credit. Community would be equally benefited, since it would have a relatively sound paper for ordinary commercial purposes.

Mr. Morris found his duties as Continental financier sufficiently embarrassing; and in the fall of 1781 brought forward a scheme for a national bank, partially embodying on a small scale the ideas of Hamilton. Congress sanctioned the plan, and the Bank of North America, the first bank in this country, was established in Philadelphia. Mr. Morris, in behalf of the general government, subscribed nearly two thirds of the capital stock of $400,000, and naturally took the entire control of the institution. The reason why individuals subscribed so little is to be found in the distrust with which paper money of all kinds had come to be regarded. Capitalists did n't believe there would be any dividends, and the people were afraid the paper would depreciate in their hands. Under these unfavorable circumstances the bank went into operation in January, 1782. Every effort was made to produce a public sentiment favorable to the credit of the bank, and its bills were the first paper handled by Americans which was convertible into coin at the pleasure of the holders. Being made receivable at the Federal and State treasuries in payment of taxes and duties, and being cautiously issued at first, the bills soon came into such circulation that the bank was able to declare dividends on its stock from twelve to sixteen per cent. per annum. Who ever heard of capitalists who could resist sixteen per cent? The bank opened its books for new subscriptions, and the stock went up without difficulty from $400,000 to $2,000,000.

We must here dismiss the Bank of North America, the parent of all our institutions of the kind, with the remark that, although it was chartered by the old Congress as a national institution, such doubts were entertained of the competency of that body to incorporate an institution within a State, that a charter was soon after procured from the legislature of Pennsylvania; and also, that its connection with the Continental treasury ceased, on the retirement of Mr. Morris from the office of financier. It continued, however, as a State bank; and it flourishes still in a green old age among the banking concerns of the Quaker City.

Till Mr. Morris's Bank of North America commenced operations in January, 1782, all the paper that had been issued in the country, whether by the colonies as such or by the central authority represented at first by the revolutionary government and afterwards by the confederation, was irredeemable paper, and illustrated the universal financial law that such paper, unless issued under very favorable circumstances and strictly limited in quantity, will depreciate in spite of everything. The bills of the Bank of North America were convertible into gold and silver at the pleasure of the holders, and they mark, therefore, an epoch in the monetary history of the country. Some silver coins had been issued in Massachusetts as early as 1652, and continued to be struck at the colonial mint for about thirty years, but the pieces all bear the dates of 1652 or 1662; and these pieces, now known and prized as the "old pine-tree coinage," were the only public coins of any description minted in the country itself until after the close of the Revolutionary war. They were shillings, sixpences, threepences, and twopences. Both silver and copper coins were, however, minted in England for the use of the colonies; and in 1722 a patent was issued by George I. to one William Wood to make coins for colonial use out of pinchbeck, in pursuance of which he had the conscience to make thirteen bright shillings, or thereabouts, out of a pound of brass. It is refreshing to add that the colonists had the sense and spirit utterly to reject Wood's money. In 1786 actual coinage of copper coins took place under State authority, in Vermont, in Connecticut, and in New Jersey. The same year witnessed the adoption in the old Congress of Jefferson's plan for a decimal currency, and the establishment of a mint under national authority, and three hundred tons of Federal copper cents were contracted to be struck the following year.

When the government went into operation under the present constitution, in 1789, besides the Bank of North America, two others had been established, the Bank of New York in New York, and the Bank of Massachusetts in Boston. These three were all, and their circulation was mostly confined to the cities in which they were located. Except the copper cents just spoken of, there was no such thing as a national currency, and the new government had not sufficient credit to make it practicable to rely on the aid of private lenders. Hamilton was now Secretary of the Treasury. In pursuance of the duty of his office, he presented to Congress in December, 1790, his celebrated report, recommending the establishment of a Bank of the United States. In this report, which at once gave Hamilton a European reputation, two points were specially argued: first, that such an institution would afford through its bills great facilities to trade and to domestic exchanges; and, second, would furnish the new government a convenient paper medium for its monetary transactions, and be a resource for temporary loans. The first point respected the people, the second the government.

There can be no doubt, I think, that in the circumstances of that time a national bank was expedient and beneficial. There was then no confidence, no credit, no currency, and no commercial relations established with foreign nations by which gold and silver could flow into the country. As an institution of loan, the bank gave credit to the extent of its means to all who had good security to offer. As an institution of circulation, it furnished a convenient, a convertible, and a national money. As a governmental fiscal agent, government could borrow of it on an emergency, and pay at its leisure from the proceeds of the imposts and taxes. The fullest acknowledgment, however, of the benefits of such an institution at that time does not at all commit one to the defence of any such institution now. Circumstances have utterly changed. *No well-established national government can afford to add to its many and higher functions the delicate duty, so much more appropriate to private bankers, of loaning money to the people on interest according to its notion of their solvency; and, in a republic especially, where hostile parties alternately administer the government, loans would be sure to be made for partisan purposes, and corruption find the bank a ready tool.

The constitutionality of Hamilton's plan was stoutly denied in Congress. The first-rate abilities and growing reputation of that eminent statesman had already awakened jealousies both in Congress and in the cabinet. Nevertheless, a bill, in substantial accordance with the views of the Secretary passed both houses by large majorities. Washington, before signing it, required the written opinion of his cabinet on the question of constitutionality. Hamilton and Knox took the affirmative; Jefferson and Randolph the negative; the President, as usual, sided with Hamilton, and signed the bill.

On New Year's day, 1853, I had the great personal pleasure of calling on the widow of Alexander Hamilton, who survived him just fifty years. Turning the conversation on her husband's connection with the government, the old lady remarked with enthusiasm, — " My husband gave you a bank. Jefferson thought we ought not to have any bank, and Washington rather thought so, too; but my husband said we must have a bank; and one day he said to me, 'My dear, you must sit up with me to-night, and write for me;' and I sat up all night, and I wrote it out with my own hand, and the next morning he carried it to Washington, and we had a bank!" This last was pronounced not without exultation. Fortunate old lady! The daughter of one of the purest and most magnanimous of the Revolutionary patriots, Gen. Philip Schuyler, and the wife of another, peerless among the statesmen of his time; who herself lived to see the complete success of the work to which her father and husband were among the chief contributors.

With a charter that was to run twenty years, with a capital stock of $10,000,000, $8,000,000 of which was subscribed by individuals, and $2,000,000 by the United States, and the whole of which was subscribed, with a surplus, within a few hours, the first United States Bank went into operation at Philadelphia, in July, 1791. Notice this feature of the stock. Hamilton had just before persuaded Congress to assume the State debts incurred in the war of the Revolution, and to fund them, together with the certificates of the public debt, into one new and compact debt. Three fourths of the subscription of individuals to the bank stock must be in these new government stocks which bore six per cent. The demand for them, thus created, brought them instantly up to par; so that the bank was made a means, incidentally, of establishing the credit of the United States, — all its paper was now at par. This splendid success of Hamilton's financial schemes, together with the unexpected income from the new tariff, accounts in part for the immense popularity of the man; and justifies the strong expression of Daniel Webster, who said, on one occasion, that Alexander Hamilton raised the public credit of the United States from the dead.

During twenty years, the term of its charter, the operation of the first United States Bank appears to have been healthful and beneficent. It furnished a paper money secured by government stocks and by cash that was current at a uniform value all over the country; its loans, under the circumstances of the time, gave a sharp spur to industry and commerce; while its dividends to stockholders never fell below eight, and frequently rose to ten per cent. It is not to be wondered at, therefore, that as the time approached for the charter to expire, the stockholders were anxious for a renewal. They applied for such renewal, offering to pay the government a million and a quarter for the privilege of continuance. It was alleged against the bank, on the other hand, that the stock was now largely owned by foreigners, which was true; and that the directors had sometimes made, or withheld, loans, for party purposes, which was doubtful. The real cause of the opposition to the renewal of the charter was this: Instead of the three State banks in existence when the national institution was chartered, there were now (1811) eighty-eight State banks, in some of which the States as such held stock. These banks and their friends supposed that it would be for their interest that the national bank should go out of being; that, in that case, they should obtain the custody and management of the national funds, and furnish the country the currency, which the national institution had furnished. The charter was defeated, in the House by one vote, and in the Senate by the casting vote of the Vice-President, George Clinton. The bank was obliged to wind up its affairs. It did so speedily and honestly. This was in 1811.

Undoubtedly the paper of the first national bank was very good money, and certainly superior to the bills of the new State banks, for the creation of which there was a sort of mania in the country so soon as it was ascertained that the national institution could not be rechartered. Many of these went into operation on the strength of little or no *bona fide* capital. They issued their notes freely, and the chasm caused by the withdrawal of the national circulation was soon filled up, and more too. As a necessary consequence, the whole circulating medium became depreciated, and the currency came into dreadful disorder throughout the country. In the fall of 1814, there was a general stoppage of all the banks in the United States, except those in New England. The notes of the New York city banks were ten per cent. below par; those of Philadelphia, eighteen; of Baltimore, twenty; of Pittsburg, twenty-five. All this illustrates the simple financial truth, that money is not a commodity of which an unlimited quantity can be absorbed by business, but is an instrument for a certain specific purpose, — namely, to facilitate the exchange of existing commodities and of services all ready to be exchanged, and only waiting for the presence of the medium to consummate the transfer; and whenever more than enough for this purpose is put out, whether it be specie or paper, the depreciation of the whole mass is inevitable; on the same principles precisely as, when the market is permanently overstocked with sewing-machines, there will be an inevitable decline in their value. Money is good for the purpose for which it was invented, and useless for any other. So are sewing-machines. When more of either is offered than enough to serve their respective purposes, in the then circumstances of society, decline in the value of both is a matter of necessity. In 1814 there was not only too much money to do the work which money was needed at that time to do, but, also, much of it was of very inferior quality. There was no sufficient genuine value behind the paper to support it.

In this state of things Mr. Dallas, then Secretary of the Treasury, recommended to Congress the establishment of a new United States Bank, modelled after the first, with a charter for twenty years, with a capital stock of $35,000,000, the bank to pay the government a bonus of a million and a half for the privilege of coming into being. It was thought that a strong central and national institution, on which the State banks, now increased in number to two hundred and forty-six, might lean for support, would enable them shortly to resume specie payments, and to go on thereafter on better principles. The bill organizing the bank was engineered through the House by John C. Calhoun. It went into operation in 1816, just after the close of the last war with England, when the reviving enterprise and enlarged business of peace seemed to open up before it a prosperous career.

The new bank was not, however, at first, fortunate in its management. It pushed its paper into circulation with reckless eagerness. In the course of one month it increased its discounts from three to twenty millions, and in nine months its discount line was thirty-three millions. The results were what might have been expected,—prices universally high, a spirit of speculation everywhere rife, and gold leaving the country by shiploads. The bank soon fell into difficulties, and public opinion turned more or less against it. Although under the abler and more careful management, first of Langdon Cheves, and then of Nicholas Biddle, the bank recovered its stability, it never enjoyed quite the same confidence and credit as the first bank.

This was not wholly its own fault; for in 1829, seven years before its charter was to expire, Andrew Jackson commenced his famous contest with the bank, which he kept up without intermission till the charter expired in 1836. Under this presidential and consequent congressional fire, the bank can hardly be said to have had a fair chance. Andrew Jackson had sworn its death by the 'tarnal—his usual oath—and Andrew Jackson was not a man to be thwarted. In his annual message in 1829, he gave the directors fair warning that there would be "constitutional difficulties" in the way of their securing any extension of their privileges, and in 1832 he vetoed the bill to recharter the bank. The next step was to remove from the custody and management of the bank the public moneys. Three years before the charter expired he requested Mr. McLane, the Secretary of the Treasury, to remove the national funds from the custody of the bank, and to place them in certain selected State banks. Mr. McLane declined to order the removal. Whereupon Mr. Duane of New York was appointed to the treasury. But Mr. Duane, no more than his predecessor, could see his way clear to remove the deposits. When made to understand that it was the determination of the President to have them removed at all hazards, he explicitly refused to lend himself for the purpose. The President removed Mr. Duane, and appointed Roger B. Taney, the late Chief Justice, as Secretary of the Treasury. He proved more flexible to the will of power, and immediately gave the required order. The consequences of this step in the circumstances were immense and mischievous. The discount line of the bank was at the moment over $60,000,000. The public deposits were $10,000,000. The sudden withdrawal of this sum affected credit and disarranged business to a remarkable degree, and caused intense excitement all over the Union.

The next movement in the "great experiment," as it was sarcastically called in the politics of the day, was the issue of the famous specie-circular, which directed the receivers of the public money to take nothing but gold and silver in payment of the public lands. Speculators and others had been making large purchases of western lands, expecting to pay in paper money. The specie-circular came upon them like a clap of thunder. Their consternation was vast, and the circular, coming as it did, shortly after the removal of the deposits, made confusion worse confounded.

General Jackson went out of office, and the second

bank went out, of being the same year; but the inaugurated movement was completed by Mr. Van Buren, who effected the complete divorce of the government from all banks and fiscal agents whatever, first, by directing the State banks which now had the keeping of the public moneys, to distribute them as surplus revenue among the States; and, by the sub-treasury scheme, in pursuance of which the United States received in payment of all dues, and paid out in all disbursements, gold and silver only. I believe in gold and silver money, or their equivalent in representative paper which can be instantly converted into them, and do not question the patriotic aims of the administrations concerned, but there was something headlong and violent in this transition from the traditional policy of the government to the new system. The successive steps fail to commend themselves to impartial men as wise. They wrought immense mischiefs at the time, contributed largely to the terrible financial crisis of 1837, and were a leading cause, no doubt, of the defeat of Van Buren in 1840, and the triumphant election of General Harrison. Such changes ought always to be carefully prepared for and gradually introduced.

From 1836 to 1862 there was no national money in the United States, except the coin; the paper currency was furnished by a number, increased at last to over fifteen hundred, of joint-stock banking companies, under the sole authority of the States. These, under various and often conflicting regulations, manufactured and issued money for the people. This money, as a whole, was never a safe, a uniform, an economical currency. It was subject to alternate contractions and expansions which spoiled it as a measure of value. It was never able to stand the shock of the commercial crises which it powerfully contributed to bring on. Money is an implement, and a costly implement, and the functions it has to perform cannot be performed by cheap, penny-wise, pound - foolish substitutes. Just as no man wants in his factory a crazy, second-hand engine, whose boiler is liable to burst, and whose gear gets out of repair, because it is cheaper, but prefers to get a good machine and pay for it, so wise and patriotic men are willing to be at the expense of getting a good, a national, a respectable, an everywhere current, and, if it must be paper, an instantly convertible money. Such a money the country at least expects to have under the new national banking law, whose origin and principal features we shall examine after casting a glance at the mint.

Two kinds of paper and two kinds of coin had preceded the issue of the bills of the first United States Bank. The first kind of paper were bills of credit issued first by the individual colonies, and then by the confederated continent, always inconvertible, and consequently always depreciating; the second kind of paper were the bills of the three State banks at Philadelphia, New York, and Boston, convertible, and so far forth excellent; but circulating mainly in their respective cities only. The first kind of coin were the pine-tree silver-pieces of Massachusetts, minted two hundred years ago, and the copper pieces struck under State authority about the time of the adoption of the constitution of the United States, simultaneously in Vermont, Connecticut, New Jersey, and Massachusetts; the other kind of coin being the copper cents nationalized by the old Congress, and which came into circulation while the convention was sitting which framed the constitution under which we live.

As soon as the new government had got fairly under way, the more pressing questions of the tariff, the national bank, the organization of the departments, being disposed of, the national mint was put into practical operation at Philadelphia. The laws relating to the mint were enacted during the session of 1792, and the first Federal coins of gold and silver were struck in January, 1795. It is to Jefferson that the country is indebted for the decimal scale of currency, so superior in convenience to all other monetary subdivisions. He had proposed a matured plan for the coinage, with the dollar for the unit, and the decimal subdivisions of dimes, cents, and mills, and the decimal multiple of the dollar, the eagle, while he was a member of the old Congress in 1785; and the Congress had adopted his plan the following year, and, as has been said, some copper cents were minted on the Federal standard; but nothing more was done till 1792, when the new Congress reaffirmed the resolutions of the old, readopted Jefferson's denominations, and put our existing mint into working order. There was a curious debate in Congress at the time as to the devices which the coins should bear. As the bill came from the Senate, where it originated, the gold and silver pieces were to have on one side the figure of the eagle, which the Continental Congress long before had adopted as the national emblem, and near this, the legend " United States of America." This was for the obverse of the coin, and so far nobody had any objection. For the reverse, the bill proposed that, in accordance with the usages of all nations from the time of the earliest known coinage, the impression or representation of the head of the President of the United States for the time being, together with his name, order of succession in the presidency, and the date of the coinage, should be stamped. This was strongly objected to in the House, as savoring of monarchy. The President's head on the coin was deemed by some a dangerous thing for the republic, and the proposal led to a sarcastic and even acrimonious debate, and was at length defeated in the House by a vote of twenty-six to twenty-two, in which the Senate was afterwards obliged to concur, and a proposition made by Key of Maryland was carried, to substitute a figure of Liberty instead of the obnoxious head of the President; but under precisely what sort of a figure to represent Liberty was then the difficulty, and at the next session Elias Boudinot of New Jersey, afterwards the director of the mint, endeavored to get substituted for the emblematic figure of Liberty the head of Columbus, but in vain; the Republican party was bound that the figure of Liberty and no other should go on to the coins, and it went, and we have here the history of that daintily seated lady, whose pretty face we used to see familiarly enough before the war, and whose acquaintance we hope to resume in the good time coming.

It may be asked how we came to have the dollar as the unit of our monetary system. The word dollar is derived from a German word which means valley, and was first applied to coins in consequence of this circumstance: in the mining region of Bohemia, at a place called Joachimsthal, (Joachim's valley,) silver-pieces of one ounce weight were coined and came into circulation about 1520 as Joachimsthaler, and then for shortness thaler; this became dalera in Spanish, and in English dollar. The thaler is still the German money of account, and the Spanish milled dollar became so famous in the world of commerce, and so familiar to our fathers in their dealings with the West Indies and the Spanish American colonies, that our Congress adopted it as the best known and most convenient unit of money. The word dime is a corruption of the Latin *decem*, ten; cent a contraction of the Latin *centum*, hundred; and mill a contraction of the Latin *mille*, thousand; so that our denominations are philosophical as well as convenient, each one in order being and being designated a tenth part of the one above.

The mint of the United States is one of the most interesting institutions in the country. It was established at Philadelphia in 1792. While it was still doubtful where the ultimate seat of the national government would be placed, the citizens of that beautiful city were strongly in hopes of being able to persuade Congress permanently to abide in their town, in which the old continental body had first met, in which independence had been declared, and which, more than any other, was popularly regarded as the headquarters of the national Union. A notable instance of log-rolling legislation, the first in our history, transferred the capital of the country to the banks of the Potomac, but the good people of the

Quaker City have nevertheless always retained the mint, as a memorial of their earlier position in the history of the government.

By the law establishing the mint, the chief officer was to be styled a director; and the ingenious David Rittenhouse, a self-taught mathematician, who had run several years before, by the help of instruments all of his own construction, the most difficult part of Mason and Dixon's line, was shortly after appointed to this post. The act stipulated that all bullion brought to the mint should be coined gratuitously; but when coin was delivered in exchange for bullion on the spot, one half of one per cent. was to be charged as seigniorage. The coins were to be the eagle, the half-eagle and the quarter-eagle in gold; the dollar, half-dollar, quarter-dollar, dime, and half-dime in silver; the cent and half-cent in copper. The weight of the eagle was to be 270 grains troy, alloyed according to the English standard, one part in twelve; and the dollar was to weigh 416 grains, alloyed one part in nine and nine-tenths. The subdivisions of these coins, gold and silver, were to be in all respects proportional to their units. At that time, in France and in Europe generally, the current relative value of gold and silver was considered one to fifteen, and the act of Congress established that as the ratio of the value of the two metals to be maintained at the mint; but, from this clause of the law, there followed important consequences, which were not foreseen, since that was not, at least in America, the true ratio of their value at that time, and being a decided undervaluation of gold, the gold coinage did not come into any circulation. It was really worth by the ounce more than fifteen ounces of silver; but, as the mint only reckoned it equal to fifteen ounces of silver, it was more valuable out of the circulation than in it, and it was therefore always exported in preference to silver, in payment of foreign balances, especially after France and the rest of Europe had changed the relative legal value to one to fifteen and one half. After that, an ounce of gold, estimated in silver, was worth three and one third per cent. more abroad than at home, and, of course, under the circumstances, it would not circulate in the home currency. The cheaper money will push out of circulation the dearer the world over. From the organization of the mint till 1817, over five millions and a half dollars in gold-pieces were coined, and very little indeed of it came into permanent circulation, for the simple reason that it was really worth more than it was counted to be worth by the regulations of the currency. It would, therefore, pay to melt it up, because it was worth more as bullion than as coin.

This state of things continued, the silver circulating freely but the gold scarcely circulating at all, till the attention of Congress was called to the subject, and a law passed substantially rating gold in relation to silver at one to sixteen. The weight of the eagle was reduced to 258 grains from 270, and the alloy increased to one part in ten from one part in twelve. This increased at one jump the legal valuation of gold $6\frac{68}{100}$ per cent. as compared with silver, which remained as before. As the former ratio was a decided undervaluation of gold, so the law of 1834 as decidedly overvalued it; and the working of a beautiful natural law became immediately apparent, by which the current of the metals was reversed, silver now passing in preference to Europe to liquidate the balances of trade, and gold coming from Europe to the United States, where it was about three and one quarter per cent. dearer than in Europe, while silver was about three and one quarter per cent. dearer in Europe than in the United States. The metals go where they have the most consideration in exchange. Between 1834 and 1837 silver was slipping out of our currency, and gold as decidedly coming in. The law of Congress went too far, and inverted the evil it was designed to correct. It endeavored to hit the true natural relative value of the two metals for the time being, but shot as much beyond the mark as the previous law fell short. Our silver coins began to be exported freely in preference to gold in payment of balances, but the tendency had not become very marked when were introduced the changes of 1837.

Dr. Robert M. Patterson, who was the director of the mint from 1835 to 1851, under whose direction the present admirably improved machinery of the mints was introduced, and who thereby developed their capacity from a coinage of $5,000,000 to $63,-000,000 per annum, drew up a new code of mint-laws, which was enacted by Congress in January, 1837, by which the previous complicated legislation was all superseded, and on which the mint has been substantially administered ever since. In the first place, the French standard of fineness of nine tenths for both gold and silver was adopted, that is to say, one part alloy in a whole of ten parts. Since its adoption by us from the French, this decimal standard of fineness has been adopted also by several other nations for their new coins, and thus some important steps have already been taken towards a most desirable end which is yet to be realized in the future, a universal currency for commerce. If the money of the leading commercial nations only contained the same quantity of alloy, and especially if the coins could be brought into decimal or other easy numerical relation to each other, as the French franc, the American dollar, and the English sovereign already are, this money would be a sort of universal money, capable of paying the balances of commerce anywhere, without the present trouble and expense of melting up and recoinage. This change in the standard of fineness necessitated a change in the weight of the silver coins, if the established relation of one to sixteen was to be maintained. Accordingly the weight of the silver dollar was reduced from 416 grains to $412\frac{1}{2}$, and the lesser silver pieces in proportion. The weight of the dollar has remained at that figure ever since, but the smaller silver coins have been, as we shall see, still further reduced in weight, and the refusal of the dollar-piece to circulate has been another good illustration for ten or more years of the universal law that the cheaper money drives our the dearer.

At different times since 1837 new denominations of coins have been added to our national series; of gold, the double-eagle, the three-dollar, and the one-dollar piece; of silver, only the three-cent piece, which has never been popular, and will be superseded by the new three-cent copper piece. In 1853 very interesting alterations were made in the character of our silver coins; up to that date the laws made both the gold and silver money a legal tender to any amount; and it was consequently optional with the debtor to pay in the cheaper metal, which ever it might be; and as experience was proving that the relative value of the two was not constant but variable, and that the legally established ratio of one to sixteen was depleting the currency of silver, it was then determined to make gold alone the legal tender, except to the extent of $5; to cease coining silver for individuals, and only coin on government account such sums as seemed to be in demand for purposes of change; and to reduce the weight of the half-dollar and its subdivisions so that their nominal value should be considerably above their real value as compared with the silver dollar, and thus their exportation be prevented. Accordingly the weight of the half-dollar has been reduced from $206\frac{1}{4}$ grains to 192 grains, and of the smaller coins in proportion. Government buys silver bullion at the market price, which has only varied for several years from $1.21 to 1.22\frac{1}{2}$ per ounce, and coins this into $1.25 of the smaller silver-pieces, thus charging a seigniorage of about three per cent. Consequently the half-dollars and lesser silver coins are overvalued in our currency, and a nominal dollar's worth of them worth $7\frac{42}{100}$ per cent. less than a silver dollar. The result of these measures has been to establish gold as the real currency of the country, and to make silver entirely subsidiary to that. The current value of the silver coin in the currency is sufficiently above its market price as bullion to prevent the exportation of the coins, and this explains the discount to which our silver has been subjected in Canada for the past three years. Instead of weighing 412½ grains, a dollar in small coin weighs only 384 grains, and therefore the Canadians with good reason have vehemently rejected these pieces at their nominal value. Their actual and proper discount as compared with the silver dollar is $7\frac{42}{100}$ per cent. It ought to be added that the gold dollar is now our unit of value, and the director of the mint has repeatedly asked Congress to bring the silver dollar out of its anomalous into a normal condition.

It now only remains to characterize the new national bank system, in its origin, structure, benefits, and dangers.

When Secretary Chase assumed the Treasury Department in the spring of 1861, the state of the country, and, of consequence, the state of the finances, were appalling. Mr. Buchanan's administration had just been trying to borrow a few millions of dollars of the people, and had only succeeded in securing a very small sum, and that at the enormous rate of twelve per cent. interest. The clouds of war which had been gathering black and sullen all the winter, soon broke in wrathful peals over the head of the new administration. The country must be defended, as well as the ordinary expenses of the government met; an army must be raised, equipped, put into the field, and paid. We do not propose to follow the Secretary in his general financial embarrassments, expedients, and resources; but it is needful to our present purpose to say that, owing to the unexpected delays and disasters of the war, and to the consequent want of confidence in the public mind, he found it extremely difficult to borrow the sums necessary to be had in order to meet the expenditures of the government; and that in his first annual report to Congress, in December, 1861, he recommended, principally for the sake of facilitating the negotiation of loans, the organization of banking associations, whose circulation should consist only of notes, uniform in character, furnished by the government, and secured as to convertibility into coin by United States bonds deposited in the treasury. It is clear that if such associations should be formed, it would make a market for the national bonds to the extent in which they should invest their capital stock in them as security for their circulation. Above all things, at that time the United States wanted to borrow money. It must borrow or perish; and therefore a national banking system, based for security on the national debt, would open a market for some hundreds of millions of the evidences of that debt, and put a corresponding sum of immediately available funds into the hands of the government.

This proposal of the Secretary, involving, as it did, the winding up of the State banks as such, found at first but little favor in Congress or among the people. The banking interests of the eastern and middle States, particularly of the State of New York, from whose State bank system the idea was mainly and by acknowledgment borrowed, were especially hostile to the scheme. In his second annual report, in December, 1862, the Secretary iterated his recommendation, and enforced it at length by arguments drawn from the necessity of effecting immediately more extensive loans, from the character of the currency for soundness and uniformity thus furnished to the people, from the convenient agencies which such banks would furnish for the deposit of public moneys, and from the firm anchorage which such a system would give to the union of the States. These arguments, which found a response especially emphatic from the Western States, coupled with the assurance of the Secretary, that, if Congress should concur in his views, though conscious of the great difficulty which vast, sudden, and protracted expenditures imposed on him, he thought he should still be able to maintain the public credit and provide for the public wants, induced Congress to frame and pass " An act to provide a national currency secured by a pledge of United States stocks, and to provide for the circulation and redemption thereof." The act was approved by the President February 25, 1863.

The fundamental idea of the whole system is the combination of national credit with private capital in the issue and redemption of money. This idea was first realized in the Bank of England. The bank is an association of individuals incorporated under the style of the " Governor and Company of the Bank of England;" and at its organization in 1694, it invested its whole capital stock of $6,000,000 (reducing pounds to dollars) in government bonds; and at various times since it has bought up more of these bonds, until now the British government owes the bank $55,075,000. This debt is the basis of the operations of the bank. It is allowed to issue notes to the full amount of this permanent debt, and to the extent of $14,925,000 more on other national securities, less permanent in their character; but for every bank-note beyond this aggregate of $70,000,-000, based on the national credit, there must be pound for pound gold and silver in the vaults of the bank. The bank-note circulation, therefore, is based first on the credit of the association of individuals called the Bank of England, which promises to redeem every note in specie on presentation, but rests back for its ultimate security on the national faith embodied in the bonds in which the capital stock of the bank is invested. Very similar is our new system. (Every bank organized under it invests its own capital stock in the bonds of the United States, bearing interest. These bonds are transferred to an officer of the treasury, called the comptroller, at Washington, (who holds them as security for the redemption of the bills of such bank) but who pays the interest on them to the bank itself, so long as the bank redeems its bills promptly and violates no provisions of the organic banking law. Ninety per cent. of the amount of such bonds thus deposited with the comptroller, provided the bonds be estimated at par value and bear interest at a rate not less than five per cent., is then furnished by the treasurer to the bank in circulating notes, engraved and registered by the United States; unless the capital stock of the bank be more than $500,000 and less than $1,000,000, in which case only eighty per cent. of the capital is furnished in notes; and if the capital be between $1,000,000 and $3,000,000, only seventy-five per cent.; and over $3,000,000, sixty per cent. These notes thus received by the banks, they issue to the people in ordinary loans and payments, and they are required by the law to keep on hand at all times twenty-five per cent. of their aggregate average circulation and deposits in lawful money of the United States, with which to redeem their notes on presentation. Thus the convertibility of the notes is dependent first on the solvency of the association, and, if that fails to redeem them, they are speedily redeemable, after certain formalities are gone through with, at the treasury of the United States; and so many of the bonds belonging to such bank, deposited with the comptroller of the currency as security for the redemption of the notes, are then to be sold as shall reimburse the United States for such redemption; so that it is almost impossible under the law that the bill-holders of any national bank can ever suffer any loss. The United States holds the capital of the bank in its own hands, and is thus enabled to guarantee the convertibility of the bills. At the same time the system secures the manifold advantages of private capital, private enterprise, and personal sagacity and integrity, in the matter of loaning money, securing deposits, and general management of the banks.

The superiority in every respect of this scheme of banking to the fast and loose system which has prevailed in this country so long, is very apparent. In the first place, perfect publicity of the affairs of every bank is provided for in the organic law, and cannot be evaded. Every bank in the principal cities must publish a statement, under oath, at the beginning of every month, of its exact condition, and forward it to the comptroller; and the other banks must do the same every quarter, and the comptroller is to publish abstracts of these reports every quarter; so that everybody can know the state of each bank in particular, as well as the state of the whole circulation. In the second place, the whole amount of the circulation cannot be increased at the will of the banks or the will of the comptroller, or in any other way except by an act of Congress authorizing such increase; so that the system is not so liable to those sudden contractions and expansions which have been the bane of our paper money hitherto. In the third place, the bills will be uniform in value all over the country, and debts can be paid by them through the post-office or otherwise, without the mediation of any bank or the payment of exchanges. In the fourth place, besides the absolute security of ultimate redemption, the ratio of lawful money actually on hand to the aggregate circulation is much higher than has hitherto prevailed in practice throughout the country. Add to these reasons this other, that the homogeneousness of the money circulating among them, in connection with a common creditorship towards the United States Government, is an additional bond binding the States and the people together, and tending powerfully to neutralize the centrifugal forces which are always at work in large societies and governments. But we shall get an idea too favorable to the new national banking system, unless we look also at

THE DANGERS.

The money which these banks are to circulate is, after all, nothing but credit money, and will be liable in some degree to the disorders which are inseparable from every form of credit. Credit is not payment, but a promise to pay. The promise may be good, it may be sure to be fulfilled; but it is not, and never can be made, the same thing as fulfilment. These bills bear upon their face the acknowledgment that they are promises to pay, and not the pay itself; and men are so constituted, and society is so delicately organized, that times are liable to come when men shall have a general distrust of mere promises, and shall desire to see them changed into fulfilment. If a panic should ever arise in regard to these notes, and a general desire be manifested on the part of the holders to convert them into cash, it is evident that many of the banks would be obliged to suspend specie payments, since they are only required to hold twenty-five per cent. of their circulation and deposits in cash, and this ratio, as a general thing, is not likely to be exceeded. It is true that their notes cannot all come back at once for redemption, nor indeed any very considerable proportion of them, since, unlike the circulation of the State banks, they will pass freely beyond the boundaries of States and sections, and become necessarily very widely diffused; yet general confidence is a thing so sensitive, and credit money is in its nature such, that an absolute freedom from panics and from supensions cannot rationally be predicted. They are liable to come: it will be strange if they do not come.

But the most imminent danger that threatens this system is this: that Congress will unwisely increase the amount already authorized to be issued before the system gets fairly settled and the resumption of specie payments takes place. This is every way to be deprecated. The system will be sound and wholesome just in proportion as Congress refuses to add to the present amount of $300,000,0000. When the war broke out, the whole paper circulation of the country, north and south, was only $202,000,000; and in the loyal States, $150,000,000; and on the first of January, 1862, in the loyal States, only $130,000,000, according to the authority of Secretary Chase. Now, we do not want an exclusively paper currency. We want a broad substratum of gold and silver underneath it to support it, control it, and redeem it. There ought to be at least as much of gold and silver in the currency and in the banks as of paper money. The English have more. That is the grand reason why the British currency is so sound and excellent; not that a part of it is credit money, but that the greater part of it is gold and silver. If Congress will only hold firm, and allow those channels of circulation which $300,000,000 of paper cannot fill to be filled up with gold and silver money, as they will be in accordance with natural laws, without the necessity of a syllable of legislation, then the banking system will stand firm, then the paper will be equal with gold, then we shall have a circulation of perhaps $650,000,000 of good money, redemption of the notes will rarely be called for, and will be perfectly easy when it is called for, and such a thing as a panic attacking the currency will be rarely or never witnessed. Let no man say that it will cost too much to maintain $350,000,000 of metallic money. The Director of the United States Mint, in his Report for 1862, tells us, as the result of careful observations and experiments at the mint, that the average abrasion of all our gold and silver coins in times of their circulation is $\frac{1}{2400}$ per annum. To maintain, then, a metallic circulation of $350,000,000 would cost $145,833 a year; we doubt whether as much paper money can be kept good for that sum, considering the losses from accident, from counterfeiting, and similar items. There is no credit in gold and silver money. It promises nothing. It represents nothing. It stands in its own right of value exactly as any other commodity, as is shown by the fact that it is worth scarcely more as coin than as bullion. The most that can be said of any paper money is, that it approximates in value and steadiness to a gold and silver money. The closer the approximation, the better the paper. Considering the likelihood that Congress will be urged to allow of more paper money, and the likelihood that they will yield to such urging, and the certainty that such action will postpone the day of resuming specie payments, and the probability that the whole system will be more or less endangered thereby, we cannot predict with any confidence the high success of the system. It is perhaps rather to be hoped for than expected.

CHAPTER XII.

ON CREDIT.

POLITICAL Economy is the science of exchanges; but there are certain exchanges which have this peculiarity, that the return service is not rendered immediately, but is impliedly or expressly promised to be rendered in the future. This peculiarity is important to be considered, and gives rise to all those phenomena which pass under the general name of Credit. The commercial use of the term credit is loose and various, denoting sometimes the reputation of a person for solvency, as when it is said, "So and So has good credit;" and sometimes denoting a general state of the public mind, in which use it is synonymous with confidence, as when it is said, "There is no credit in a time of commercial crisis;" and sometimes denoting also the paper evidences of an obligation resting on some party to render a return service for some service already received. Credit, in general, may be defined as an exchange in which the return service is delayed, and which usually gives birth to a written evidence that such service is due. In order that this form of exchanges may be common, it is of course needful that there should be a general confidence in the public mind; in other words, a general expectation that such debts will be promptly paid.

As indicating a common honor and financial ability among business men, and as facilitating the production of services of all sorts, this state of general confidence is so desirable in the sphere of exchange that great pains should be taken that nothing occur to destroy it; — the destruction of confidence and credit being usually caused by the undue extension of the one, and the excessive multiplication of the evidences of the other. We will first look at the principal forms of credit, and then at its advantages and disadvantages.

(1.) Book Accounts. A charge in a trader's books is both a current and a legal evidence that the person charged has received a certain service, and has virtually promised to render the sum charged as a return service. This is the most common of the forms of credit; and if the person charged fails of his own accord to complete the exchange thus commenced, the law, in the absence of any proof to make the charge suspicious, collects it, if possible, and forcibly completes the exchange. The convenience of this form of credit is so great that it is not likely ever to be disused; and as between people who deal much with each other is very useful, inasmuch as their respective book accounts are set against each other in settlement, and only balances are required to be cancelled in money. It is for the benefit of both creditor and debtor, however, that such credits should be short in time, and such settlements frequent, since thus only does the creditor realize the gains of the exchange, and the debtor keep fair his mercantile name. If it be difficult or impossible to follow strictly the excellent financial maxim, "Pay as you go," the next best thing to that is, "Go and pay." The gains of an exchange are lessened, or its terms become more onerous, just in proportion as delay in its completion is experienced or expected. Book accounts are subject also to this disadvantage as compared with other forms of credit, that their number and amount as against any person are less likely to become publicly known, and therefore he is more likely to be trusted in this form by others beyond the point of his solvency and their safety.

(2.) Promissory notes. These are issued by individuals, corporations, and nations. They are usually on interest; and in this case, if the principal be considered secure, and the interest be promptly paid, the element of time is comparatively a matter of indifference, because the interest is compensation for delay, and is frequently the motive on the part of the holder of the note for rendering that service of which the note is evidence. Bank-bills are a form of promissory notes not on interest, and the bank issuing them really borrows of the people, and has the use of that amount of money, without paying interest, but offers, as a kind of compensation for this privilege, to convert its notes into coin on demand of any holder. It is this proffered convertibility into coin that enables the promissory notes of a bank to circulate as money, while the notes of other corporations and individuals equally solid and solvent do not circulate as money. It must be borne in mind, however, that the offer to convert them into cash does not essentially alter the nature of bank-notes; they are a form of credit; and although they are commonly issued against another form of credit, namely, against the interest-bearing notes of individuals who resort to the bank for discount, this only complicates the exchange without changing its nature. It is an instance of exchanging one form of credit for another which happens to have a greater currency or validity than the first, and for this superiority of the bank credit the individual credit pays an interest, in other words, is discounted; and such exchanges of one form of paper credit for another, with or without a premium, may go on indefinitely; as credit money, such paper may serve as a medium in many exchanges; but ultimately, and before the entire series of transactions is closed, such paper is to be exchanged for something that is not paper; it is redeemed in cash, or gives a claim to something no longer credit which is in reality the return service for the original service rendered. When such promissory note, or other form of credit, is payable to bearer, it may run a devious round, may play a part in many a transaction; but it is in reality nothing but a general warrant entitling the holder, in view of some original service of the claim for the return of which he has become in some manner possessed, to take his satisfaction for that service whenever he will. It is like the land warrants, given by the United States, entitling the holder, in return for military service rendered, to locate his acres on any unoccupied national land within the national boundaries. As a warrant, its function ceases so soon as the acres have been chosen. Credit passes into payment. Thus bank-bills are redeemable in coin. The national legal-tender notes are fundable in government bonds, another form of credit, but whose principal and interest are payable in gold. The private notes of individuals and corporations are payable in money, and if in credit money, this itself ends in something that is not credit, and thus the circuit of exchange is completed.

When the United States borrows money, it gives the lender a promissory note on interest at a certain rate, both principal and interest being payable at certain specified times. These notes are called indifferently bonds, stocks, or funds. The government has issued in the past four years nearly $2,500,000,000 worth of them, in return for money loaned to it by the people, and they bear interest at rates varying from 5 to $7\frac{3}{10}$ per cent., and are payable at periods varying from three to forty years. The bonds designated as "five-twenties," bear gold interest at six per cent., and the government reserves the right to pay the principal in five years, and pledges itself to pay it twenty years from date. So of the "ten-forties." The "seven-thirties" are so named, not from the time of payment, but from the rate of interest, which is $7\frac{30}{100}$ per cent., payable in legal tenders for three years, when the principal is payable in the same, or fundable in six per cent. gold-bearing bonds, at the option of the holders. So ready have the American people been to loan money to their government for the past two years, and take these bonds as security, that the treasury has experienced very little embarrassment from the want of money, although the expenditures have been at times over $3,000,000 a day. In the course of one week in the spring of 1865, ninety and odd millions of dollars were subscribed to a national loan. It is believed that the history of national borrowing presents no parallel with the late success of the United States in realizing money in the way of loans. The largest English loans ever made were made in 1812 and 1813, during the wars with Napoleon and the United States. In these two years the British exchequer borrowed $534,000,000, being an average of $22,250,000 a month, and pronounced that a wonderful financial achievement, as it was; but, from an aggregate of national wealth not larger than England's then was, though from a larger population, the United States has realized in four years from loans a sum about five times as large as that, and at an average rate of interest but little higher than England then paid, which was five per cent. and a fraction.[1] The national debt of England in March, 1863, was $3,915,000,000, on which the average rate of interest was three and one half per cent. The national debt of France, which is rather more than half as large as England's, pays rates of interest varying from three to four and one half per cent. The entire debt of the United States, Oct. 1st, 1865, was $2,744,947,726; and the total interest upon it, $137,529,216.

(3.) Bills of exchange. A bill of exchange is a written instrument designed to secure the payment of a distant debt without the transmission of money, being in effect a setting off or exchange of one debt against another. Thus, suppose A in Boston owes B in New York $1000, and another party, C in New York, owes A in Boston a like sum; it is not

[1] Appleton's Annual Cyclopædia, 1863. Article, "Finances."

necessary that A should send the money to B to cancel his debt, and C send the money to A for a like purpose; the two debts, by means of a bill of exchange, are set off against each other, and both transactions are closed without sending any money from one city to the other. A draws a bill upon C, directing him to pay B $1000, and sends this bill to C, who, if that mode of payment be satisfactory to him, accepts it by endorsing his name upon it, which completes the transaction between A and C, and then presents it with payment to B, which completes the transaction between B and A. A is called the drawer of the bill, C the drawee until he has endorsed, and then the acceptor, and B is the payee. Sometimes the bill passes through several hands, which may either be by successive endorsements, specifying to whom payment is to be made, or by what is called an endorsement in blank, by which is meant that the payee or subsequent holder, to whom the bill has been endorsed, merely writes his own name upon the bill, which is equivalent to making it payable to bearer. The remarkable convenience of bills of exchange in adjusting debts between distant places has already brought them into very general use wherever the necessary basis for them in commercial integrity is supposed to exist; and every year is witnessing an extension of their use in all commercial countries. Bills of exchange are either payable at sight, or after an interval fixed in the bill itself; and are either inland or foreign bills. Bills which have some time to run before maturity are frequently discounted by bankers or other moneylenders, that is to say, the payee transfers the bill to them, receiving the amount, minus interest for the time it has still to run; and the bill thus serves the important function of enabling a debt due from one person to be made available for obtaining credit from another. It is a principal part of the business of banks to buy in this manner bills of exchange, either real bills, or accommodation bills, so called, which only differ from the others in that there is no real debt between the drawer and drawee, and collect them at maturity, thus securing bank interest on all money paid in purchasing such bills. The bills are discounted on the joint credit of the drawer and acceptor. It is evident that the use of bills of exchange, especially those which pass from hand to hand by endorsement, dispense with the use and transmission of large amounts of money, and, as between distant places especially, are one of those economizing expedients of credit which are the birth of modern civilization and a sound mercantile honor.

Very similar are foreign bills of exchange in their functions and usefulness. Commercial relations between two countries, say for example, France and England, always give rise to a mutual indebtedness of their merchants, and if these debts were all to be paid by the actual sending of money to and from, there would have to be a constant and expensive outward and inward flow of the precious metals in respect to each country, which necessity is neatly obviated by the use of bills of exchange, and coin is only transmitted to settle the balances on whichever side there is an excess of debt. French dealers are always sending goods to England, and English dealers goods to France; and for what they send to England the French merchants draw bills on the parties to whom the goods are consigned, and the English merchants draw similar bills on their debtors in France; these bills are bought up by bankers or brokers in either country, and exposed again for sale to any parties who may have debts to pay in the other country. Thus bills on London, in other words, on English debtors, are always for sale in France; and bills on France, that is, on French debtors, are always for sale in London; the mutual debtors of the two countries, therefore, instead of sending coin to cancel their debts, buy and transmit these bills. As I wish to make the course and par of international exchange very plain to my readers, I will give a particular illustration. Suppose Pierre & Co., of Paris, send a cargo of wine to Barclay & Co., of London, worth £5000; the London firm thereby becomes indebted to the Paris firm to that amount, and Pierre & Co. draw a bill on Barclay & Co. for £5000; if they themselves have no debt to pay in London, they sell this bill to a Paris broker (if the exchange be then at par) for its face, minus interest for the time it has to run; and this broker is now ready to sell the bill again to anybody in Paris who has a debt to pay in London; and the person in London who receives it in liquidation of a French debt to him, presents it at maturity to Barclay & Co. for payment. A bill drawn in London for a cargo of hardware sent to Paris, is similarly negotiated with a London broker, and finds its way similarly to France, in payment of some English debt, and ends its career when it reaches the French firm on which it was originally drawn. We are now in position to understand clearly what is meant by the par of exchange. The merchants in Paris, who have debts due to them in London, draw bills of exchange for the amount of these debts, and, through the agency of middlemen or brokers, go into the market to sell these bills to other Paris merchants who have debts to pay in London. If the former set have a larger amount to sell than the latter have occasion to buy, in other words, if there be a larger amount of debts due from London to Paris, than from Paris to London, then the competition of the sellers of bills on London will lower their price somewhat in the market, in order, as usual, that the supply and demand may be equalized. In this case the par of exchange is disturbed, a bill on London for £100 may not sell for over £99, and the exchange is then said to be one per cent. against London, or, which is the same thing, one per cent. in favor of Paris. The par of exchange, therefore, between two countries, depends upon the substantial equality of their mutual debts; and if an exchange unfavorable to either continues long, and especially if the discount on its bills be sufficient to cover the charges of the transmission of specie, gold will begin to flow from the country against which the exchange has turned, and the equilibrium of payments, and hence the par of exchange will be restored. Also, the par tends to restore itself, without the sending of specie, in this way: if bills on London are at a discount in Paris, for the same reason that they are so will bills on Paris be at a premium in London, and therefore there will be a direct encouragement to the extent of the premium for exportations from England to France, because on every cargo sent bills can be drawn and sold in London for a premium; but the more bills on Paris thus offered, the more the premium disappears, and the par of exchange is restored so soon as the debts thus contracted by France are equal to the debts due her from England. At the same time, and so long as the discount on London bills continues, there is a discouragement to further exportations from France to England, because the bills drawn in virtue of such cargoes can only be sold below par. Here is another instance of a magnificently comprehensive law by which Nature vindicates her right to reign in the domain of exchange. It is through this law, stimulating exportations on the one side, and slackening them on the other, that most of the casual disturbances of the par of exchange are rectified; but if, notwithstanding this, the disturbance continues obstinate, it indicates one of two things as true of the country against which the exchange has turned : it has either made over-purchases of the other country beyond the power of its ordinary exports to cancel, or the money in which the bills drawn on it are liable to be paid is an inferior money. In the first case, the only proper remedy is an export of gold to pay off the old scores, and a more prudent method of purchasing in the future; in the second case, which is well exemplified in the instance of Amsterdam, cited in a preceding chapter, the remedy is to raise the currency to a good specie standard. When the rates of exchange were first established between England and the

United States, the pound sterling was reckoned as equal to $4.44 of our money; since then the weight and fineness of our gold coins have been reduced, and the real par of exchange is one pound for $4.87; the old nominal par however remains as the standard, so that the exchange is really at par when it stands in the quotations as $109\frac{1}{2}$, or $9\frac{1}{2}$ per cent. above par. Our gold dollar contains 23.2 grains of fine gold, and the English sovereign 113 grains and a fraction, and the true par therefore is 4.87 for 1. The par of exchange between France and the United States is 5 francs 17 centimes for $1; and between France and England, is 25 francs 20 centimes for £1.

(4.) Checks. Formerly, in England, and in other countries as well, every considerable dealer kept his strong box, and when he had occasion to make payments, told down the solid cash upon his own counter. Afterwards, the goldsmiths of London solicited the honor of keeping in their vaults the spare cash of the merchants, who in their payments among one another came to employ checks drawn on the goldsmiths, and at the shops of the latter the principal payments in coin were effected. The later introduction of banks brought along with it the custom, now continually widening in commercial countries among all classes of people, of keeping one's funds with a banker, and making payments by orders, or checks, upon him. When the person making the payment and the person receiving it keep their money with the same banker, there is no need of any money passing at all in the premises, the sum being merely transferred in the banker's books from the credit of the payer to that of the receiver. The banker is quite willing to do this business for nothing, and even to allow the depositors a low rate of interest on all balances remaining in his hands, in consideration of the privilege he enjoys of loaning such proportion of the sums as he deems safe to other parties at a higher rate of interest. In the large cities, by an arrangement called "the clearing-house," substantially the same benefits are secured as if all the people of the city kept their cash at the same bank; inasmuch as all the checks drawn on each of the different banks, and passing in the course of the business day into other banks, are assorted before evening at the clearing-house, and set off as far as possible against each other, leaving only balances to be adjusted in money. So long as the banks are strong and solvent, the safety of such checks is only surpassed by their convenience, which itself is enhanced by the facility with which they pass by endorsement from hand to hand, perhaps a dozen times in a morning, making payments equal to their face as often as they are transferred, and thus dispensing with the use of large masses of coin.

Some of the advantages of credit have been already anticipated in the discussion of its principal forms; but it is important to be observed that credit creates nothing except the paper embodying the evidence of it, but either, first, transfers the ownership of a return-service already in existence, and ready to be rendered at any time, into other hands; or, second, anticipates a return-service not yet ready to be rendered. Thus, when I deposit an $100 with a sound banker, and afterwards draw a check for the amount, which check passes by endorsement through a dozen hands before being presented for payment, there is a simple transfer by means of credit of the ownership of a service all ready to be rendered at any time, and the check does more conveniently, perhaps, exactly what the $100 in cash would have done, if, instead of depositing it at all, I had paid it out to the man to whom I paid the check, and he to the second, and so on through the dozen. The twelfth man in either case, and each in turn in the last case, receives an $100 in cash, the proprietorship of which, in the case of the check, passed from one to the other. But when I loan a poor artisan an $100 to buy stock with, and take his note, which is to be paid from the proceeds of his year's work, the return-service is wholly anticipated, and the element of time comes in, as well as the element of risk. Indeed, the element of time is the only basis of the distinction in hand. Credit in its nature is always the same thing, is always an exchange in which the return-service is contingent, and although the probability that it will be rendered is susceptible of all the degrees from a wellnigh certainty that it will to a wellnigh certainty that it will not, that is a matter which must be judged of from the character and condition of the party who is bound to render it, and nothing needs to be said about it in this connection; but time is a more calculable element in credit, and since credit is substantially delay and not power, since it only transfers capital from hand to hand and creates nothing, it follows that for the safety of both creditor and debtor, the time of credits should be short. Some people, seeing men prosper on borrowed capital, seeing the undoubted benefits of some forms of credit, have jumped to the conclusion that credit is a positive productive agent, a thing to be put on a level with labor and capital. No. Labor united with capital will work wonders, and the nature of capital is not altered by the fact that it has been borrowed, and when skilfully used by the borrower will net him a profit besides paying back principal and interest; but it is a strange jumble to ascribe to the credit, which merely transfers the capital for a time, the efficiency which is due to the capital united with labor. Let the nature of credit be distinctly understood at the outset, and it is impossible that there should be any confusion in the premises. Both parties to a credit exchange undoubtedly expect to be benefited thereby, otherwise it would not be made; and the party who parts with money, or labor, or whatever is rendered, gives over to the other in consideration of a promised equivalent, a positive power, which would doubtless have been somewhat efficient in his own hands, but which is expected to become more efficient in the hands of the other. Its whole efficiency, therefore, obtained in the hands of the borrower, is not due to credit, but only that surplus efficiency over and beyond what the loan would have had in the hands of the original holder, or rather, over and beyond what must be rendered by the borrower to the original holder. It is only in this sense that credit can be said to have efficiency at all; and, short times being presupposed as essential, since the gain of the creditor is not in the promise but in the fulfilment, it is precisely here that we are to look for the first class of advantages which a general credit system can offer.

There are some men, and particularly young men, who have integrity and industry and skill, but no capital; and when such men are enabled to borrow money to start themselves in business, or to enlarge a business already in successful operation, the general interests of production, as well as their personal interests, are subserved by such credit, because in all probability capital thus passes from hands which are less to hands which are more able to use it productively. Those who are best able to make capital tell are generally those who are most desirous to obtain it, and frequently those who can offer the best security for its replacement. Nothing is to be said against, but everything in favor, of such a loaning of capital as shall bring it, under safe conditions, from the hands of the idle, the aged, those indisposed, or those incompetent to use it productively, into hands at once competent and honest. Such credit is a benefit, and only a benefit, to all the parties concerned, and to society at large. The operators retain something of profit after replacing the capital with interest; the lenders receive more than if their capital remained idle, or they employed it themselves; and society is benefited by a more complete development and rapid circulation of services. Despite all the instances of broken faith, it is still an honor to human nature that men do so gain by good character the confidence of their fellows that they are, and ought to be, trusted with capital on their simple word or note; and it is the glory of free political institutions, that under their influence, more than elsewhere, young men with no other dower than integrity and purpose do rise, by the help of so slight a stepping-stone as this, in crowds, to the high places of opulence. In the point of view, that thus all the available capital of the community is brought out into productive activity, too much can scarcely be said in favor of joint-stock companies, whose managers are known to be men of probity, which gather up the driblets of unoccupied capital here and there, and, combining them, enter upon paths of profitable production, which individual enterprise cannot tread. Too much cannot be said in favor of savings-banks, which take the surplus earnings of the poor, and not only keep them safely, but pay a fair interest on each deposit, and loan the aggregate at a higher rate on choice securities, thus stimulating frugality in a wide circle of depositors, and at the same time aiding production by opportune loans to the best class of borrowers. Here too come in life-insurance companies, which illustrate the advantages of credit in a most gratifying light, and whose action I hope to see extended to larger and larger classes of men, since it tends to transmute low and selfish cares into a noble care for those who are to come after, who might otherwise be left penniless dependants, and by elevating and enlarging the views of men, to make them better producers and better citizens. In this category of the advantages of credit come also the ordinary bank discounts, made for short periods only, holding the debtor to the strictest rules of payment, only professing and only enabled to help customers over the transient hard places in their business, and not to furnish the funds on which the business is mainly conducted. Sums drawn from the banks on credit should only form a part of the circulating capital of a business, and never be put into the form of fixed capital. The passing necessities of a business having an independent basis of its own can be safely and conveniently met by bank discounts. A bank is essentially a loan-office, a combination of money-lenders who put their funds together for the better lending of them, a convenient institution at which lenders and borrowers come together, and in which there is a better knowledge of the reputation of the borrowers for solvency than the individual lenders could separately hope to obtain. So far as the capital stock is made up of small subscriptions, it has the advantage just spoken of, of calling otherwise idle sums into activity; and so far as no undue privileges are accorded to it by law, there is no branch of industry more legitimate and beneficial than banking. It is no essential part of the functions of a bank, that it manufacture and issue money; the money it loans should be the national money; and if that, unfortunately, be credit money, the element of credit in the money should be sharply discriminated in the public mind from that element of credit by which the bank loans it to its customers. Bank credits are good, but that does not prove that credit money is good; and it was one ground of the viciousness of the late banking system of the United States, that the different kinds of credit involved in it were inextricably interwoven with each other in the common apprehensions, and when the money failed utterly, as it did repeatedly, to answer the purposes of money, people could not exactly tell whose fault it was.

There is another class of advantages in credit, which do not depend so much on the transfer of capital from less to more productive hands, as on the facilities which credit affords in economizing the general operations of exchange. Here the advantages are derived from the convenience of settling accounts arising out of exchanges, rather than from the character of the exchanges themselves. Look, for example, at bills of exchange. They serve to settle up the accounts arising from the commerce of two continents, with but little transmission of money from either, and with but little loss of time. Bills drawn in New York on London are usually payable at sixty days' sight; and the merchant dispatching a ship is able to realize at once the value of her cargo, minus interest for the time his bill has to run; he is indeed still liable in part to see that his bill is ultimately paid by his drawee; but the commercial integrity of the leading houses in all countries is with justice so firmly believed in and acted on, that on the whole but little anxiety springs from this source. It is one of the noble things in international commerce that men trust each other across the oceans, and lay millions of value on the faith of a single firm. Inland bills of exchange equally facilitate settlements within the country itself; and checks contribute to the same end even more simply, passing readily in payments wherever the parties are known, and, though credit, doing the work of money more conveniently, and within certain limits as safely as money itself could do it. It is not strange that some thinkers and writers, seeing these unquestionable benefits of credit even within the peculiar sphere of money itself, have come to think and to teach that credit might answer all the purposes of money, and, like Herbert Spencer, would leave the largest liberty to all men to issue money if they choose, and such money as they choose, and as much money as they choose, supposing that only that which is good in quality and sufficient in quantity can gain currency. The trouble with these writers, every one of them is, that they neglect the second and more delicate function of money, namely, that it is and ever must be a measure of value, and treat it only as a medium of exchange. Their scheme is inadequate therefore, and never can be realized. The very advantages of credit itself, which have now been explained, are dependent on this, that there be underneath it, to support and limit it, a solid basis of value-money, in whose denominations value can be reckoned, in whose coins the balances of credit can be struck, and whose security everywhere by natural laws only can enable fulfilment to join hand in hand with promise. If ever credit should usurp the whole domain of money, a tolerable standard of value would be no longer possible, credit itself would lose its foothold, and the vast balloon of promise, sailing for a while through the blue, the joy of projectors and the wonder of credulous spectators, would come down to the earth flapping, and floundering, and ruined.

There are some natural disadvantages in credit. The first is, that when it is much given by dealers to consumers, the reverse results take place from those already characterized, and capital passes out from the hands of productive operators and becomes temporarily unavailable as capital. When an industrious artisan or merchant has trusted out $1000 to dilatory customers for six months or a year, it is so much withdrawn for so long from his active capital, and to make up the consequent loss of profit there must be an addition to the prices of his wares, and besides some bad debts belong to such a system, and there must be an additional price to compensate this, and thus the customers who pay promptly bear a part of the proper burden of the delinquents, who at least do not wholly escape, inasmuch as they ultimately (if they pay at all) pay a price enhanced by their own delay. If the current profit of capital be ten per cent., and the merchant sells and gets returns five times a year, something less than two per cent. profit may be charged to each article, but if he only gets returns at the end of the year, ten per cent. must be put upon everything. Hence the excellent maxim, " Quick sales and small profits."

But the principal disadvantage of credit is seen in its action on prices through increased demand, and in its consequent tendency to produce commercial crises; and this chapter will be concluded by a presentation of this subject, together with a sketch of the three great commercial crises that swept over this country in 1837, 1847, and 1857.

The cause of commercial crises is, in general, an undue expansion of credit; or, to use an equivalent expression, a disproportion between the amount of debts and the available capital in the loan-market, or elsewhere, to meet those debts.

A man's whole purchasing-power is made up of

three things: first, the property in his possession; secondly, the value that is owed to him; thirdly, his credit. He can buy value with these three things; and his power to buy is exactly measured by the sum of these three things. But while the first two are limited and ascertainable, the third, credit, is in a certain sense unlimited. Being based upon confidence, which is itself a variable quantity, a man's credit at one time may be vastly greater than at another, compared with his real property; and, if he have the reputation of doing a safe and regular business, and is favored by circumstances, he will find himself sometimes able to buy on credit to an extent perfectly enormous compared with his capital. Instances are given of dealers, who, in times of speculation, have effected purchases to an extent seventy or even one hundred times greater than their capital. And on the other hand, in times of panic, men of known character and of financial solidity find it impossible to borrow a dollar.

Now money acts upon prices only by being offered in exchange for commodities; but we have seen that commodities may be purchased by credit as well as by money; when, therefore, credit is offered and received for commodities, it has the same influence upon prices, as when money is offered and received for them. The form which the credit assumes to effect the purchase is a matter of indifference, whether bank-notes, checks, bills of exchange, or book-credits, what acts upon prices is the credit, in whatever shape given, or whether it gives rise to transferable paper or not.

It follows from this, that whenever there is an extension of credit for the purpose of purchasing, there will be a corresponding rise of prices. He who employs both his cash and his credit in purchasing, creates a demand for the article to the full amount of his money and credit taken together, and raises the price proportionally to both.

There might be a simultaneous rise of price in several commodities, and a considerable spirit of speculation manifested in these, if there were no such thing as credit and all business were done by ready money; but there could not be a general rise of prices as to all commodities; for, while men spent more money on the few commodities, and they rose in price, they would have less money to spend on other commodities, and these would not rise, but rather fall. It is only when credit can be used freely, and increased purchases can go on in all departments at once, that there can be a rise of prices as to all commodities, and a universal spirit of speculation.

At such times, and while prices are still rising, men seem to be making great gains; those that sell while the fever is on do make great gains; and they not only use their credit freely, but they really have more credit to use, from the very fact they seem to be prosperous. Everybody wishes to extend his operations to the utmost limit, in order to realize the greatest possible gains. Everybody wishes to use not only all his money, but all his credit. Everybody desires accommodation, and accordingly everybody gives accommodation. All forms of indebtedness are greatly increased. Promissory-notes, bills of exchange, book-credits, are indefinitely multiplied in all directions.

It begins now to be perceived in certain quarters, that the thing has been overdone; speculative purchases cease; prices begin to fall; holders of commodities are anxious to sell; this very anxiety makes the price decline still further; holders rush into the market to avoid a still greater loss; and, as nobody wishes to buy when a market is falling, prices go down, down, down. Their inflated wealth collapses in the hands of the holders; a panic often sets in, more unreasonable, if possible, than the previous overconfidence. Men must realize something from their property; they sell it therefore, frequently, at almost any sacrifice; but the small amounts of money thus realized, and all the loans which can be extorted for enormous rates of interest, now when credit is almost destroyed, are totally inadequate to meet the immense mass of debts contracted when confidence was high. Property for which a man gave his note for $10,000 is now worth but $1000, but that fact does not annihilate his debt, or erase his name from the unlucky paper; he is still bound for the $10,000. And as the mass of paper, greatly augmented during the period of excitement, comes to maturity, how can it be met? It cannot be met. There is not disposable capital enough in the loan-market to meet it, even if it could be made available. But those who have capital hold on to it. They do not know whom to trust. Everybody seems to be losing, and many are failing all around them, and they will not loan. Those men therefore who have these debts to meet have no resource. They could borrow indefinitely a few months before, but now they cannot borrow a dollar. They besiege the banks with which they deal, sometimes piteously, and sometimes bitterly, for accommodation. But the banks cannot help them. These men must fail. There is no help for it. Thousands do fail in every revulsion. Distress, more or less extensive, is the invariable consequent of the series of events called a commercial crisis. That series is constituted somewhat in this manner: first, business a little brisk; second, confidence and credit enlarging; third, a spirit of speculation; fourth, a vast increase of all forms of debt; fifth, the revulsion, or what may be called the cascade of discredit; sixth, stagnation and distress.

Such is the general course and history of a financial crisis; let us now, as was proposed, take up the three great crises in their order.

The crisis of 1837 was characterized by a more reckless spirit of speculation, and by more general distress among all classes of people, than has been witnessed in the country since. The reason of this was, and it is the grand peculiarity of that crisis, that the trouble originated in the currency; and we have already sufficiently learned that any disorder in the currency intensifies and repeats itself in all other directions.

In his annual message to Congress in 1829, General Jackson observes : — " The charter of the Bank of the United States expires in 1836, and its stockholders will most probably apply for a renewal of their privileges. In order to avoid the evils resulting from precipitancy in a measure involving such important principles and such deep pecuniary interests, I feel that I cannot in justice to the parties interested too soon present it to the deliberate consideration of the Legislature and the people. Both the constitutionality and the expediency of the law creating this bank are well questioned by a large portion of our fellow-citizens, and it must be admitted by all that it has failed in the great end of establishing a uniform and sound currency."

It must be said, in justice to General Jackson, that he gave the friends of the national bank a fair warning. He served a notice on them to "quit" seven years before their charter expired. Year after year in his annual messages he reiterated the charges against the bank; and when, in 1832, he vetoed the bill to recharter it, and, a year later, removed from its custody the public deposits, everybody knew that the national bank would expire with its charter.

In anticipation of this event, State banks sprung up like mushrooms, each anxious to obtain a share of the circulation which the national bank was about to vacate. There was an over-issue of bank-bills. One inevitable effect of a currency inflated in this way is to enhance prices, start speculation, expand credit, and prepare the way on the rising side for a crisis. Another effect, just as necessary, of such over-issue, is to turn foreign exchanges against a country, and drain away the very gold on which the bank-bills are professedly based. When the inclined plane of speculation and expanded credit has been gradually ascended in accordance with the first effect, the cascade of discredit is accelerated by the second effect.

Just so it was in 1837. Large numbers of banks came into being with very little scrutiny into their resources. Whether they had capital or not, they issued their bills as freely as the oldest and best-established institutions; and the banks, in which the United States funds were deposited after their removal, were expressly enjoined by the government to make loans freely, especially to importing merchants.

In such a state of things, every man could borrow, and did borrow. A spirit of speculation set in, which was not confined, as usual, to business men and dealers, but attacked all classes alike, — farmers, mechanics, and even clergymen. Under the influence of floods of paper money prices went up prodigiously.

At the same time, the depreciation of the currency was indicated, as it always is, by the fall of the exchanges, and the unwonted importation of foreign goods. We imported in the year 1836 one hundred and ninety millions, while we exported less than one hundred and twenty-nine millions. Gold flowed from the country, of course it did, until thirty millions of specie had been drained from the reserves of the banks. To say the very least of it, $30,000,000, in the ordinary state of the currency at that time, drawn from the bank reserves, would withdraw $100,000,000 from circulation. Just imagine the effect of withdrawing $100,000,000 from the circulation at a time when the mass of debts is enormous, when everybody must have money or fail, and when gold has largely left the country. You will have, I think, a commercial crisis with a witness; — a state of things described by Daniel Webster, when he speaks of the country " as overwhelmed with irredeemable paper, mere paper, representing, not gold, nor silver. No, sir, representing nothing but broken promises, bad faith, bankrupt corporations, cheated creditors, and a ruined people!"

On the 1st of January, 1837, the Secretary of the Treasury estimated the state of the currency as follows: — Bank bills in circulation $120,000,000; specie in circulation, $28,000,000; specie in the banks, $45,000,000. Besides the drain of $30,000,000, which was shipped to Europe, there was a still further drain on this reserve of $45,000,000, in consequence of two governmental regulations. The first was the operation of the specie-circular. All public lands must be paid for in gold and silver. This produced frequent and sometimes large drafts from the banks of specie. The second was the order issued from the Treasury Department to distribute the surplus funds of the United States among the several States. Those State banks which had received the public deposits on their removal from the national bank supposed that the money would be left with them until the exigencies of the government should require its expenditure. They had therefore treated these funds as so much capital on which they could make loans. Judge then of their consternation, when they received an order directing them to distribute these funds in specie among the several States. Their loans must be at once, and very largely, curtailed.

Then came the reaction. The failure of a single bank, in one of the Middle States, created a panic, which raged till every bank in the country, without exception, stopped payment. Even the banks favored with the national deposits suspended with the rest, and the wheels of government were brought to a stand-still.

An extra session of Congress was called, and what

did the President, Mr. Van Buren, propose? To revoke the specie-circular? Not at all. To postpone for awhile the distribution of the surplus funds? Not at all. The Message had no remedy to propose, no relief to offer. The doctrine was for the first time advanced, that all the government could do, or was designed to do, was to take care of itself, and could not be expected to legislate with reference to the monetary concerns of the people.

The revulsion of 1847 was different in several respects; neither was it so severe in this country as it was in England; but so far as it prevailed in each country, it seems to have resulted from a similar set of circumstances in each. The currency did not play so important a part among the causes as we are compelled to assign to it in the crisis of 1837, nor as it undoubtedly did in 1857. Neither was the amount of credits so much enlarged beyond their usual or average amount as is generally the case before a revulsion.

The circumstances were briefly these. While credits continued about as they were, or were slightly increased by railroad speculation, the capital in the loan-markets which had supported these credits from time to time, and on which they depended, was largely, and somewhat suddenly, drawn off to be put into the form of fixed capital. All great public works, such as railroads, canals, and so on, take more or less money out of the loan-market, and convert it into fixed capital, and thus make it unavailable for future lending. This happened in 1847. Railroad-building was then at its height. The continual demands on the loan-market by these railroad-calls diminished the loanable fund to such an extent, that they who had been accustomed to rely on it in carrying forward their business, and whose own capital had become temporarily or permanently unavailable, found it impossible to command that perpetual renewal of credit, which had previously enabled them to struggle on. Very large numbers failed. In England the mischief was so extensive, and the panic so great, that the government resorted to the expedient of allowing the Bank of England to violate its charter, and increase its loans beyond the point to which it is restricted by law. The chief interest of this crisis is, that it illustrates the principle that circulating capital may be transformed into fixed capital too rapidly for the general interests of production.

I pass now to consider briefly the last crisis of 1857. And here a significant fact must be placed first and foremost. On the first day of January, 1856, as is shown by the bank-returns for that year, there was in circulation in this country $195,000,000 of bank-notes; and to support this enormous circulation, there was at the same time less than $19,500,000 of specie in the vaults of the banks; that is, in the whole country, the circulation of bank-bills exceeded the specie reserves in the proportion of ten to one; while in particular States the disproportion was still greater; in Vermont more than eighteen to one, and in Mississippi, (Jefferson Davis's State,) nearly forty-two to one. It is obvious that the banks of the country, as a whole, were insolvent; they could only pay one dollar in ten of their legal obligations; these represented not gold and silver, but debts due to the banks, bonds, mortgages, and private notes, and however sure it may be that such credit money will ultimately be redeemed, it is totally unfit for currency.

And if the principles in regard to over-issue, which we have so often explained, are correct, and they are the settled doctrines on that point, it follows that we had in 1856 a largely depreciated currency; and it might have been expected, and it was expected and predicted, that that depreciated currency would produce its legitimate and necessary fruits. "It caused the rapid expansion of estimated values for almost every description of property, and thus made the anticipation of still larger values a ground of credit. High prices tempted speculation; large returns accruing from almost every species of investment, tempted merchants and business-men to become borrowers on a large scale."

They borrowed to carry on their own business, and invested their real capital in stocks, in railroads, in Western lands. The promise and the prestige of large dividends seduced capital from its safe and accustomed channels and tended to expand the credit of individuals and corporations far beyond the basis of their actual property; for, it is important to notice, that, at such times, credits are based not only on every species of actual property, but on reputed property, future property, possible property.

Thus while a mass of debts was being accumulated, and credit-paper of every name was multiplied to an unwonted degree beyond the convertible value of property in hand, the gold of the country was being shipped away, as it always tends to be where a depreciated currency prevails; and the quantity of

ON CREDIT. 345

imported goods was vastly increased, as it always tends to be in such circumstances.

Such was the state in which the country found itself in the summer of 1857, largely indebted both at home and abroad.

In the mean time, much of the property on the strength of which these debts had been contracted, begun to decline in value. It begun to be discerned that there was a difference between reputed property and actual property. Real estate at the West, city lots and wild lands, begun to collapse from their state of inflation. Railroad property of every kind had depreciated down to the neighborhood of actual value; while a decided fall in the price of manufactured and imported goods was inevitable.

The materials for a panic were thus in readiness, when an event occurred which sent a shock through every limb and fibre of the immense credit-system. This was the failure of the " Ohio Life and Trust Company." It was a corporation that had enjoyed the utmost of public confidence, into whose hands many a poor man had passed over his hard earnings for safe keeping, and whose branches established in all the great cities had widely connected it. A large number of persons all over the country were interested in it, either as stockholders, or depositors, or holders of its obligations. Occurring too just at that critical time, its failure was a signal everywhere. Merchants and business-men came home from their summer resorts and watering-places with a rush. Confidence was gone. Every man was suddenly called on to pay, but looked in vain for a place where he might borrow. Extensions and new loans it was impossible to obtain. Prices of all kinds of property went down to a minimum. Assets of debtors dwindled, till they could no longer sustain credit or furnish liquidation. As by a touch, property shrivelled from the dimensions imparted to it by universal confidence and anticipated profits, to a mere skeleton. To complete the disaster, the panic attacked the currency, and the banks suspended. I am not altogether without hopes that the one just characterized will be the last of the series of great national commercial crises.

CHAPTER XIII.

ON FOREIGN TRADE.

The principles which determine the question of foreign trade have been already unfolded in these pages. It is only because their application to the wider field of international exchanges has been contested by some persons, while conceding their validity within the boundaries of the individual nations, that it is now needful to bestow upon the subject a separate treatment, to demonstrate that the laws of exchange are universal and not partial, and to attempt to answer with candor and thoroughness the objections that have been raised to the conclusions established by the almost unbroken unanimity of political economists who have written during the last hundred years. Here, as everywhere else within the science, the safe appeal lies to the common sense of men. A writer whose simple object is to reach the truth, and who has no interest, real or supposed, in defending or overthrowing a dogma, will not confuse the understanding of his readers, and his own, by leaping at once into the most complicated phenomena which the domain of exchange exposes to the observation of an intelligent science. He will take the simplest cases first, will display familiarly the principles applicable to them, and then with the clue well in hand, will pass on, and can be followed through the most intricate portions of the subject. It is not owing so much to any inherent difficulties of the subject-matter, that the question of foreign trade has been the vexed question of the late centuries, as it has been owing to a false method pursued in discussing it; a method which, however favorable to the apparent establishment of current maxims, and however approved by men of interested views, can never be made useful in the investigation of truth. It may be considered as a point already well settled by experience, that no man's sagacity is sufficient to guide himself or others to any sound conclusions on this field, who takes his stand at the outset amid the whirl of interlocking phenomena, and then endeavors to work himself out through the entangling meshes which surround him at every step. Happily, there is no need of any such procedure. Man is man, motive is motive, and exchange is exchange; and the apparent chaos of commerce can be resolved through these alone into harmony and order.

In our third chapter it was put, I believe, beyond the reach of controversy or cavil, that the only reason why men ever exchange services at all, is on the ground of a relative superiority at different points. This relative superiority at different points was shown to depend in individuals partly on natural gifts, partly on concentration of mind, or muscle, or both, on a single class of efforts, and partly on the use and familiarity in the use of the gratuitous helps of Nature aiding that class of efforts. The tailor makes the blacksmith's coat, and the blacksmith shoes the tailor's horse, for no other reason in the world, except that each has a relative advantage of the other in his own work, and therefore there is a mutual gain in their exchanging works. To pretend that there would be any exchange between them, in case the blacksmith could make coats as well as the tailor, and the tailor shoe horses as well as the blacksmith, would be to assert that man acts without a motive, and that exchanges take place without a gain. It was also shown in the same connection, that the greater the difference of relative advantage, the greater the gain of an exchange, because each purchases the service of the other at the rate of his own highest efficiency. To recur to the same example, while the efficiency of the tailor and the blacksmith each in his own trade remained at 6, the efficiency of each in the trade of the other being at 5, there was only a gain of 2 to be divided between them; but when by concentration and application the efficiency of each in his own trade rose to 15, his efficiency in the other remaining at 5, there was a gain of 20 to be divided between them. When the relative superiority of each over the other in his own trade was low, the gain, though sufficient to justify the exchange, was small; but when the difference of relative advantage increased, just in that ratio did the exchange become more profitable to both. The obvious inference from this, then drawn, and now repeated, is, that every person who exchanges with others is directly interested in the highest efficiency and success of their efforts as well as his own. The diversity of relative advantage at different points exhibited by different nations, and consequetuly the gains of international exchange, were expressly reserved at that point to a later stage of our inquiry. That stage is now reached.

The various countries of the earth have received from the hands of God a diversity of original gifts, in climate, soil, natural productions, position, and opportunity. This diversity exists for a good design, and can never be substantially reduced by man, even if there were, as there is not, any good reason for desiring to reduce it. Besides original diversity in these respects, there has been developed in the history of the inhabitants of these countries, a diversity of tastes, aptitudes, habits, strength, intelligence, and skill to avail themselves of the forces of Nature around them. These differences are somewhat less inherent and more flexible than the others, but they exist, and always have existed, and in a greater or less degree always will exist; and it is on these diversities, original, traditional, and acquired, that international commerce depends; it never would have come into existence without them, and it would cease instantly and completely were they to fade out. Men do not engage in foreign trade for fun; they engage in it for the sake of the mutual gain derivable to both parties; they desist from it so soon as that mutual gain disappears; and there is no mutual gain in any series of exchanges, unless each party has a superior power in producing that which is rendered, compared with his power in producing that which is received. We will suppose a trade between England and France in cottons and silks, England sending cottons to France, and France sending silks in return. When and how long will this be a profitable trade? Then, when efforts bestowed in France upon silks will procure, through exchange with England, more of cottons than the same amount of efforts bestowed in France upon cottons will produce of cottons directly; and then, when efforts bestowed upon cottons in England will procure more of silks, through exchange with France, than the same amount of efforts bestowed in England upon silks will produce of silks directly. So long as there is a difference of relative efficiency in the production of the two commodities in the two countries, so long, setting cost of carriage aside, may there be a profitable exchange of the two. To make such an exchange profitable to both parties, it is not at all needful that the cottons exchanged for the silks shall have cost the English as many days' labor as the silks may have cost the French; or that the silks shall cost the French as much as the cottons cost the English; it is not a question of the absolute cost of either commodity to the parties producing it; but a question of the relative cost of that produced in either country compared with what would be the cost of the other commodity were it to be produced in that country. The question for the Frenchman is, Can I get more cottons by working on silks for a month, and then trading with England, than I can get by a month's work on cottons at home? And the question for the Englishman is, Can I get more silks by making cottons, and then trading with France, than I can get by trying to make silks at home? As this point is fundamental, and determines the whole matter of foreign trade, it shall be illustrated arithmetically. Suppose that cottons costing $100 in England exchange for silks costing $80 in France: is that a losing trade for England? Not necessarily. Is it a remunerative trade for

France? Not necessarily. It depends simply upon this: whether $100 expended in England in the manufacture of silks will produce as many and as good silks as can be obtained for $100 by exchange with France? If it will, depend on it, that $100 will never go to France to buy silks. If it will not, and silks are in demand in England, then, clearly, the trade is advantageous to the Englishman. If the cottons costing $100 in England, and obtained in exchange for silks which cost but $80 in France, can there and then be made for $75, France makes a losing trade (but only by supposition), though she gets what cost $100 for what cost but $80. My readers will perceive, that it is not the absolute cost of commodities to the countries producing them that determines their value in foreign trade, but that cost relatively to what would be the cost of the return commodities were they to be grown or manufactured there. A demand in each country for the product of the other is of course presupposed in the illustration.

If this general representation be just, and I think every thoughtful person will concede it, then it follows, that, setting aside a greater cost of carriage, foreign trade presents no elements peculiar to itself, but only the same elements which domestic trade presents; and consequently, that the same laws and limitations applicable to domestic exchanges are applicable also to foreign exchanges. As in every other exchange, so here, there are two efforts, represented in this case by the cost of the respective commodities, — the cottons $100, and the silks $80; there are two desires, — the desire of the Englishman for silks, and of the Frenchman for cottons; there are two estimations, — the estimation of the Frenchman of the effort in silks required to obtain the cottons by exchange compared with the effort required to obtain them directly, and the Englishman's estimation of his effort in cottons necessary to procure the silks in exchange, compared with what would be the effort needed to manufacture the silks in England; and, finally, as always, two satisfactions.

Now let us further suppose that while the cottons cost $100 in England, it would cost $120 to manufacture there as good silks as can be made in France for $80; and that while the silks cost but $80 in France, it would cost $96 to make cottons there as good as the English can make for $100. On this supposition, France can make both silks and cottons at a cheaper absolute cost than England can. But does that destroy the motive and the gain of an exchange between the countries in these two articles? Let us see. By exchange with England, France gets for $80 in silks, cottons which would otherwise cost her $96, — a handsome gain of 20 per cent.; England gets for cottons costing her $100 silks which would otherwise have cost her $120, — another handsome gain of 20 per cent. Though France can make each commodity for less absolute money than England can make either, there is a diversity of relative advantage, and therefore there might be in this case, as there is actually in many such cases, a profitable trade. The efficiency of France in making silks, relatively to that of England in making silks, is in the ratio of 80 to 120, — a difference of 50 per cent.; while the efficiency of France in making cottons, relatively to that of England in making the same, is only in the ratio of 96 to 100, — a difference of 4¼ per cent. In the majority of cases, doubtless, foreign trade takes place in articles, in the production of one of which each of the respective countries has an absolute advantage over the other, but an every way advantageous trade may be carried on in articles in the production of both of which one nation shall have an absolute superiority over the other, provided only that this superiority be relatively diverse in the two articles, as has just been shown. This is an effectual answer, as I take it, to the clamor of some, who object to importing articles which might be made at home for the same sum of money as foreigners expend in making them; admitted, that they might be so made; does it follow that the country importing them would get them as cheaply by making them itself? By no means does that follow. By the supposition, the importing country has an efficiency in making those articles equal to that of the foreign country; but it may also have a superiority absolute or relative over that country in the production of other articles which that country wants in exchange; if so, the exchange complained of may go on to the manifest profit of both parties. Our general supposition a little changed will put this case in its true light: France can make cottons for $100 which it costs England also $100 to make; shall she give up her trade with England in silks and cottons, because she can make cottons as cheap as England can? She had better not. Let the exchange go on; for $80 in silks she gets cottons which would otherwise cost her $100, — a gain of 25 per cent.; England gets silks for $100 which would otherwise cost her $120, — a gain of 20 per cent. as before. Let no nation be in haste then to drop a trade, because it thinks it can make the article received in exchange as cheaply as the other nation makes it, so long as it has an advantage over the other, absolute or relative, in making the article rendered in exchange; and when that advantage ceases, the trade will drop of itself.

What will be the extreme limits of the value of cottons and silks in a trade between England and France under the conditions supposed? And when will a third nation be able to undersell either in the ports of the other? The extreme value of French silks in English cottons, will be 80 and 96; they cannot fall below 80, because they cost the French that to produce them; they cannot rise above 96, because at that rate the French can make cottons, and there would be no gain in exchanging. Nations, no more than individuals, will get themselves served at a greater effort than that at which they can serve themselves. If a given effort does not realize more through exchange than it would directly, then the exchange ceases of necessity, as fire goes out for lack of fuel. The extreme limits of the value of English cottons in French silks, will be 100 and 120, for reasons precisely similar. Therefore the highest profits possible to both nations, under the conditions of the trade, are 20 per cent. each. France would be glad to take the cottons at a return of 80, at which rate her gain would be 20 per cent.; and she cannot under any circumstances offer quite 96, at which rate her gain would disappear. No third nation, therefore, in a trade of silks for cottons, can expel the French from the English ports, until it is prepared to offer nearly 96, or more, in silks in return for English cottons; that is to say, until its efficiency in making silks relatively to that of England in making them, differs more than that of France does, from the efficiency of France in making cottons relatively to that of England in making the same. A greater difference of relative advantage, and nothing else, will enable a third nation to undersell France in such a trade. England would be glad to take the silks at a return of 100, at which rate her gain is 20 per cent.; and she cannot possibly offer quite 120, because at that rate her gain would wholly vanish. She could be undersold in the French ports, under similar conditions, and not otherwise, as the French in her own ports, as just now indicated. We have seen that the difference of relative efficiency in the production of the two articles in the two countries is in the ratio of 50 to $4\frac{1}{6}$; and no nation can take away the silks of France from the English, or the cottons of England from the French, either with other cottons and silks, or any other commodity, unless its efficiency in the production of the commodity whatever it be, relatively to the efficiency of the two countries in the production of the two commodities, presents a greater difference than 50 to $4\frac{1}{6}$. Here is the whole doctrine of one nation's underselling another in the ports of a third. It can do so under conditions of greater relative efficiency, and not otherwise.

So far we have considered only their relative cost of production as determining the value of articles in foreign trade. But we know that the element of desires also helps to determine all value. We come now to illustrate what is sometimes and properly called "the Equation of International Demand."

If the demand for French silks in England just answers to the demand for English cottons in France, so that the silks offered by France just pay for the cottons offered by England, then, cost of carriage aside, the gains of the trade will be equally divided between the two nations, each will realize 20 per cent. profit, because neither will have any motive to lower the value of its commodity below its highest value; France, from its point of view, will offer 80 in silks and get 96 in cottons; England, from her point, will offer 100 in cottons and get 120 in silks. Demand and supply are equalized at a point of value most favorable to both parties, and really determined by the relative cost of production. This case of equalization, though possible, is likely rarely to occur in practice. On any terms of exchange first offered, there is likely to be a stronger demand in one country for the product of the other than in this country for the product of that. This will lead to a change of value, and a new division of profits. The product for which the demand is less will find its market sluggish, and in order to tempt further and brisker exchanges, will be compelled to offer more favorable conditions. He who enters a market in quest of what is more in demand with a service in return which is less in demand, will have to lower his terms, or not trade. The equalization of supply and demand will only be reached in this case, by quickening the demand for the commodity now less in demand, through an offer of better terms in trade.

Thus, if the demand for French silks in the English ports be slack, in comparison with the demand for English cottons in France, at the rate of exchange first established — 80 for 96, the French merchant has no resource, if he wishes to continue the trade, but to offer more silks for the same amount of cottons, say, 85 for 96. If this reduction prove sufficient to cancel the account in cottons with the account in silks, then the trade will go on on this new basis for a while, the equalization of supply and demand has been reached through a new valuation of the commodities, and there is now a different division of the profits. France gains now only 13 per cent. by her trade with England, while England gains $27\frac{1}{2}$ per cent. in her trade with France. Under these new terms of exchange, it is possible that silks may again become heavy in reference to cottons, and a new decline take place in their relative value. If the French are obliged to offer 90 for 96, in order to obtain the cottons they want, their profits will sink to $5\frac{2}{3}$ per cent., while the English profits will rise to 35 per cent. If, in any contingency, the French were compelled to offer in the neighborhood of 96 in silks for 96 in cottons, the trade would cease of course, just as every other transaction ceases when the motive for it ceases. Of course, the cottons are just as likely to become dull in reference to silks, as the silks to cottons, and in this case England must lower her demands, and thus surrender a larger share of the profits to France. By the play of supply and demand, within the outermost limits drawn by the relative cost of production, is the value of articles determined in foreign trade; and no degree of complication in the variety of articles, or in circuitous exchanges, affects, for substance, these fundamental principles. For example, if, instead of one article, as cottons, England sends two articles, or ten, to France in payment for silks, she will send in preference that article in which her labor is relatively most efficient, so long as the French demand will receive it; then, when obliged to lower on that down to the point at which her next most available article stands, she will send that in quantities regulated by the demand for it; and so on to the end. No matter whether the articles be one or many; no matter whether the trade be a direct, or an indirect, trade; the profits in all cases will depend, first upon the ratio of the cost of what is rendered to what would otherwise be the cost of that received; and secondly, upon the relative intensity of the two demands. The greater the relative efficiency of any nation in producing an article of export, and the stronger the demand for that article in foreign ports, the more profitable does the trade become to that nation. The precious metals, whether produced at home, or obtained from other nations by another series of exchanges, stand here in the same relations as other commodities, and are frequently the most profitable articles that a nation can export. The terms of international exchanges, then, between any two nations, are so adjusted, as to equalize the demand for their respective products, and cancel the debts mutually incurred.

It follows from all this by a necessary inference, that what a nation purchases by its exports, it purchases by its most efficient labor, and consequently at the cheapest possible rate to itself. Only those things, for the procuring of which a nation possesses decided advantages relatively to other nations, and relatively to its own advantages in producing directly what is received in return, are ever exported; and hence, the return cargoes, no matter what they have cost their original producers, are purchased by this nation as cheaply as if they had been produced by its own most advantageous labor. This is a wholly impregnable position, and the advocates of restricting foreign trade are challenged to try their hand a little at its defences.

We see also, at this point, what to think of those people who deem it needful that each nation should be able to "compete" with other nations in everything. Why are not these people consistent enough to apply their favorite doctrine of "competing" to domestic exchanges also, and demand that the clergyman shall have facilities for "competing" with the lawyer, the tailor with the blacksmith, the farmer with the manufacturer, the publisher with the author? Will these people never learn that all exchanges, domestic as well as foreign, depend on relative superiority at different points, and that a nation which should try to make its success in production equal at all points, would be as foolish as an artisan trying to learn and practise all trades at once? Suppose the nation to succeed, what then? It would supply its wants at a certain average efficiency of effort; whereas, by a thorough development of all its own peculiar resources, it could command by exchange the products of the world at a cost not exceeding that of its own most productive and efficient exertion. In one word, whatever justifies individuals in selecting diverse paths of production according to their capacities and opportunity, the same justifies the nations in fully drawing out their own best capabilities under the conditions in which God has placed them, and then, exchanging what costs them little for what would otherwise cost them much, in enjoying all that the world offers at the least expenditure of irksome effort. Such action promotes the common good of all the nations, and makes the best of all accessible to all, and arms each with the power of all; while the opposite action, by lessening the diversities of relative advantage, so far forth incapacitates all for exchanges which are at once profitable and stimulating.

Closely connected with the one just cited, is another narrow and superficial notion, happily less prevalent now than formerly, namely, that new improvements in machinery, or other enhanced facilities of production, realized in any nation, are a disadvantage to other nations in their trade with that nation. Let us examine this point. Suppose France, by new methods of silk culture, to become able to make the silk which before cost $80 for $50, cottons in France, and silk and cottons in England, remaining in natural cost as before, does France alone gain the entire advantage of the increased cheapness of silk? We will see. The production of silk in France is greatly quickened by the cheaper methods, more is produced, more is carried to England to buy cottons with, but at the old rate of 80 for 96 the English will not take any more silks, and the French, who can now abundantly afford it, since their nominal 80 is really 50, will offer more silks for 96 in cottons, in order to tempt a brisker and broader sale. They offer, say, 96 in silks for 96 in cottons, and if that reduction of value of silks in cottons be enough for the equalization of the respective demands, the trade will go on on that basis, at least for a time; and as there is now a larger difference of relative advantage than before, there will be, as always in such cases, larger profits to be divided between the two parties. The 96 now offered in silks to the English is really only 60 in cost to the French, so that the French gain in the trade is largely increased; they now get for what costs them 60 what would otherwise cost them 96, a clear gain of 60 per cent. Before the new methods of silk culture were introduced they gained only 20 per cent. But the English have also gained largely by the ingenuity and diligence of their neighbors. Before, they gained only 20 per cent. in the trade at best; now they get for what costs them $100 that which otherwise would cost them $144, a clear gain of 44 per cent. Indeed, it might easily happen, through the changes in international demand, that even a larger share of the benefit of the French improvements should accrue to the English than to the French themselves; the share of the French all the while being large, and much larger, than if, greedily endeavoring to keep all the benefit, they refused to trade at all. Thus we reach again, from another outlook, a grand doctrine of exchange, that each party is benefited by the progress and prosperity of the other. The only way in which all nations can share in the benefits of the thrift and enterprise of each other, is through mutual international exchanges; and when each nation sees to it that it has a few commodities at least for which there is a strong demand among foreigners, and in the production of which themselves have a strong superiority, it may rest assured that it buys all it buys from abroad, gold included, at the cheapest rate to itself, and shares a part of the prosperity of every nation with which it trades.

It is now time to look at the cost of carriage, thus far allowed to sink out of sight for the sake of greater simplicity of view. This is an important element in international exchanges, and one which must not be neglected, although Mr. Carey unduly enlarges upon it with a view to prejudice a free exchange. Certainly, it costs something to carry any goods abroad, and to bring back a return, and we may be assured that if such return goods could be procured as cheaply without incurring such expense, the expense would never be incurred. The fact that all expenses connected with carriage are gladly borne by the merchants who carry on the trade, shows that the gains of the trade are so great as not only to pay freights and insurance, but also to leave a good margin for profits. Mr. Carey does not get around this stubborn fact. What use is it to pile up calculations to show that the expenses incurred in carriage, if applied to production at home, would secure as good goods and more of them? If they would, why don't they? Have n't men common sense? Is n't self interest a tolerably strong motive-power? Is it needful to invoke the mighty arm of law to compel men to act in accordance with their pecuniary interests? Mr.

Carey would restrict foreign trade, because it costs so much to carry on. Is that wise, provided the gains after all largely overbalance the cost? If they did not overbalance it, would the trade go forward? If the cost be large, as it is, that is a good reason to desire its reduction, if possible; to labor for increased facilities of transportation, for cheaper freights, and better rates of insurance; but to argue for forcibly stopping a trade by legal enactment, because it costs those so much who freely undertake to carry it on, does not strike me, and, I believe, will not strike my readers, as a sound argument. Which nation, a party in foreign trade, pays the costs of carriage? Or does each pay them in equal proportion? The aggregate cost of transportation to the foreign market is so much added to the cost of production, and is a deduction of so much from what would otherwise be the whole gain of the exchange; but it is not true that each party necessarily pays the whole of his own freights, and therefore, that the party carrying bulky articles is at a disadvantage compared with the other. He may or may not be at a disadvantage. That will depend on the effect of the new expense, however divided, on the demand in the respective countries. Suppose, that in the outset England pays the whole cost of carrying cottons to France, and France the whole cost of sending the silks to England; but as cottons are many times more bulky than silks proportionably to value, a larger bill of freights would fall to England; and cottons would therefore fall relatively to silks; but cottons and silks both have risen absolutely, that is, with reference to a given effort, or with reference to a money standard. Suppose that France, instead of 80 for 96, now has to give 82 for 96, and England, instead of 100 for 120 now has to give 105 for 120. The French gain in the trade is reduced by cost of carriage from 20 per cent. to nearly 18, and the English gain from 20 per cent. to nearly 14; but it is by no means certain that the trade would go on on these terms; the enhanced price of silks might well deaden the demand for them in England, more than the relatively less enhanced price of cottons in France would affect the demand for them. Silks have risen in England 5 per cent., but cottons have risen in France only 2½ per cent.; it is therefore every way likely that thereafter the demand for cottons will be stronger than the demand for silks, and if so, the French will have to offer better terms, or, what is the same thing, be obliged to pay a part of the English freights; so that there is nothing in the true state of the case to justify the conclusion jumped at by some people that they who carry heavy goods are at a disadvantage compared with those who carry light goods. That will depend on the equation of international demand. Nothing in the nature of things hinders, that each party shall in effect pay the freights of the other, or one even really pay the freights of both.

These, then, are the essential principles of foreign trade, brought out, it is hoped, as clearly and consecutively as the relative and complicated nature of the transactions will allow; and in the light of these principles it is very clear that foreign trade is just as legitimate as domestic trade; that it rests on the same ultimate principles in the constitution of man and in the providential arrangements of Nature; that the profit of it is mutual to both parties, or it would never come into being, or, coming into being, would cease of itself; that to prohibit it, or restrict it, otherwise than in the interest of morals, health, or revenue, must find a justification, if at all, outside the pale of Political Economy ; that to say to any body of men who wish to render purely commercial services to foreigners, to receive back similar services in return, that such services shall neither be rendered nor received, is not only to destroy a certain gain, but also to interfere with a natural and inalienable right.

Unfortunately, the old mercantile system, which was so wise as to believe that gold and silver were the only objects of real value, taught also, in coincidence with its fundamental belief, that foreign trade ought to be so regulated and restricted as to bring in the largest possible quantity of the precious metals; that each nation ought to sell much and buy little in order to grow rich; that bounties ought to be given to exporters to encourage them to sell, and prohibitions laid upon importers to prevent their buying; and that the introduction, through exchange with foreigners, of articles which might be produced at home, should be by all means prevented by law, no matter what advantages for producing them foreigners might have, or what advantages the nation itself might have in producing that which the foreigners would be glad to take in exchange. The mercantile system as such, is long ago dead and buried, but it has left one of its progeny behind it, of no better birth than its parent, which has not yet found its predestined death and burial. This is the doctrine sometimes euphoniously and courteously denominated Protection to Native Industry, a designation however not in the least indicative of its real nature. This doctrine, now utterly expelled from England and Germany, still lingers feebly in some other parts of Europe, and, though steadily declining in the United States, is still strong enough here to control the present national-legislation. It has been reinforced, of late years, by the very respectable authority of Mr. Carey, some of whose points will be considered in the sequel; and by one or two other persons whose opinions are entitled to a respectful consideration; and the prevalence of the doctrine in the popular mind, particularly in New England, is still such that I deem it useful to examine the topic at some length, preferring to do so in the way of replying to the main objections urged against the opposite doctrine of a free commerce, especially as Protection so called acts at present wholly on the defensive. Some of the objections are of a popular character, and I shall feel at liberty to subject them to a popular refutation; while such as profess to be scientific, will, it is hoped, be met by a scientific method at least equal to their own.

It may be proper to mention at the outset, to avoid misapprehension, as a matter purely personal, that I have no prejudices in favor of Free Trade. I was brought up in the old Whig school, and accustomed from my boyhood to hear and to repeat the current arguments in favor of what is called Protection. I remember with perfect distinctness the

Presidential campaign of 1840, in which this was a main plank of the platform; and when, ten years later, as a student, I commenced to study Political Economy, I supposed that a protective tariff was a corner-stone of commercial prosperity. A careful study of the principles of this science, with a noting of the records of experience in the premises, and nothing else, has convinced me, as thousands have been convinced before and since, that the doctrine of Protection is based wholly upon the fallacies of the Mercantile System; and since these fallacies have been abundantly exposed, no logical ground is left for a doctrine of restriction and prohibitions. And it is worth while to notice, in passing, how much the doctrine in question has gained by the use of the very attractive word " Protective." This word, so agreeable to our minds from its association with security of person and property, is not properly descriptive of the system. The system is one of restraint and prohibition, and, of necessity, so far as it is applied, both diminishes in amount the commerce of the world, and diverts it from its own freely chosen channels. If the correct but prosy epithets "restrictive," "prohibitory," had been applied to the doctrine, instead of the less accurate but agreeable "protective," the hold of the doctrine itself upon the general mind would, I imagine, have been far less tenacious. Let us remember that a word never yet changed the essential nature of anything.

The first main distinction to which I call attention, is that between a protective tariff and a revenue tariff. Upon this point a great confusion exists in the common mind. It is not at all the doctrine of Free Trade that no duties shall be laid upon imported goods. Duties ought to be laid upon imported goods, because that is a convenient and unexceptionable mode of raising a part of the taxes by which government is supported. Very high duties may be properly laid upon luxuries that are imported, such as wines and plate, for example, because they who buy such things are able to pay liberally for the support of the government. Free Trade has nothing to object to any duties that are laid with a simple view to equitable taxation. A tariff for revenue, therefore, as a mode of taxing the people for the support of the government, a tariff honestly adjusted for that purpose, has nothing whatever in conflict with the broadest doctrine of Free Trade. England, for example, which has adopted a complete system of freedom in her foreign commerce, still levies duties on imports, and will continue to do so, for purposes of revenue merely. She raises on the average about thirty-five per cent. of her aggregate revenue from this source.

But the idea of a protective tariff is totally different. Here duties are laid upon foreign commodities, so high, as either to exclude them altogether, and thus give the domestic manufacturer or grower the complete monopoly of the home market; or, if the duty be not so high as to be entirely prohibitory, it is made high enough to raise the price of the foreign article to the point at which the home manufacturer is desirous of selling his own. The effect that is designed, and that actually follows, is to raise the price to all consumers, in order that a factitious advantage may accrue to certain home manufacturers. When most successful, the effect is to transfer money from the pockets of all consumers, to the pockets of a few manufacturers. I do not stop at this point to demonstrate the economical folly of this, my object now being to show the idea that always underlies protective duties. We have seen already in the first chapter, and shall recur to the subject in the next, how the doctrine of protection grew immediately out of the Mercantile System, the so called "Balance of Trade." Restrictive duties have never been laid in any age or country except for the purpose of securing, either a more favorable "balance of trade," or else certain supposed advantages to home manufacturers or growers.

Now, the interesting question arises, which has been much agitated in this country, whether these two ideas of revenue and protection, which are so distinct and apparently incompatible, can be combined together? Whether a revenue tariff can be so adjusted as to afford incidental protection? Defeated as a general theory, and no longer able to stand upon its own merits, Protection, in this country, only asks the privilege of leaning upon revenue. It is conceded that Protection for Protection's sake is improper; but it is claimed that there is no harm in having as much protection as may incidentally result from a tariff framed for revenue. This shows how the general doctrine of Protection has declined, and seeks at last a compromise with freedom. There is no sound basis for such compromise; and why? Because revenue is only received on those goods that come in, and protection is only secured when the goods are kept out. You get no revenue, except as you let the things in; you get little protection except as you keep the things out. The two ideas are opposite and incompatible; one cannot rationally combine them; a revenue tariff with incidental protection is a solecism. But it may be said, that a moderate duty that shall lessen, but not prevent importation, will raise the price of the foreign article, and thus enable the home manufacturer to realize the same price. This is true. But just look at it. The government gets a revenue only on that part that is imported; the high price has to be paid upon all that is consumed. The government makes the people pay much, in order that the treasury may receive little. I think that that is no desirable way of raising a revenue.

It follows, that the principles on which a revenue tariff should be framed are very different from those that should rule in protective tariffs. If the object be revenue, the duties should be low, so as not to discourage importation, or very sensibly increase prices. Low duties on all imports, except high-priced foreign luxuries, which are used only by the rich, and which may be taxed heavily without discouraging importation, will infallibly yield the largest aggregate revenue. The reason for this is, that society is like a pyramid standing on its broadest base: each horizontal section of it is more extended than the one above it. So in society: the number of those able to purchase an article at five dollars, is more than twice as numerous as those able to purchase it at ten; and those who are able to buy it at one dollar are probably more than ten times as many as those who would buy it at five dollars. The official list of incomes for the year 1864, in the Tenth District of Massachusetts, lies before me, and selecting one town at random, I find in its list one income over $40,000, three over $30,000, seven over $20,000, nine over $10,000, thirteen over $5000, twenty-nine over $2000, and seventy-eight over $1000. A lower duty, therefore, on any article is likely to bring it within the reach of a much wider circle of consumers; and for many to pay a low duty is better for the revenue than for a few to pay a high duty. Of course, the exact limitations must be found out by experience; but Alexander Hamilton long ago, in one of the papers of "The Federalist," called attention to the fact in this connection, that a large multiplier will not of itself make a large product. The multiplicand is also a factor. During the late high prices, I was told by a prominent merchant, that the people not only did not buy as much tea as formerly, but also that they did not spend as many dollars for tea as when the article was cheaper.

As between foreign nations, an interesting experiment is now going forward under the treaty of commerce between France and England. In 1861, this principle of low duties was embodied in the mutual tariffs of the two nations, and the results thus far have delighted the friends and confounded the enemies of a free commerce. Not only has the amount of commodities exchanged prodigiously increased, but the increase of the revenue for England on the imports from France for the first three months of the new system, over the corresponding quarter of the previous year, was $1,430,000; and the increase for France on the imports from England for the same three months, $7,382,000. Thus do facts corroborate principles, and make us sure that we stand upon the rock.

(1.) I shall now attempt to answer some objections. One of the most common of these has been, that Free Trade is a theory: "It is all very well in theory, but it will not work in practice"; as if there could be a good theory that worked ill in practice! A theory that does not work in practice is a bad theory. That is the very way we determine whether a theory is good or bad, — Does it correspond with facts, — does it work well when applied? If it does not, it is condemned, it is worthless. There is a palpable sophism in this expression, " Good in theory, bad in practice." What makes a theory good? Simply because it corresponds with and explains the facts. Newton's theory of gravitation is a good theory on this ground, and no other. If a man objects to any theory, let him bring facts, principles, any truth whatever, to disprove it, and he shall be welcome; but don't let him delude himself and others by supposing that he can concede the theory to be good, and then save himself on the practice. A theory is good because it is good in practice, and for no other reason.

There have been so many unfounded theories broached on all subjects, that the term has fallen into some reproach, and it is for this reason that the charge is brought against Free Trade, of being a theory: but there is nothing in the world more respectable than a good theory proved by solid arguments and verified by facts. I am prepared to show, however, that the charge of being a theory falls with far greater force against the doctrine of protection than against the doctrine of freedom. Free Trade can hardly be said to be a theory at all. It is the natural state of things. If you and I wish to exchange commodities for our mutual benefit, there is no theory or doctrine in the premises; we exchange, and that is the whole of it. If a Massachusetts fisherman wishes to exchange his dried cod with a West India sugar planter, and the trade is mutually beneficial, what theory is involved? They exchange, each is richer than before, and that is the whole of it.

If now some one steps in between you and me, or between the fisherman and the planter, and says, " You shall not trade!" he is bound to tell the reason why. The burden lies upon him. Let him bring forward his theory of restriction, and justify it. Let us hear the arguments and see the grounds that justify the prohibition of an advantageous trade! You see the burden of proof lies upon the advocates of restriction. It is the advocates of restriction that drag in a theory which interrupts the play of natural laws,—which says to men who wish to trade, " You shall not trade!" Commerce is no game of grab, of fraud, of overreaching. Its benefits are reciprocal and mutual; otherwise there would be no commerce. The freights of the navigating interest, and the gains of the merchants, are but a very small part of the benefits of commerce; the variety of commodities and of comforts which every commercial nation enjoys, by exchanging its own surplus products for the surplus products of its neighbors, is the substantial advantage of trade. When now this beneficial interchange is going forward, or, if the artificial barriers were thrown down, would be going forward, who is he that takes upon him to curtail and to prohibit it? Who is he that thinks himself competent to manipulate the unchanging laws of trade?

It is conceded by everybody that a free exchange of commodities within the same country is highly beneficial: what makes it suddenly cease to be beneficial as between foreign countries? Does the mutual benefit of an exchange depend upon the accident that the parties to it are citizens or subjects of the same government? The south end of Vermont trades freely and advantageously with its neighbors across the line in Massachusetts; is there any good reason why the north end of Vermont should not trade just as freely and advantageously with its neighbors across the line in Canada? These are questions which the theory of protection, in my opinion, cannot satisfactorily answer.

(2.) I pass to a second current objection, namely, that if we admit foreign goods freely, we thereby employ the labor of foreigners, and so far diminish the wages of our own laborers. Let us see if this is so. Foreign articles are certainly wrought by foreign labor; do we, then, by buying them employ foreign labor, to the prejudice of our own laborers? We are obliged to pay for everything we buy,— are we not? In what do we pay? Clearly, in the products of our own labor. We employ our own laborers to produce the articles which we exchange for foreign articles. We pay for our imports by our exports. Our exports are created by home labor, and the only possible way for us to obtain the results of foreign toil, is to offer in exchange the results of domestic toil. A commercial nation, therefore, not only does not, but it cannot employ foreign labor. The more it buys of foreigners, the more home labor it must employ to create the articles with which it pays for what it buys. We must remember that the exports, taking the years together, must and do balance the imports. Free Trade, therefore, can by no possibility discourage home labor, or diminish the wages of laborers; and, as a matter of fact, labor is best rewarded, other things being equal, in the freest commercial countries.

I deem it important thoroughly to demolish this objection, for it has been considered the stronghold of the advocates of Protection. I admit that a protective tariff may stimulate a certain branch of manufacture, may concentrate capital in it, may call laborers into it, and even for a time increase the wages of those laborers. But competition will very speedily reduce wages in that department to the average level in other departments, and unless it can be shown that restriction increases the general wages-fund of a country, — that fund that is set apart for the payment of labor, — it is in vain to claim that it can increase the general wages of labor. Capital and laborers may indeed be withdrawn from one employment to another by artificial stimulus, but is there any general gain in that? While the one is stimulated, is not the other depressed? I have seen upon the ocean the wind blow up a wave, but I always noticed a depression behind it. The general level of the ocean is not raised, however high the waves rise.

Now how can the free interchange of commodities lessen the demand for labor or the rewards of labor? You are employing a hundred men. You wish to obtain a certain quantity of cutlery. Does it make any difference to you or to the wages of your men, whether you employ them directly in making the cutlery, or in making buttons with which you can purchase the cutlery from abroad? If, by employing them in making buttons you can purchase more and better cutlery, (and if you cannot, there is no temptation to an exchange,) is it not plain to reason that it is better for you, and that you can afford to pay them better wages, than if you employed their labor less effectively directly upon cutlery? This is but an instance, but it involves the principle. There is, there can be no discouragement to domestic labor in the freest international exchanges. Every foreign purchase necessitates the employment of domestic labor to create that with which the purchase is made, thereby enlarging the demand for laborers, and thus tending to increase their wages. The tendency of Free Trade is directly the reverse of that alleged in the objection; because the varied objects of use and elegance offered to our desires by international commerce, stimulate labor to create that with which to buy them.

We know now how to answer those who say, that if we should trade freely, with England, for example, we should bring down wages in this country to the English standard. This is too hollow a bugbear to frighten sensible people any longer. To say nothing of the principles just explained, and others equally conclusive, that combine to scout it, the facts in the case would seem to settle the whole question. We have traded with England for eighty years, largely, increasingly, and from 1846 to 1861, almost freely, and yet wages have been constantly rising in America, and never stood at a higher figure than when the Morrill Tariff was passed in 1861.

(3.) But if the doctrine of Protection be so false, and have no single solid argument in its support, why have so many nations acted on it, so many great men, among others, Daniel Webster, believed in it? This objection I am bound to notice, for it has had no small influence. To estimate its force rightly, two things must be remembered: first, that the doctrine of protection is an inheritance from the remote past, an outgrowth from a confessedly false dogma, which, being then universally received and acted on by the nations, has given this, one of its corollaries, whatever validity custom and prescription can give; and, secondly, that there has always been a rich and influential class of men in the commercial countries who have supposed that their interests were subserved by the practical application of the doctrine. In respect to Daniel Webster, the first great speech which he made in Congress, a speech that foreshadowed his great fame, was delivered in 1814 on the tariff. It was a free trade speech throughout, unequivocal and complete in its advocacy of commercial freedom. There he stood, in the pride of early manhood, impregnable. If he left, fourteen years later, this high ground of truth and principle, to occupy the lower ground of what he deemed expedient, it was because the hostility of the South to the growing commerce of the North contributed to bring upon the nation a high restrictive tariff, and Northern capital, thus prohibited the seas, embarked in extensive manufactures; and then the South, jealous again, proposed to reverse its policy and abolish the inducements under which this capital had been embarked. It was thus that Mr. Webster became the champion of manufacturing interests which he deemed were unjustly and factiously attacked. He never justified restriction as a principle; his commercial instincts were too strong for that; he always attempted to justify his course by peculiar and factitious circumstances; almost half of his congressional life had passed away, before he could be brought to vote for levying high duties; and although he afterwards brought forward, in defence of the position thus assumed, arguments which Political Economy pronounces unsound, and although there doubtless mingled in with his motives a desire to gratify powerful constituents and friends who were directly interested in high duties, there is abundant reason to believe that his defection from sound principles was never so radical as has been commonly supposed.

It is not difficult to see why there have always been so many advocates of the system of restriction. It is an old system. It is a system some of the arguments for which are superficially plausible. Above all, it is a system which many enterprising and prosperous men have considered as essential to their pecuniary interests; and when such men demand a champion, eloquence and arguments are never long wanting. As a matter of fact, the legislation of the world has been largely controlled by such men, and that too, not always in the interest of the masses. It is more than doubtful whether manufacturers as a whole class have ever been permanently benefited by protective duties, or rather, it is certain that they have not been; but they have supposed that they were, and some of them have been, prodigiously benefited; and they have acted, and are acting, on that supposition, and the power of such men over public opinion is very considerable. As a class, they are intelligent and rich, and can easily combine to influence opinion and legislation. But even if they were benefited, as a whole, by protective duties, what sort of justice is it to take money out of my pocket and put it into theirs? I object to that. My mickle, and your mickle, and our neighbor's mickle will make a very pretty muckle, — a small tax on all consumers of protected goods will reach a very handsome sum; but what valid claim can the manufacturers lay to it? They are a very deserving class, and consequently prosperous; but it may be respectfully submitted that they do not need unequal legislation in their behalf. They are not a needy generation, but are well to do. The list of incomes on which a United States tax is paid, now annually published throughout the country, puts this fact beyond the shadow of question. In most sections of New England, they are the only men of large incomes. Now, it is no objection to these excellent men that they are rich, and getting richer; they are rather deserving of all honor for their enterprise and vigor and success; but it is conclusive on this point, that they no longer need, even if they ever needed, any special protection from the government. Let them stand on the same level of advantage with other men, let them enjoy no unequal privileges, and everybody will rejoice in their prosperity. At present, they occupy a false position, fatal to their own genuine self-respect, and to the hearty congratulations of their fellow-citizens. By far the larger part of the industrial interests of the country have no special protection at the hands of government; and is it possible that these shrewd and able men who own and run mills and foundries, are willing to acknowledge they alone of their fellow-citizens are unable to render valuable and remunerable services to society without an artificial and governmental prop at their back?

(4.) This brings us to another objection, namely, that, were it not for protective duties, our manufactures would collapse, or as it is sometimes phrased, other nations would take all our manufacturing away from us. The first thing to be said about this is, that we do not manufacture for the sake of manufacturing, but for the sake of the product, — it is not the process that we care about, but the product; and even if it could be shown, as it cannot, that free trade would lessen the manufacturing, that would not be so deplorable, provided we obtained by it for the satisfaction of our wants as many or more manufactured products. Satisfactions, and not efforts, are ultimate in the field of exchange. In the second place, it is needful to look at the meaning of the word, manufactures. So far, I have used it in the loose popular way by which it has come to mean practically in this country the processes by which cotton, wool, and iron, are rendered available for various human uses. These more prominent interests are currently meant under the terms manufactures and manufacturers; but of course the terms properly include a wide range of efforts beyond these, indeed almost all forms of industry not agricultural, and not primarily mental. Now to say, in the broad sense, that protective duties are necessary in order that manufactures may succeed, is to make a statement which can be shown to be false. What is the magic of a protective duty? This, that it says to men who would otherwise come to our shores to trade, " You shall not bring those commodities you were about to bring, nor take away those commodities you were about to take in exchange." People commonly look only at the first part of what is said, and console themselves by thinking, if foreigners are not allowed to bring those goods, somebody will make them at home for us. But this is only half of it. Those branches of manufacture, or of agriculture, as the case may be, which were furnishing the goods wherewith to pay for those commodities about to be imported but now prohibited, lose their market. If we will not buy, of course we cannot sell. If we prohibit importations, we thereby necessarily prevent exportations; that is to say, we take away their market from those who manufacture or grow the goods which would be exported. We depress a profitable branch of manufacture by taking away its market, for the sake of introducing or fostering a branch which is by supposition and confession unprofitable.

The advocates of protection do not claim that branches of business which would otherwise be profitable and self-supporting should be protected, but only the weak and less profitable kinds; and so to bolster up these, protective duties virtually destroy other branches of industry, which only ask that their natural market shall be let alone, to maintain an independent and profitable existence. It is impossible to characterize in terms of respect so short-sighted and miserable a policy. How can a free commerce depress manufactures, when every nation must manufacture or grow a dollar's worth at home for every dollar's worth imported from abroad? How can high duties foster manufactures as a whole, when their very first effect is to cut off from their market all those manufactures which would otherwise have gone abroad with a profit, and their second effect merely to stimulate up to the general level of profit those which it is claimed will not otherwise yield a profit?

The French manufacturers in 1861 were afraid that if the barriers of restriction were thrown down, as proposed in Mr. Cobden's treaty, their business would suffer from English competition. The result has shown how futile were their fears. A large part of the manufactures of either country are admitted into the other with perfect freedom, and the duties on most of the rest very materially reduced; and the French manufacturers have found, as the American at no distant day will find, that there is nothing which stimulates manufactures so much as a broad market, — not merely a home-market, but a world-market. The French sent to England, in 1863, 1,076,-000,000 francs worth of goods and received back within a trifle as much in return, which was almost a quarter of what they sent and received to and from the rest of the world. It is as the friends and not the enemies of manufactures that we demand the abrogation of restrictive duties. Manufactures as a whole can never reach their point of just expansion, until this professedly discriminating, really repressing, and only at a few favorite points stimulating, system shall be abolished.

But it is said, that England can work up cottons, and Germany wools, and the North of Europe irons, cheaper than we can. Those who have followed me thus far through this chapter, now know that absolute cost of production has little to do directly in foreign trade. But if it be true that these commodities, or any others whatsoever, can really be obtained by us by a less expense of effort through exchange than directly, is there a decent reason why we should prefer to get them by the hardest when the easiest way is open? We may be assured that we shall not get them without being obliged to pay for them, and to pay for them will require a fair expenditure of effort and skill. If foreigners have the advantage over us in some things, we have the advantage over them in many things, and all exchange and the profits of it depend on relative superiority at different points.

(5.) I pass to an objection much urged by Mr. Carey, and others, namely, that the United States, without the aid of protective duties, will be confined to agricultural pursuits, and no diversity of employments, so essential to full social life, will come into play. But the truth is, diversity of employments is rooted in human nature, and in the circumstances amid which God has placed men, and so far is it from law being necessary to foster this diversity, that law is powerless to prevent it! While we were colonies of Great Britain, the laws were very strict against domestic manufacturing of almost all kinds, and yet long before the Revolution, the various branches of manufacture were introduced and prosecuted in spite of the laws: clothiers' mills went up along the mountain streams; wool and woollens were exported to the West Indies and elsewhere; iron was smelted and rolled and slit and plaited, and the manufacture of steel was attempted, and the germs of many diverse employments were expanding, notwithstanding the hostility of the law.[1] Parliament felt itself called on to pass laws again and again prohibiting under severe penalties these incipient manufactures, sometimes making them liable to summary destruction as "nuisances." As soon as a branch of industry becomes profitable, and suitable to the conditions in which a community is placed, nothing but extreme vigilance can prevent its springing into being. Men naturally, spontaneously, under the pressure of necessity render to each other such services as are in demand, and as are possible to be rendered in the state in which they are placed. Foster manufactures artificially? They will come in naturally and inevitably just so fast and so far as they ought to come in. They are as natural to men as agriculture. They require capital indeed, and on a large scale, a large capital. So does agriculture. Capital is the growth of time and of frugality. No

[1] See Hildreth, *passim*.

new society can come at once into all the forms of industry which adorn an old established State; there must be a gradual growth of capital and of skill, and as these increase, one branch of industry after another comes in, and finds a stable foothold; and as capital further increases, and the rate per cent. of capital goes down, it becomes profitable to do many things which it would be sheer folly to do at an earlier period. When every dollar of the capital of a country can realize a clear gain of ten per cent., is there any sense or reason in withdrawing a part of it into occupations which can only yield six per cent.? " But we must have diversity," says Mr. Carey. Certainly, we want diversity, but only a natural diversity, in which each branch can stand on its own legs, and not find it necessary to tax all its neighbors in order that its own profits may equal the average of theirs. The theory of a protective tariff is this: that certain unprofitable branches of business shall be cared for by the State, that is to say, the citizens shall be taxed to bring up the profits of these to the general standard of profits. Is a diversity, thus secured, a profitable diversity? Would it not be better for all concerned not to enter at present upon forms of industry that by confession do not pay? " But," urges the advocate of protection, " if they do not now pay, they will pay by-and-by." How do you know that they will? The fact that they do not now pay, is not of itself good proof that they ever will; and at any rate, it strikes a good many people that it would be better to wait till that time comes, and to enter upon branches of industry just as fast as they become profitable, and no faster.

It seems strange to me, that Mr. Carey, whose general confidence in man and in nature is so justly strong, should find his confidence desert him just at this point; should show so much impatience with a natural progress of diversity and association; and should vehemently invoke the assistance of law to help on diversity within a sphere for whose general freedom he is a distinguished champion. He is less consistent than the famous charioteer, who, when his horses ran away down the hill, trusted in Providence until the breeching broke, and then gave all up for lost. Mr. Carey trusts in Providence, and does well; but all at once, when to other passengers as clear-sighted as himself there are no signs of anything giving way, he shrieks out that the breeching is breaking, Providence is inadequate, we must have recourse to Protection.

The idea that the United States, with a greater variety and abundance of natural resources than any other country on the globe; with an industrious, and enterprising, and skilful people; with mountain streams which leap to the wheels of industry with a song; with forests and coal-fields, and mines; with marts and markets, and navigable lakes and rivers; with a genius for traffic, and a keen eye to profit,— the idea that the United States is to be reduced to a mere farming country, unless government can be coaxed to tax foreigners and citizens in behalf of some branches of manufacture which are asserted to be otherwise unprofitable,— is too ridiculous for serious refutation. Why, no nation of the earth has such facilities for manufacturing: the raw materials are here; the food is here in abounding measure; the instruments are here in water, wood, and coal; cattle and horses and pastures are here; everything is here which a nation can ask for with which to produce either directly that which is wanted, or directly that with which to purchase at the cheapest rates what is wanted from abroad; and if God shall give us grace to mind our own business, to avoid entangling alliances with our neighbors, and unnatural wars with foreigners, to rise above the silly jealousies which have hitherto restricted trade, we shall yet be the beehive of the nations, the chosen home of the industrial and civilizing arts.

(6.) But Mr. Carey endeavors to discover a distinction between commerce and trade. He says: " The words commerce and trade are commonly regarded as convertible terms, yet are the ideas they express so widely different, as to render it essential that their difference be clearly understood. All men are prompted to associate and combine with each other, — to exchange ideas and services with each other,— and thus to maintain commerce. Some men seek to perform exchanges for other men, and thus to maintain trade."[1] This attempted distinction plays a very important part in Mr. Carey's system; he is returning to it perpetually; and according to it, commerce increases as trade declines, the trader is a foe alike to commerce and society, and lives "by appropriation," and restrictions ought to be laid on trade in order "to establish perfect freedom of commerce throughout the world." He complains that hitherto "commerce has been sacrificed at the shrine of trade." Now, I have no hesitation in affirming that this for-

[1] Social Science, Vol. I. p. 210.

midable looking distinction is for the most part destitute of any basis of difference. Let us examine it. They who exchange services with each other, says the distinction, practise commerce, while they who perform exchanges for other men are mere traders. The distinction is made to turn on the ownership of the services exchanged: if the principals exchange for themselves, that is commerce; if they employ agents to do it for them, that is trade; if a merchant freights his own ship with his own goods and takes them to a foreign port, and takes care to exchange there with real owners only for what he wants in return, that is commerce; but if he employs a supercargo to manage his sales and returns, then it is trade. If a middle-man buys the cargo outright, and sells to another middle-man on the other side who is real owner of the return services, that is commerce under the definition; while in domestic exchanges all bargains mediated by employees is trade under the definition. This, to say the least of it, is putting a fine point on commercial transactions; and, so far as I can see, is totally irrelevant in a general doctrine of exchanges. Exchange is exchange, and the laws of exchange and the profits of exchange remain unaffected by any such distinction. *Qui facit per alium facit per se.* If I employ an agent to do any portion of my business for me, it is because I think it profitable to do so, and there is an exchange of services between him and me for that purpose, but the exchanges which he effects in my name as principal are in nature the same as if I effected them myself. If Mr. Carey wants to say that exchanges would be more profitable if there were no costs of carriage, no clerk hire, no intermediate services of any sort, there is nobody to dispute with him; but since exchanges cannot be carried on to any extent without these agencies, what is the use of quarrelling with Nature and Providence? The transporter is just as much of a producer as the grower or transformer,— he renders a valuable service, and must be paid for it of course. As soon as his services can be dispensed with, and no loss accrue, they will most assuredly be dispensed with; but to say that people shall not employ such an agent if they think their interests subserved by employing him, can hardly be reconciled with any adequate notions of freedom or of exchange. All sorts of services are in order in exchange. All sorts of talent are available. If a man has not capital to do business for himself, let him begin by doing business for others. If a man can furnish a ship, but cannot freight her, there is no mortal objection to his furnishing a ship. Let the merchant freight her, and let them divide profits on the return. If a distinction between commerce and trade be allowed, for which I see no ground whatever, each, at any rate, is swallowed up in the higher unity of exchange, and becomes amenable to the principles already unfolded.

It is in this connection, that Mr. Carey exalts the policy of Colbert, the famous finance minister of Louis XIV., who certainly did much for the prosperity of France, and well deserves the fame which posterity is so ready to accord. But to refer the immense industrial impulse which France received at that time in any considerable degree to the restrictive duties laid by Colbert on foreign trade, is an instance, by no means single in Mr. Carey's books, of a fallacy called by the logicians *post hoc ergo propter hoc*. It is most unsatisfactory and illogical to be told that one thing came after another and therefore was caused by it. Colbert did many things much better worth the doing than to lay prohibitory duties. He swept away, so far as lay in his power, all the obstacles to the freest interchange of commodities within the realm of France. He abolished the interminable internal tolls and duties. He simplified and reduced the taxes. Says Henri Martin, — "We are struck with admiration to see Colbert begin by reducing an impost thirty-three per cent., on the increased product of which he founded in great part his hopes. Trampling on the routine of the exchequer, he had comprehended that consumption increases in equal or even greater proportion to the abasement of duties that weigh on consumable objects, and that the public treasury does not lose what the well-being of the people gains."[1] He abolished superfluous offices, and introduced economy, and, as far as possible, honesty into every department of the State. He emancipated the Communes from their old burdens, and forbade their incurring new debts. He renovated the whole industrial and financial system; and France began mightily to prosper. But he was also in part, unfortunately, a disciple of the mercantile system. He laid heavy duties on foreign goods, which of course provoked foreigners to lay similar duties on the products of French industry. Martin himself, with whom Colbert is a hero, acknowledges this consequence. It has never been proved, and never can be, that the high duties contributed to the then prosperity of the

[1] History of France.

French; the weight of bare authority is about evenly balanced on the question; but he who follows reason and science in the premises will not hesitate in his decision.

(7.) Mr. Erastus B. Bigelow of Boston published in 1862 a quarto volume, entitled " The Tariff Question, considered in Regard to the Policy of England and the Interests of the United States." About a hundred pages of this volume are letter-press; and the remaining hundred and fifty contain statistical and comparative tables, designed to illustrate and confirm the positions taken in the text.

Mr. Bigelow is an inventor, and as such deserves well of the country and of the world. He has invented a power-loom for the weaving of two-ply and three-ply carpets,— a mechanical feat, which, before he accomplished it, had been pronounced an impossibility. In consequence of his inventions and improvements the carpet manufacture in this country has received a vast expansion, — fabrics which before were produced from hand-looms at the rate of 3 to 8 yards per day being now produced of better quality from the power-loom at the rate of 18 to 30 yards per day. Lowell and Clinton in Massachusetts, Thomsonville and Tariffville in Connecticut, have had flourishing carpet establishments under the Bigelow patents.

As these tabular statements and statistics make up much the larger part of Mr. Bigelow's book, so they constitute also its most valuable part; and as I propose in these paragraphs to make some strictures upon the arguments and positions of the book, I wish to acknowledge, at the outset, in the amplest manner, the accuracy and value of these statistics. Some of them were compiled, with great labor, from sources that are inaccessible to most people, and the whole together make up a set of tables exceedingly valuable for reference.

Let Mr. Bigelow state his fundamental position in his own words: " Let it be understood, then, that the protective policy here advocated, is not a policy that seeks to favor a particular interest at the expense of some other interest, or which would build up one section of the country to the detriment of other sections. A scale of duties which should place our manufacturers on a level with their competitors in countries whose wages and interest are lower and capital more abundant than with us, could have no effects nor tendencies which would not be beneficial to all classes and to the whole nation. In the selection of objects there would be need, certainly, of a careful discrimination. It is clearly unwise to foster by legislative aid any branch of industry or business for the prosecution of which our natural advantages are decidedly inferior. Some strong and peculiar necessity can alone justify such a course. But in regard to all those pursuits for which we have the requisite endowments, and need only the acquired advantages of capital, skill, and position, in order to compete successfully with other nations, I hold it to be not only proper but necessary that so much of governmental aid shall be afforded as will raise our industry to a footing of equality. To do this effectually, our duties should be so established as not only to meet and equalize the differences just mentioned, but also to counteract that occasional application of foreign capital by which our market is sometimes designedly flooded with cheap goods, at a loss it is true, to the producer, but with still greater damage to some struggling manufacture of our own, if not indeed to its utter prostration."

Let us look for a moment at this passage. In the first sentence he disclaims "advocating a protective policy that seeks to build up a particular interest at the expense of some other interest." But, unluckily, he fails to tell us anywhere in his book how that thing can be done, — how a particular interest can be fostered by protective duties except at the expense of other interests. Who pays the enhanced price caused by the duty? Clearly, all consumers pay it. This is universally admitted. Mr. Bigelow does not deny it. Unless then, it can be shown that the enhanced prices of commodities are paid at nobody's expense, that the consumer pays two dollars as easily as one, then it is in vain to talk about a protective policy that fosters one interest without depressing others. It is an omission fatal to his argument, that our author does not show how this financial miracle is wrought. We cannot indeed blame him for not showing what is impossible to be shown, but we do blame him for bringing forward an argument the whole validity of which depends on one premise, without attempting to prove that premise. This proof is utterly wanting in the book before us. The argument falls therefore of itself to the ground. It is an easy thing to say: " Let us have a protective tariff here that shall stimulate artificially certain branches of industry, and nobody be any the poorer." Is it impertinent for us to require of those who say this, that they shall tell us how these branches of industry can be thus stimulated and nobody be any the poorer?

But the second sentence is still more extraordinary. It contains the surprising assertion that a scale of high restrictive duties "could have no effects nor tendencies which would not be beneficial to all classes and to the whole nation." Let us look at some of these "effects and tendencies," and see if they be so universally beneficial. First, commerce is lessened by the restriction. Some people who used to come to your shores to trade, to bring their surplus products and to take off yours, no longer come. You have flung your fist into their face, and they prudently stay away. In consequence, those home commodities you formerly exchanged with them no longer find a market, that is, their best and freely chosen market. Perhaps they do not find a market at all. Home labor is so far discouraged, and home products are so far less valuable. Is there anything in this beneficial "to all classes and to the whole nation"? Again, your action leads the other nation to adopt or perpetuate similar restrictions. You are thrust from her ports just as you thrust her from yours. You fail to get her commodities which you formerly enjoyed. There are fewer exchanges here, and fewer exchanges there. Commerce thus receives a double blow, first on one cheek, then on the other. Is there anything in this "beneficial to all classes and to the whole nation"? Furthermore, in consequence of these restrictions, the prices of all commodities that are exchanged, stand at a much higher figure, and every consumer must pay these enhanced prices. Is there anything in this beneficial to all classes and to the whole nation? The truth is, this assertion is very loose, and very wide of the facts, and Mr. Bigelow would find it difficult to justify his language to intelligent and candid people.

But besides this the sentence under review contains a fallacy which has been again and again exposed, but which deserves another faithful exposure, and shall receive it. We must have a restrictive tariff, says Mr. Bigelow, because other nations have a lower rate of wages and interest, and more abundant capital than we. But it is fair to presume that Mr. Bigelow knows that foreign trade depends only very remotely on the absolute cost of the articles exchanged. It is relative efficiency, not absolute, that determines foreign trade. If any person does not know this, then he is ignorant of the one fundamental proposition of commerce, and his reasoning, as a matter of course, cannot reach correct conclusions. If, on the other hand, a writer be familiar with this fundamental proposition, he should see that any reference to lower wages and lower interest of money is, in this connection, entirely irrelevant. It is a matter of indifference to us what the goods we buy from abroad cost their producers, whether they paid high wages or low wages, high interest or low interest; we do not care about the absolute cost of production of anything we buy; the question of interest for us is how much of the home commodity must we give for it, and what does the home commodity cost us. The simple question that determines foreign trade is this,— would the commodity, if produced here, cost more than that commodity with which we buy it? If it would, then we profitably import it; and this, without any reference to its cost to the foreign producer. Whether he pays high wages or low wages, high interest or low interest, whether capital is abundant there or scarce, has little to do with this question of a profitable* exchange of commodities, and justifies, in no conceivable manner, the restrictive system. California has much higher wages and a much higher interest than New England; does she need, therefore, to prohibit New-England ships from entering the Golden Gate? Is it for her interest to put restrictions on New-England goods? Does New England, because wages are lower here, get more than her share of advantage in the California trade? If not, no more would England or India in a trade with us. We trade with all the world: some parts have a higher rate of wages and interest than we; some parts have a lower rate; so far as that matter is concerned our trade may be equally advantageous with them all.

To this law of foreign trade there is, however, a single not unimportant exception. When two nations go into the market of the world with the same commodity, to buy gold and silver, then the absolute money-cost of that commodity is, as between the two, an important question. That one of the two nations whose wages are lower, and whose rate of interest is less, in the manufacture of the common commodity will, in a trade for gold, under-sell the other — that is, can afford to give more of its commodity for an ounce of gold, because its commodity has cost less in gold. This is clear, and it is the only case where foreign trade is determined by the absolute cost of production. But our author can get no crumb of comfort here; for in the first place, the commerce of the world is not a commerce for gold and silver, but a commerce of commodities, in the exchange of which relative cost is the only principle. And in the second place, when two nations go into the market of the world for gold, they rarely carry the same commodity, but carry, each its own peculiar commodities, in the production of which it has the greatest advantage. They have a strong motive to do this always, for that which they have the greatest advantage in producing will buy all other commodities, gold included, at the cheapest rate. Here too the relative cost decides. And in the third place, if two nations do carry the same commodity into the same market to buy the same gold, and the nation whose wages and profits are higher is thereby at a disadvantage in the trade, how is a restrictive tariff at home to help that matter? The true remedy is to cultivate our own peculiar advantages to the highest point, and carry those commodities abroad to buy our gold, and not endeavor to compete with our neighbor in the same commodity. High wages and high profits are a vast national advantage; restrictive systems tend certainly to reduce them; but shall we throw away a great advantage enjoyed by all laborers and all capital in all departments, in order to compete with less fortunate nations in a single trade with a single commodity? The folly of this is patent; especially as the United States is a gold-producing country, and not only supplies herself with gold, but half the world besides. All this talk therefore about high wages and high profits putting us at a disadvantage in foreign trade, and making restriction necessary, is moonshine of the purest sort, — is, in every case, irrelevant.

In the next sentence of the extract quoted, Mr. Bigelow really, though unconsciously, concedes to us the whole question in dispute. "It is clearly unwise," says he, "to foster by legislative aid any branch of industry for which our natural advantages are decidedly inferior." But if our natural advantages are not decidedly inferior, why do we need any legislative aid at all? Or, to translate this euphonious expression "legislative aid" into plainer English, why should everybody be taxed to maintain a branch of industry whose natural advantages are not inferior?

If the natural advantages are inferior, it is clearly unwise to protect, says Mr. Bigelow; but if the natural advantages are not inferior, what is the need of protection?

What hinders the establishment of a branch of industry in any country whose natural advantages for that branch are not inferior? Clearly two things can hinder it: lack of capital and lack of skill. If all the capital of the country is now taken up by branches of industry already existing, of what advantage is it to introduce a new branch which can only come into being at the expense of the old by withdrawing capital from the old? The capital is already taken up. Let it abide in its freely chosen channels. If the capital of the country is not all taken up, then certainly new branches of industry will come in, will come in of their own accord; you cannot keep them out. Every kind of business, which, under present circumstances, is profitable, will be carried on, and those that are not profitable we do not want.

If the restrictive system could increase the capital of a country, then it might with some show of reason be defended, but it would be a difficult task, I think, to show how the capital of a country can be increased by stopping a profitable commerce.

And just so of skill. If the new branch of manufacture for which skilled labor is wanted is carried on abroad, the laborers can be easily imported. An assurance of higher wages and constant employment has brought and will bring again skilled laborers from every country in Europe. Restriction, cannot give us skill, since all experience has shown, and common sense testifies to the same point, that skill will be best developed under the freest competition — under circumstances where everything depends on relative skill, rather than where very little depends on it; where a high price, artificially created, is sure, whether skill be exercised or not. The sharp spur of emulation added to the keen impulse of interest, will most assuredly carry skill to its highest point. Since, then, Mr. Bigelow would not employ protection where natural advantages are inferior, and since where they are not inferior the only obstacles to new branches of business are the want of skill and capital, which skill and capital restriction has no tendency to increase, where is the ground for protection at all?

In the last sentence quoted Mr. Bigelow betrays, what is indeed betrayed in various parts of the book, that he had never studied with sufficient care the nature of commerce in its simple elements. It would have saved him, as I think, from some mistakes, and from many fallacies, if he had thoroughly reflected that commerce is nothing but an exchange of commodities for commodities for the mutual advantage of the parties, and that exchange is always a reciprocal act; when a man sells he buys, and when he buys he sells. If a foreigner brings goods to our shores he always carries away in effect a corresponding value from our shores. He sells to us, and in the very act he buys from us: we buy from him and in the very act sell to him. It is a reciprocal act. The only motive he has to bring anything hither is that he may carry something hence. When therefore Mr. Bigelow says in the sentence referred to, that foreigners will sometimes, as he expresses it, "flood our markets with cheap goods at a loss to themselves, for the purpose of strangling some business of ours," he holds up a bugbear, which, I am inclined to think, under the laws of commerce and the laws of human nature, never could become a reality. Certainly until some well-authenticated case is given of foreigners who were willing to submit to a present and positive loss in the hope of a gain uncertain, problematical, and future; until some well-authenticated case is given of a rising manufacture, adapted to our circumstances and profitable in itself, being ruined in this way; until a well-authenticated case is given of a magnanimous manufacturer sacrificing his present gains for a future and uncertain benefit to accrue to his fellow-manufacturers, freighting ships to America to bring nothing back, — until the case is given, I shall beg leave to think that a thing so contrary to the interests of capital, to the laws of trade, and even to the principles of human nature, has not occurred in the past, and is not likely to in the future.

(8.) One further objection to free trade remains to be briefly considered. It is this, and it has been urged with some plausibility and much pertinacity, namely, that every nation ought to be independent of others in all the more essential articles of life; and therefore protective duties ought to be laid in order to compel the nations to make or grow all the articles of prime necessity for themselves. The objection divides itself into two parts, the postulate and the inference, and it shall be considered in that order and relation. First, every nation ought to be independent of others in respect to the supply of its more necessary wants, such as food, clothing, means of defence and offence, and so on. But what is it to be independent? I suppose it means, in this connection, to be sure of getting what is wanted under all contingencies. But is an individual man to be regarded as "dependent," and as likely to lose his bread, unless he devote himself to the growing of food directly? If he only has wherewithal to buy food, I take it that he is just as "independent," just as likely to get it, as if he produced it himself; and so a nation which has products to offer which are in demand in the world without, is very sure of getting whatever it wants, provided it is anywhere to be bought, and is, in my apprehension of it, in a very "independent" position. Protectionists have degraded language and degraded exchange by trying to make it appear that a man and a nation are reduced to conditions of dependence whenever they find it for their interest to buy;

but the truth is that there is nothing dependent in buying and selling; the parties stand on a footing of perfect equality towards each other; each is at the same moment buyer and seller; one is as independent as the other, and nobody can be more so than either, except the savage and the hermit, who live in a state of isolation. Moreover, every nation does of course devote itself directly to the supply of its principal wants, and always continues to do so, unless it appears that it can supply those wants more cheaply through exchange. If it can supply them more cheaply through exchange, it becomes, in my judgment, more "independent" by doing so; more independent of irksome effort, and more sure of getting its wants supplied, since now it draws its supplies from a wider surface, from any point in the wide world where such supplies are to be had and where its own products are in demand. So far as food is concerned, this objection sounds but poorly in the mouths of protectionists, who are the men perpetually bemoaning the prospect that every nation, unless it follow their advice and lay protective duties, will be exclusively agricultural.

But the inference is even less defensible than the postulate. Let it be admitted, for argument's sake, that to buy is to be dependent, and that every nation loses a part of its independence by every act of foreign exchange by which it obtains its necessary supplies; does it follow that protective duties are the true remedy? No. Prohibition is the barrier to hold up before the waning independence of the nation. Why allow a thing to go forward under more onerous conditions, which under less onerous was proving fatal to independence? If for the citizens to import freely be so disadvantageous to their independence, how disastrous must it be to have the importations still go forward under a tax in addition, which the citizens must pay!

The late insurgent States of this country furnish a capital illustration of the fact that war and a stringent blockade cannot prevent exchanges from going forward, when there is wherewithal at home to pay for goods, and goods abroad which are wanted at home. The United States maintained a thousand vessels, more or less, along the coast of the insurgent region, to intercept all trade; but there was cotton within which the English wanted, and goods without which the insurgents wanted, and the exchanges went on, with great hazards and frequent losses indeed, but went on for four years, to an immense amount of transactions.

It is always pleasant to be able to confirm one's reasonings with facts, to clench the nail driven home by a logical process, with a blow or two from the hammer of actual experience. It is fortunately possible to do this in regard to free trade. All the leading commercial nations, the United States alone excepted, have been relaxing of late years their commercial systems: the United States decidedly relaxed hers in 1846, and again in 1857, but in 1861, alone of nations, and in the face of principles, she took the back track, and prejudiced thereby as well the revenue, which we have sorely needed in our time of trial, as the cause of Freedom itself, which was represented by rebel emissaries abroad as of a piece with the craft which so little appreciated the dawn of an era of universal freedom as to mark its opening by a restrictive and irritating tariff.

England many years ago abandoned for substance the doctrine of protection, but only within a decade did she abolish the last vestige of the system in the discrimination till then maintained in favor of her own ships over those of foreigners in her own ports. There is nothing now to hinder American ships from competing on equal terms with English vessels in the coastwise carrying-trade of England itself. The English tariffs are adjusted with a view to revenue merely; and in the late special commercial treaty with France, the duties were thrown off entirely from a portion of French manufactures, and materially reduced on most of the rest. England claims, through the mouth of her responsible ministers and statesmen, to set before the nations an honest example of free trade; and invites them, as I believe, in good faith, to follow her in the path which she has opened up for herself. The force of this example is frequently sought to be parried by alleging that England reached through protection a point of prosperity at which she was well able to dispense with protection. This is neither ingenuous nor true; since the men who have persuaded the English government to abandon the principle of protection, are the men who have demonstrated the economical folly of the principle under all circumstances; and have shown that England maintained the policy so long at a loss to herself as well as her neighbors. Other nations can say, if they please, "We will maintain protection as long as England did, and then follow her example in giving it up." But if they do this, they will do it at a loss, as England did, and too late bemoan their folly, as England does. Said Mr. Gladstone, Chancellor of the English Exchequer, in 1856, — " There is one domestic feature which I wish it were in our power effectually to exhibit to the governments and inhabitants of foreign countries. They know by statistics, which are open to the world, the immense extension which our commerce has attained under and by virtue of freedom of trade, and the great advancement that has happily been achieved in the condition of the people; but they do not know what it has cost us to achieve this beneficial, nay, blessed change; what time, what struggles, what interruptions to the general work of legislation; what animosities and divisions among the great classes which make up the nation; what shocks to our established mode of conducting the government of the country; what fears and risk, at some periods, of public convulsion. *These were the fine and penalty we paid for long adherence to folly.* We paid this fine and penalty upon returning to the path of wisdom, which too late we wished we had never left. It is not easy to calculate its amount, but if it could be exactly reckoned, and fully exposed to the eyes of other nations, our juniors in trade, it might supply them with a timely warning against imitating our former errors, and with the best encouragement to the adoption, before they become entangled in the creation of artificial interests, of our recent and better example."

But it is said, as if that were sufficient to condemn free trade, that England adopted it out of pure selfishness. Of course she did; and other nations will also adopt it from the same motive. No other motive is appropriate in the premises. The idea, disseminated by protectionists, that it requires a millenium for free trade to work in, is wholly fallacious; it requires an enlightened selfishness, and nothing more; and it is one of the grand wonders of Providence, that the elements of society are so wisely prearranged, that, within the sphere of exchange, the welfare of all is promoted through the enlightened selfishness of each. Trade is always selfish, just as much so under freedom as under protection; it is a sphere all whose operations are subject to the legitimate control of conscience, but it is not, and never was designed to be, a sphere of sympathy and benevolence: these have a sphere of their own, above and beyond the sphere of exchange. When a man gives, let him give, and enjoy the luxury of doing good; when a man buys and sells, let him honestly, but with an eye to self-interest only, buy and sell and get gain.

The Zoll-Verein, or Revenue-Union of the German States, presents a splendid example of the prosperity which follows in the train of free exchange. The system commenced with Prussia in 1818, and has been gradually extended by the voluntary acceptance of it on the part of all the German States, except Austria, the free cities of Lübeck, Hamburg, and Bremen, and two or three of the small northern duchies. All interior custom-houses and barriers are swept away within the territory included in the Zoll-Verein; and a series of duties, not to exceed in any case ten per cent. *ad valorem* are laid on foreign manufactures, of which nothing is prohibited, the proceeds going into a common treasury, and then distributed among the various members of the union on the basis of their population. The rate of imposts on foreign goods is varied from time to time by the Zoll-Verein Congress, but ten per cent. is the maximum, and the interests of the revenue are consulted in adjusting the rates below that: since 1851 the raw materials coming from abroad are admitted free, or nearly so. Whether these facts justify Mr. Carey in regarding the Zoll-Verein as affording an example of protective duties, the intelligent reader must judge. I call these conditions, under which 34,000,000 of people are allowed to trade with absolute freedom among themselves, and with all the world outside at rates never exceeding ten per cent., very free conditions of trade; and if Mr. Carey is content that such rates as these, which he calls "protective," should be established for the United States, where at present the average rate on dutiable foreign goods falls scarcely if at all below fifty per cent., nobody will quarrel with him about the word. Germany is prosperous beyond all precedent under the stimulating influence of free exchange. Every State, without exception, now receives a larger revenue than it did before it joined the Zoll-Verein, and the production of the great staples of industry has prodigiously increased. The production of iron increased from 3,708,432 cwt. in 1850, to 10,207,098 cwt. in 1858; and the importation of foreign iron increased within the same dates from 2,455,000 cwt. to 6,587,000 cwt.; an interesting proof that the free introduction of foreign articles does not depress, but rather stimulate, the production of the same articles at home.

I have dwelt the longer on this question of free trade, because it is a practical one now in this country, for whose right solution every citizen should be anxious. Some additional light will be thrown upon the subject in each of the three remaining chapters.

CHAPTER XIV.

ON THE MERCANTILE SYSTEM.

THERE have been three epochs in the progress of the science of 'Exchange. Each of these has been marked by a theory of its own, of which the two earlier were radically incorrect, yet prepared the way for the third and true system. We have already sufficiently considered the first of these theories, which assumed that gold and silver are the only wealth, and, consequently, that the only way for a nation to grow rich was to foster the importation and prohibit the exportation of the precious metals. The second commercial theory was more refined and complicated; we have already spoken of it as the Mercantile System, and partially explained its fundamental principle. The principle was to preserve the balance of trade, to make the exports greater than the imports, so that the balance should come back in gold and silver. The whole system is based on the absurd supposition that a merchant will carry abroad goods worth at home a certain sum, merely that he may bring back goods and money worth as much. Why, on that principle, should he carry forth goods at all?

The nature of trade, as mutually advantageous, was not understood. After every fair mercantile transaction, both parties are richer than before. The

ON THE MERCANTILE SYSTEM. 411

more genuine exchanges there are between two countries the better, because the motive for an exchange is always and everywhere the mutual interest of the parties. The benefit of the exchange is shared by both, otherwise there would be no exchange.

But the Mercantile System led each nation to suppose, that, by manœuvre and finesse, it could obtain more than its natural share of advantage. England, for example, in her trade with France, found that, by natural tendency, she bought as much of French wines and silks as she sold France of hardware and woollens. Instead of being satisfied with a legitimate and mutually advantageous trade, the English, under the promptings of the Mercantile System, say, " This will never do. This will never do. There is no balance in our favor. We must sell to France more than we buy of her, or else we get no balance of trade." Accordingly restrictions are laid on some French goods. Their introduction is either prohibited, or heavy duties are levied on them, in order to lessen the quantity imported. This is done in the hope of selling to the French as much as before, but of buying less, this is, less French goods; so that the difference must be paid in gold and silver.

All that was mighty well! But unfortunately the gold and silver, even if they should get it, was no whit better than the French goods, and would probably go right back to France in the purchase of such goods. And unfortunately also the French were adepts in the Mercantile System; they wanted a favorable balance too. They must sell more than they buy. Their exports must exceed their imports. Why not? And accordingly they prohibit some species of English goods, or burden them with a heavy duty: the English retaliate by new restrictions on the products of French industry, and are again in turn retaliated upon. Thus they go on tinkering and tormenting trade in the vain hope of some imaginary balance!

Because England and France are adjacent, and because their natural productions and acquired industry are so very diverse, they are naturally to an immense extent mutual buyers and sellers. France is gifted, perhaps as much as any country upon earth, in point of soil, climate, and natural productions. She produces with the greatest facility, and in the greatest abundance, wines and the cereal grains; and has unusual advantages also for the culture of the mulberry and the manufacture of silk.

England is not thus blessed by Nature; but she has freedom, and industry, and energy, and skill; these have made her for centuries the greatest manufacturing and commercial country in the world. She has always had those things to sell which France wanted to buy, and has always wanted to buy those things which France has had to sell. Exchanges between two such countries are natural and inevitable. If the governments undertake to forbid them, then the business will be done by smugglers, though with hazard and loss.

Now, the Mercantile System disturbed and well-nigh destroyed this natural and profitable trade. To be sure, England could buy her wines of France much cheaper and of better quality than of Portugal; but then, the balance of trade with France was supposed to be less favorable than with Portugal; and therefore the French wines were prohibited, and the monopoly of supplying the English market was given to the Portuguese. The English drank poorer wines at a greater expense. If this were all, it would not have been so bad; but the French, to retaliate and to restore the balance, prohibited English woollens. Thus the English were not only obliged to regale themselves on poor wine at a high price, but to lose an excellent market for woollen goods. The French lost not only the best market for their wines, but must purchase their woollens elsewhere at an enhanced cost. It was a dead loss all round — a gratuitous loss without any compensation whatever.

So far has this regulating mania been carried at times, that almost all legitimate commerce ceased between the two countries. Adam Smith tells us that, in his time, that is less than a hundred years ago, smugglers were the principal importers of British goods into France, and of French goods into Britain. So reluctant was England to buy of France, so fully were her statesmen under the influence of the prejudice that the prosperity of her neighbors was incompatible with her own, that Parliament, as late as William and Mary's time, decreed that the French trade was a nuisance.

(1.) This laying extraordinary restraints on the importation of goods from those countries with which the balance was supposed to be unfavorable, was one device of the Mercantile System to increase the quantity of gold and silver. It was unfortunately not the only nor the worst one. The great idea was, you perceive, to discourage importation and to encourage exportation, in order that the country might grow rich by the stream of gold and silver which, it was supposed, would pour in to pay the balance between the large exports and the small imports.

(2.) An obvious expedient was to prohibit altogether, or to burden with very high duties, the introduction of all such goods as could be produced at home. If we can produce the articles at home, then we shall not have to import them, and that will help the balance. Under the influence of this feeling, England, damp and cold, in the very teeth of Nature's protests, undertook to rival France in the culture of silk. Heavy restraints were laid on foreign silks, and the monopoly of supplying the home market was given to her own manufacturers. Certainly, silk can be made in England, of a somewhat inferior quality and at a somewhat greater cost than in sunnier climes. To overcome these disadvantages, what was needed was the healthy stimulus of competition. If things had been left to take their natural course, and foreign silks had been admitted freely, the home manufacturers would have been put upon their mettle to discover improved processes, to invent machinery, to make up the disadvantages of Nature by expedients of Art. The plant never becomes hardy and strong that does not root itself amid the breezes of heaven; so neither does a branch of business grow up into self-sustaining and vigorous life without the stimulating breezes of competition. Of this the case in hand affords an excellent illustration. For more than a century the silk manufacture of England, fenced round and protected, as it was called, by these restrictive and prohibitory duties, languished, pined, and at times almost expired; for the simple reason that the manufacturers, instead of relying upon their own invention, skill, and energy, looked to the government for support, and to an artificial monopoly; and when at length in 1826 this foolish system was abandoned, and the silk interest was told that it must look out for itself, and the ports were thrown open to foreign silk, then first the English silk culture began to thrive; it has thriven from that day to this, until now we are told that in the plainer and firmer kinds of silk the English surpass the French, and that there is a considerable exportation of these English silks into France itself.

As an illustration of the mischiefs which the Mercantile System everywhere introduced into the realm of industry, let us look at this instance a little more closely. During the continuance of the monopoly, the English consumers of silk were obliged to pay a very high price for an inferior article. To whose benefit did this high price accrue? It was designed to accrue to the benefit of the home manufacturer. The sole object in laying the prohibitory duties was to prevent importations, and to leave the home market entire to the home manufacturer. Precisely at this point we see how the whole doctrine of Protection grew out of the Mercantile System. The Mercantile System wished to repress importations for the sake of the balance of trade; but if needful articles cannot be imported, they must be made or grown at home; and in order to be made or grown at home, the makers or growers must be encouraged. The monopoly of the home market was precisely this encouragement; and it is owing to this single circumstance that influential classes in every mercantile community have supposed themselves benefited by this monopoly, that the doctrine of Protection has lingered so long in the general mind. It is easy, however, to see that this benefit is in most cases wholly imaginary; and that the high prices paid by the consumers do not, on the whole, strengthen the manufacture, as has been supposed. If the government had gone further, and given those who had already commenced the culture of silk the monopoly against their own countrymen as well as against foreigners, so that nobody could engage in the manufacture except those already engaged in it, then, indeed, these would grow rich at the expense of their countrymen. Government would take money out of the pocket of every consumer of silk, and put it into their pocket, and the whole benefit of the high prices would accrue to the manufacturers alone. But governments have rarely gone so far as this. They have excluded foreign competition, but not prohibited home competition; and the result has been, that the high duties which excluded the foreign goods, and the consequent high prices of the domestic product, have drawn many men and much capital into that business, in the hope of an 'extraordinary profit. The business has been artificially stimulated, and capital has been thrust into it which would not have gone of its own accord. The thing has been overdone; and the feverish home competition, in its anxiety to reap monopoly prices, has brought down prices far below the paying figure. The business has collapsed from its very inflation; and thus alternate chills and fever have shaken the life out of it.

But the Mercantile System, and the restrictive policy that sprung from it, obtained universal currency. The statute-books of every nation in Europe are defaced by the absurdest laws and regulations respecting manufactures and commerce. It was ordered, for example, by an act passed in England in 1678, that all dead bodies should be wrapped in woollen shrouds! This, you must know, was for the encouragement of the woollen manufacture!

The artisans in the cities and towns were formed into guilds, that is, incorporated societies, and to each guild was given the monopoly of the market, in its branch of industry. No man could practise the art of a shoemaker in Antwerp or London without the consent of the guild of St. Crispin; and the guild itself determined the number of apprentices to each artisan, the years he should serve, the conditions under which he might become a master; in short, determined everything respecting the trade by constitution and bye-laws. The governments, justly regarding these artisans as the most industrious and deserving of their subjects, granted them many privileges, which, however, were no less contrary to sound principles than the rest of the system. That they might obtain cheap provisions, the export of corn was forbidden; and thus agriculture was prevented from selling its products in the best market, wherever that market might be found. That they might obtain the raw materials of their manufactures cheap, the export of these was strictly forbidden. The tanner and currier, for example, must sell his product to the "gentle Craft of Leather," and had no other market.

The general doctrine of fostering exportation was infringed on in these instances, because it was thought that there would be a greater ultimate export of manufactured products, if the raw materials of these were forbidden to be exported, and cheap provisions were secured to the artisans.

In order to encourage agriculture, most European countries, in accordance with the doctrines of the Mercantile System, passed corn-laws forbidding the importation of foreign grain, each nation wishing to raise its own subsistence from its own soil. The consequence of this was that the landholders secured the monopoly of supplying the home market with food; which of course greatly enhanced the price to all consumers, especially in times of scarcity. The increased price of bread, which rich and poor must pay alike, was but a part of the evil consequences. No nation is so sure of its subsistence, when it endeavors to raise the whole of that subsistence at home, as when it leaves the channels of importation open for foreign supplies. When the trade in corn is free, the dearth in one country is instantly supplied by the superabundance of another, and that by natural laws as beautiful and invariable in their operation as the laws that govern the heavenly bodies. Interference with natural law in no direction is so mischievous and culpable as in this. Is it not plain to common sense that that nation is most likely to obtain its food with regularity and in plenty which draws its supplies from the widest surface? Massachusetts, for example, does not begin to feed its own population; but does any one suppose her people are any more likely to starve on that account? She can buy food with the products of her industry. Her calicoes and cassimeres, her hardware and cutlery, her nick-nacks and notions, will buy wheat not only in the marts of the West, but in Poland and Russia as well. She is sure to be fed, because she has wherewithal to buy food; more sure to be fed than if she compelled the industry of her people to abandon the more profitable mill-stream and factory, shop, and foundry, to extort from these rocky hill-sides the reluctant grains.

England, too, in 1849, removed the last vestige of corn-laws from her statute-book, and now imports flour freely from the Black Sea and from the Baltic, from France and from the United States. Who supposes that, if England did not raise a kernel of wheat, she would not be as certain of her daily bread as the people of Poland or of Michigan? But one may say, in case of war, she had better raise her food at home. But it is absurd to suppose that any nation would be at war with all the world at once; and we may be assured that the portion not belligerent would be eager to furnish the supplies. And besides, plenty of wheat would enter England if the English only wanted it, though all the navies of the world should blockade the fast-anchored isle. Every creek and headland would be alive with the silent and secret but busy agents of a clandestine trade.

The simple consideration that condemns this second expedient of the Mercantile System, namely, the prohibiting the importation of such commodities as can be produced at home, and the Protective policy inseparably connected with it, is, that it involves a dead loss to the productive powers of the world. There is in the world a certain amount of capital and a certain amount of industry. These, if left to their own keen sense of interest, will make the aggregate amount of production in the world as great as that amount of capital and industry can make it. If, then, a free commerce distribute this aggregate production over the earth in accordance with the simple law of supply and demand, we shall have not only the greatest production, but the most perfect distribution.

But if now government steps in, and withdraws capital and industry from their freely chosen posts of activity, prohibits exchanges that would otherwise be made, and commands commodities to be manufactured or grown in localities where they would not naturally be manufactured or grown, then certainly the aggregate production of the world is lessened, and its distribution is less perfect.

(3.) The Mercantile System had two other expedients which were frequently employed to subserve the ends of its grand principle. For the sake of increasing the exports, and thus improving the balance of trade, bounties were given to encourage the export and sale of native fabrics in foreign markets. A bounty, we understand, is a sum of money paid outright by the government to the exporters of native fabrics, in order to enable them to sell their goods as cheap or cheaper than their rivals in the foreign market. England, for example, was so anxious to sell her goods to foreigners, that she regularly paid her merchants for selling the goods at a loss. "The price of these goods in that market," says the merchant, "will not reward my capital with the ordinary profit." "Never mind," says England, "sell away, and I will make up your loss by a bounty!" Was not that a rare and brilliant way of enriching the country? By natural laws, a branch of industry ceases as soon as it becomes unprofitable; but by the system of bounties a trade was perpetuated of which the expense was greater than the returns, of which every operation destroyed a portion of the capital employed in it. The loss was made up to the operators by government; in other words, the people were taxed to pay it.

(4.) The fourth and last expedient of the Mercantile System was to help the balance of trade by founding colonies, that the mother country might enjoy the monopoly of their trade, and force them to resort exclusively to her markets. All the English colonies on this continent were bound by the rigid fetters of this colonial system. Up to the date of American Independence, Virginia and Massachusetts must buy all they wished to buy in English markets, and carry all they had to sell to English ports. Spain and France extended the same colonial monopoly, with even more of inflexibility, over their American and West India settlements; and it was considerations growing out of this colonial policy which gave birth to the American Revolution; and that war was waged not more for the interests of humanity than for the freedom of trade.

CHAPTER XV.

ON AMERICAN TARIFFS.

So long as the United States were colonies of Great Britain, their commerce was bound in the rigid fetters of the Mercantile System. We have already seen in the last chapter that colonies were one of the devices of the Mercantile System to secure a favorable "balance of trade." If the maxim be to sell as much as possible and buy as little as possible, then colonies, which could be compelled to receive the goods of the mother country, must be commercially valuable. Accordingly, all the commercial countries of Europe, and particularly Spain and England, adopted a colonial policy that sprung directly from this fundamental maxim. They valued their colonies as affording broad markets for the sale of products, and also because they could monopolize the articles produced by the colonists themselves. In general, the colonists were compelled to sell all they had to sell to the mother country, and to buy all they had to buy of the mother country; even though the articles thus bought were not the produce of the mother country, but must first be imported there and then exported thence to the colonies. Until the Revolution, a Boston ship, for example, could not sail directly to China for teas, but the teas must first be brought to England in British ships, must pay a duty there, and then be reëxported to the colonies.

As early as 1650 this monopoly system was entered upon by the then republican Parliament of England. The colonies had already overcome the difficulties incident to their first settlement, had begun to increase rapidly in wealth, and their commerce had become so considerable as to afford a temptation to restrict its freedom and to endeavor to make it peculiarly advantageous to the mother country. In the year named an act was passed restricting the export and import trade of the colonies to British ships and to ships built in the colonies. No foreign keel could enter a colonial harbor, either to buy or to sell.

Ten years later, that is in 1660, the famous "Navigation Act" was passed, which with small modifications continued to be the maritime law of England down to 1815; which was essentially modified in 1825; and the small remains of which have only recently been expunged from the statute-book.

This Navigation Act is of great interest to Americans, because the American Revolution grew directly out of it. Says Bancroft, "American Independence, like the great rivers of the country, had many sources; but the head spring which colored all the stream was the Navigation Act." It was enacted that certain enumerated articles, which included all the principal productions of the colonies, could not be exported directly to any foreign country, but must first be sent to Great Britain, and there unladen, before they could be forwarded to their final destination. It amounted to the same thing as prohibiting all exports except to the mother country. The chief products of their industry the colonists could not export to any place but Great Britain, not even to Ireland; neither sugar, nor tobacco, nor cotton, nor wool, nor indigo, nor ginger, nor dye-woods, nor molasses, nor rice, nor peltry, nor ore, nor pitch, nor tar, nor turpentine, nor masts, nor yards, nor bowsprits, nor coffee, nor cocoa-nuts, nor whale-fins, nor hides, nor ashes.

Nor was this all. England constituted herself not only the sole market for American products, but also the sole storehouse for American supplies. The colonies must not only sell exclusively in British markets, but they must also buy exclusively in British markets. It was enacted, that " no commodity of the growth, production, or manufacture of Europe, shall be imported into the British plantations, but such as are laden and put on board in England, Wales, or Berwick-upon-Tweed, and in English-built shipping, whereof the master and three fourths of the crew are English."

The preamble to this statute, which was supplemental to the Navigation Act, is curious, and assigns as the motive of the restriction, " the maintaining a greater correspondence and kindness between the subjects at home and those in the plantations; keeping the colonies in a firmer dependence on the mother country; making them yet more beneficial to it in the further employment and increase of English shipping and in the vent of English manufactures and commodities; rendering the navigation to them more safe and cheap; and making this kingdom a staple, not only of the commodities of the plantations, but also of the commodities of other countries and places for their supply; it being the usage of other nations to keep their plantation-trade exclusively to themselves."

In close connection with these commercial restrictions, it was a leading point in the colonial policy to discourage all attempts of the colonists to manufacture for themselves. "That the country which was the home of the beaver might not manufacture its own hats, no man in the colonies could be a hatter or a journeyman at that trade, unless he had served an apprenticeship of seven years. No hatter might employ more than two apprentices. No American hat might be sent from one plantation to another. America abounded in iron ores of the best quality, as well as in wood and coal; slitting-mills, steel-furnaces, and plating-forges, to work with a tilt-hammer, were prohibited in the colonies as nuisances." Similar restrictions existed in respect to wool and weaving; no wool, or any manufacture of it, could be carried across the line of one province to another; and a British sailor, wanting clothes in a colonial harbor, was forbidden to buy there more than forty shillings' worth. To print the English Bible in the colonies would have been a high-handed infringement of the law; and while that book was reverently read around almost every hearthstone in the land, not a copy of it was printed here till we became an independent nation.

So fully were British statesmen trammelled by the ideas of this colonial system, that Lord Chatham himself, the best friend the colonies had in England, did not hesitate to say from his place in Parliament, that in a certain probable contingency, he would prohibit the colonists from manufacturing even a hobnail or a horseshoe. And Lord Sheffield, at a later period, said, "The only use of American colonies is the monopoly of their consumption, and the carriage of their produce."

From this degrading commercial vassalage the Revolution set us free. You will have observed that the economical consideration that condemns the colonial policy is, that it violates this sound commercial doctrine, namely, that men should buy in the cheapest market and sell in the dearest, wherever those markets are to be found. If the mother country finds it necessary to employ prohibitions to draw the colony-trade to herself, it proves that that trade, if left to itself, would have found other and more profitable channels. If Great Britain could have furnished us with all commodities as cheaply as we could procure them elsewhere, then there was no need of prohibitions and penalties — we should have gone to her of our own accord, as unerringly as the needle points to the pole. If she could not furnish us as cheaply as others, we were wronged — it was a tribute and a tax. She made us buy in a dearer market, when a cheaper one was open.

So, if she could pay as much for our commodities as we could get for them elsewhere, there was no need of compelling us to sell to her; we should, in that case, sell to her inevitably. If she would not give what we could get elsewhere, then we were wronged; she made us sell in a cheaper market, when a dearer one was open. Her prohibitions then were either needless, or they were pernicious.

But it may be said that our loss was her gain;

that what we paid extra as consumers, was to them extra profit as manufacturers and merchants. But where is the justice of taxing one set of subjects or citizens for the benefit of another set of subjects or citizens? And how is the wealth of the whole to be promoted by a transfer of gains from one part to another part?

A deeper consideration condemns the colonial policy. Every country has certain advantages, which, if properly improved, enable that country to defy the competition of the world in certain branches of industry. If England could not sell as cheaply as others in the colonial ports, then she was employing her capital and labor at home less profitably than she might have employed them; for if she had employed them upon those branches of production for which she had natural and acquired advantages, no nation could have undersold her; and therefore, if a forced market in the colonies encouraged her to continue branches of industry that would otherwise have been abandoned, it was a permanent loss to her own productive power.

I do not believe that colonial monopolies ever enriched a mother country, on the whole. So perfect and compensating are economic laws, that the losses of one country can never contribute to the permanent gains of another. The highest commercial prosperity of one country implies and demands a corresponding prosperity in other countries. Commerce is exchange. The richer your neighbors are in all products, the richer you will become by your dealings with them. England's hereditary jealousy of the prosperity of France has been as economically foolish as it has been bitter and persistent. It is true of the family of Commerce, as it is of the family of Christ, "If one member suffer, all the members suffer with it."

A good commercial system was not one of the immediate fruits of the American Revolution. The first government established in this country, the government of the Confederation, which lasted from 1781 to 1789, was not gifted by the people with the power "to regulate commerce." This was one of the reserved rights of the States, which immediately began to use it in accordance with their own views of their own interests. Each State laid its own tariff, and undertook to regulate its own trade. The results were most disastrous. Great Britain, seeing that, as a nation, we were helpless commercially, not only refused to negotiate a commercial treaty with us, but by an Order in Council, peremptorily excluded our ships from her West India possessions, between which and the United States there had grown up, partly through some relaxations in the Act of Navigation, and partly in violation of that Act, a large and most profitable trade. We were in no position to retaliate. As a nation, we had no power to exclude her ships, and thus force her to a position of reciprocity.' The States passed various and conflicting laws. If Massachusetts, for example, laid a duty on certain goods, and Rhode Island did not, very little revenue would Massachusetts draw from that source; the goods were imported into Rhode Island, and then smuggled across the border. Thirteen independent States regulating the commerce of our seaboard, induced endless confusion, and there was no power to remedy it. Our commerce, such as it was, was ruined.

To consult upon a remedy for this state of things was the specific purpose of the meeting at Annapolis, in 1786. Alexander Hamilton was there as a delegate from New York. He persuaded the delegates to decline entering upon the subject of commerce, inasmuch as it was connected with other great defects of the Confederation, to which their powers did not reach; and drew up an Address to Congress to call another Convention, with ample powers to go over the whole ground, and to devise a system adequate to the exigences of the country.

Thus was summoned the Federal Convention of 1787, which framed the Constitution under which we live, and which gave to Congress, that is, the nation, the needful power "to regulate commerce."

The new House of Representatives, under the Constitution, commenced at once to discuss and frame a uniform national tariff. It passed in 1789; and, with some modifications and additions passed in subsequent years, constituted what I shall call, for convenience, the Hamilton tariff. I name it so, because Hamilton, as Secretary of the Treasury, made an elaborate Report to Congress on the subject, and the tariff, as finally adjusted, bore in almost every part the impress of his moulding hand. This tariff lasted for twenty-five years. It was very successful. It admitted the principle of protection, indeed, but mainly as subordinate to revenue, and rarely for its own sake, and the general rate of duties laid was very low. For instance, in the original bill as passed, cotton goods were charged 5 per cent., iron goods

7½ per cent., and woollens 5 per cent. These duties were afterwards somewhat, but not largely, increased.[1]

Now under this low tariff the revenue steadily increased, year by year. There was almost no fluctuation, but a steady annual growth of income from 1790 to 1808, when the Embargo was laid, which, of course, interrupted everything. During these eighteen years, the revenue gradually rose from $4,000,000 in 1791 to over $16,000,000 in 1808; and, what is of greater consequence, the ratio of income to population is still more striking. The revenue begun at the rate of about $1,000,000 to 1,000,000 of people, and steadily rose during the eighteen years to about $2,500,000 to 1,000,000 of people.

If now we compare these eighteen years of a low revenue, tariff with the eighteen years of the protective tariff, from 1816, when the new system was entered upon, to 1832 when it was partially abandoned again, we shall find, in the first place, great fluctuations in the second period, instead of the great steadiness of the first. Here it is, — $26,000,000 one year, $17,000,000 the next, $20,000,000 the next, $15,000,000 the next, $13,000,000 the next, $23,000,000 another, $17,000,000 another. Thus it was, up and down, an irregular teeter. Not only no steady increase, but no steady diminution, — nothing steady about it. In reference to the population, the product of the new duties never rose higher than the old ratio of 1808, namely, $2,500,000 to 1,000,000 of people, but sometimes sunk down to $750,000 to 1,000,000 of people. Thus do facts and figures show,

[1] Hildreth's United States.

independent of irrefragable reasoning, that the earlier system was the wiser.

But while I praise the Hamilton tariff, in comparison with those that came after it, I do not forget its defects. It borrowed from the old Navigation Act of England, and made unwise discriminations between foreign bottoms and American ships. Duties were 10 per cent. higher on goods imported in foreign ships. Tonnage was 6 cents per ton on American ships; 30 cents per ton on ships American-built but owned by foreigners; and 50 cents per ton on all others. These discriminations have long since disappeared. It cannot be wise to put obstacles in the way of foreigners coming to our ports to trade. Neither do sound principles approve even the moderate margin yielded in this tariff to protection. The duties indeed were low, — they were scarcely a burden upon industry, — but neither on the other hand did they aid it. All above the best revenue figure was needless. If, with the great advantage of being able to escape the costs of transportation, together with the abundance of raw material, and the endless resources of agriculture, any branch of industry could not live without artificial help, then the proof is complete that it ought not to have been entered upon, and could not have been prosecuted, except at a permanent loss.

Our second tariff, passed in 1816, I shall designate as the Calhoun tariff. Then first we entered upon the protective system as such; and it is a curious instance of how times change and men change with them, that Mr. Calhoun, who afterwards became the champion of Free Trade, strenuously advocated this tariff, while Mr. Webster as strenuously opposed it. Till then the tariff question formed no element in our politics; if I may say so, nobody knew that we had any tariff unless he chanced to read the statute-book; and it was an evil day for this country when a purely scientific question became mixed up in passions and politics, and adhesion, on one side or the other, to what not one voter in a thousand ever begun to comprehend, was made a test of party. From that day to this, no tariff question has ever been decided on its merits. Interests, sections, passions, have influenced every bill; and it is a part of the punishment, I believe, for prosecuting an artificial and false system in any department, that it is hard work to get out of it. New England generally opposed the Calhoun tariff, and the principle of protection embodied in it; so did a majority of the Southern members; but South Carolina, seeing the growing value of cotton, and anxious for a home market for the raw material, united with Pennsylvania and the Middle States in securing the high duties, especially upon cottons and iron. The duties were increased, on an average, 42 per cent. above the old rates preceding the war. Imported articles were divided into three classes: 1st, Those of which a full domestic supply could be produced; 2d, Those of which only a partial domestic supply could be afforded; and 3d, Those produced at home very slightly, or not at all. On the first class, the duties were fixed substantially at 35 per cent. *ad valorem.* On the second class, including cottons and woollens, the duties were 25 per cent., to be reduced after three years to 20 per cent. On the third class the rates were mostly fixed with a view to revenue only.

In connection with the tariff, we copied again, and more largely, from the English Navigation Act. Importations by foreign ships were limited to the produce of their respective countries; and the coasting-trade, hitherto open to foreign vessels, was now restricted to those American owned and built. In one word, we entered fairly and squarely upon the career of restriction.

Our third tariff, that of 1824, we may call, if we please, the Clay tariff. That gentleman, though Speaker of the House at the time, took an earnest part in the debates, and was regarded as the most prominent advocate of what then first began to be called the "American System," that is, the system of high protective duties. Mr. Webster still opposed this system, made an elaborate speech in reply to Mr. Clay, and voted against the bill.

The bill increased the duties on protected articles very considerably; and is an excellent proof that interests that are petted, and legislatively protected, do not long remain satisfied with what they receive, but are soon clamorous for more protection. The Calhoun tariff gave these interests large protection; eight years run on, and they call for more; they get it. Are they satisfied? Why should they be? Instead of being taught to rely upon themselves, they have been taught to lean upon the government. Certainly they will ask for more still.

Four years after the Clay tariff, that is in 1828, was passed the "Tariff of Abominations," so called, in the politics of the time. The manufacturers of course had asked for more protection; but the opposition to the system was now strong; it could not prevent the passage of the bill, but it loaded it down with all manner of objectionable features, to make it as distasteful as possible to its advocates. A political design to make the protective system unpopular appeared, and was indeed avowed; but the friends of protection, in view of the higher duties on many articles, came to the conclusion to support the bill notwithstanding its odious features. They swallowed the whole with the best grace they could. Daniel Webster, after strenuous but fruitless efforts to reduce its "abominations," for the first time in his life voted for a bill involving the principle of high protective duties. This was in John Quincy Adams's administration.

Four years later Mr. Clay went into the Presidential canvass against General Jackson upon the avowed platform of protective duties. He was beaten. The country seemed to indicate its preference for another system; and accordingly in 1833 our fifth tariff, called the "Compromise tariff," became a law. It adopted a sliding scale in reference to all duties that were over 20 per cent., providing for their gradual reduction on each alternate year, till 1842, when and thereafter the uniform rate on all these goods should be 20 per cent. on the home valuation. Mr. Clay himself brought forward this bill as a "compromise;" it was approved by Mr. Calhoun, and it passed both Houses by decided majorities.

During the next nine years the attention of the country was occupied by the great questions of a National Bank and the currency. On these and other questions the administration of Van Buren became unpopular and broke down; and the Whig party, coming into power, passed what I shall call the "Whig tariff" of 1842. It was a high protective tariff. The average of duties was perhaps 50 per cent., instead of the 20 per cent. of its predecessor. Under it, millions of capital were seduced into manufactures, particularly of iron; and when the high duties were abolished, as they were a few years later, hundreds and thousands of persons were pecuniarily ruined. It is impossible to speak in terms sufficiently deprecatory of an artificial system that inveigles capital and laborers into branches of industry in which they never would have embarked of their own accord. Our whole course of legislation on this subject cannot be properly characterized in terms of respect. Congress has alternately inflated, and then punctured, the bubble. Nothing injures commerce so much as to tinker it. A constant changing of the terms on which foreigners are permitted to trade with us disgusts them and injures us. Even a bad tariff persisted in, is a good deal better than a series of good and bad ones together.

In 1846 was passed what we will call the "Walker tariff," from Robert J. Walker, then Secretary of the Treasury. It reduced the duties on imports down to about the standard of the "Compromise" of 1833. It discriminated however, as the Compromise did not, between goods that could be produced at home and those that could not. It approached, in short, more nearly than any other, in its principles and details, to the Hamilton tariff, although the general rate of duties was higher. From that time up to 1857, there was a regular and large increase in the amount of dutiable goods imported, bringing in a larger revenue to the government. The surplus in the treasury accumulated, and large sums were expended by the government in buying up its own bonds at a high premium, for the sake of emptying the treasury. Under these circumstances the "tariff of 1857" was passed, decidedly lowering the rates of duties, and largely increasing the free list. The financial crisis of that year diminished the imports, and the revenue fell off $22,000,000. It rallied, however, the next two years, but owing to the large increase in the free list, not quite up to the old point.

It only remains to speak of the "Morrill tariff" of 1861. It is the ninth in order, and our present tariff. The difficulties growing out of the war ostensibly united all parties in the view of obtaining, if possible, more revenue to the government; but there was no agreement as to the means by which more revenue could be obtained; and the protectionists in Congress seized the opportunity of the withdrawment of the Southern members for discriminating in favor of the articles in which they were interested, even to the extent of diminishing the revenue by practically prohibiting the importation. They did another thing which imposed at the time on many people, and which can hardly be characterized in too severe terms. At the moment when the great need of the government was revenue, they added largely to the free list, taking care to put upon it many articles which are used in manufactures, and which thus escape taxation altogether. They put the duty on protected articles so high that little or no revenue is received on them, and at the same time withdrew, by means of the free list, all revenue from many articles especially used in protected manufactures. The new tariff therefore has not produced the revenue expected from it. It is not honestly adjusted for that purpose. To put articles on a free list is no boon to free trade; especially when it is accompanied, as in this case, by very high duties. The present duties are very much too high, and many things are exempted from duty which ought to pay duty for the sake of revenue. The present tariff therefore rests on false principles throughout, and it cannot be permanent. They who feel themselves benefited by it may as well make up their minds to dispense with it. The Western States will not tolerate it. Political Economy denounces it. To relax commercial systems and not to restrict them is alone in accordance with the spirit of this age. The state of the country demands its abolition. The claims of the public debt require a larger revenue from customs. $86,000,000 were received in the year closing on the 1st of July, 1865. We may well receive $125,000,000 from a tariff which is framed in accordance with the true principles of exchange. In 1831 the ratio of free goods imported to dutiable goods was as 33 to 100, $71,130,351 free and $218,180,191 dutiable; and in 1862, the ratio was as 40 to 100, $52,721,648 free and $136,683,123 dutiable; instead of this there should be a low revenue duty upon the entire imports; and this would doubtless have doubled or trebled the revenue of those years. The idea of protection and the idea of taxation are very distinct ideas; and a recommendation to abandon the one by no means carries along with it a recommendation to abandon the other.

CHAPTER XVI.

ON TAXATION.

IF the general views maintained throughout this book are conceded to be correct, we shall now reach with very little difficulty the true principles of taxation. Value resides in services exchanged; and since government is an essential prerequisite to any general and satisfactory exchanges, since it contributes by direct effort to the security of person and property, it justly claims from every citizen in return a compensation for the service thus rendered to him. I do not mean to say that government exists solely for the protection of person and property, or that all the operations of government are to be brought down within the sphere of exchange; government exists as well for the improvement as for the protection of society, and many of its high functions are moral, to be performed under a lofty sense of responsibility to God and to future ages; but the matter of taxation, by which government is outwardly supported, and by which it takes to itself a part of the gains of every man's industry, seems to me to find a ready and solid justification in the common principles of exchange. A tax paid is a reward for a service rendered; and because the service may have respected another generation as well as the present, it is sometimes proper that the tax also shall be passed over in part to another generation to pay. The services which government renders to production by its laws, courts, and officers, by the force which it is at all times ready to exert in behalf of any citizen or the whole society when threatened with evil, are rendered somewhat on the principle of division of labor, one set of agents devoting themselves to that work; and, notwithstanding some crying abuses of authority which no constitution or public virtue have yet been found adequate wholly to avert, are rendered on the whole economically and satisfactorily. Taxes, therefore, demanded of citizens by a lawful government which tolerably performs its functions, are legitimate and just on principles of exchange alone.

The questions now arise, in what proportions shall the citizens contribute to the fund necessary to be raised by taxation? And in what manner shall these contributions be paid?

The common notion has been that, since every man's person is supposed to be equally protected by the government, a uniform poll-tax assessed on all citizens alike is right, and that for the rest, a man should be taxed according to his property. But what is property? No word has received a greater variety of definitions, or is less settled in definite meaning in the minds of men. The lawyers make a distinction between real property and personal property; and the law at present, though a man have neither real estate nor movables, yet taxes him on his income, on the rewards of his daily industry, regarding that as a species of property. And this too is just; because, as I think, the ultimate idea of property is the power and right to render services in exchange. Robinson Crusoe, while solitary upon his island, did not and could not have property, in the true sense of that word. It is not the fact of appropriation that makes anything property; it is not the fact that a man has made it or transformed it, that makes anything property; it is not the fact that a man may rightfully give it away, that makes anything property; but it is the fact that a man has something, no matter what it is, for which something else may be obtained in exchange, that makes that something property, and gives government the right to tax it. In other words, property consists in values, in a purchasing-power, and not in possession, or in appropriation, or in the esteem in which a man holds anything he has as long as it is his own. The test of property is a sale; that which will bring something when exposed for exchange is property; that which will bring nothing, either never was, or has now ceased to be, distinctively property. This view may not seem to be as novel as it is, or it may be prejudiced by its very novelty, but at any rate it carries along with it that strongest of the criteria of truth, that it simplifies and illumines a confused section of the field of human thinking; and at the same time justifies a practice which governments have reached, as it were through instinct, but which is continually a subject of cavil and complaint, the practice, namely, of taxing men who have neither real estate nor chattels, on their incomes from industry. Within a month an intelligent man was heard to inveigh against the injustice of the law which taxes the industrious man who works and gains an income, but takes little or nothing from the man unable or too lazy to work. Nevertheless the law is right in its action, and my neighbor was wrong in his strictures.

To the general question, then, in what proportions shall the citizens contribute in taxes to the support of government, the general answer comes, that they ought to contribute in accordance with the value of the services which they either do or might render to their fellow-citizens. Under the expression "might render" is not included any personal services not actually rendered, but only those forms of material property which might be exchanged for other forms if the owner saw fit to exchange them, but which he prefers for the present to keep in his own possession. It would not be fair, for example, to tax a professional man on services which his neighbors, or any other authority, think he might render, were he less indolent or more capable; but it is fair to tax any man on those forms of material property in his possession with which he may at any time he chooses render services in exchange. The right to tax on the part of the government is connected with the right to exchange on the part of the citizens, grows out of this, and is limited by it. This consideration, though it may exclude the propriety of a poll-tax, is consistent with all other forms of taxation, and gives unity to them.

I do not think that the common sense of mankind falls in with the opinion ably advocated by Mr. Mill and others, that persons of a large property or of a large income should pay taxes higher than the due proportion of their properties or incomes to more moderate properties or incomes. The transaction between the government and a tax-payer is itself a kind of exchange, and if the ground of it be, as I think it is, that government facilitates by way of protection all his other exchanges, then ought he to pay taxes proportionably to the amount of his exchanges actual or possible; and a man should pay on an income of $10,000 ten times as much, and no more, as a man with an income of $1000. Mr. Mill regards equality of burden as the true general principle of taxation; and as a rich man can pay more than his proportional share with perhaps less sacrifice than the poor man, therefore he ought to pay more than his proportional share. This principle is embodied in the present United States law by which incomes are taxed; incomes over $600 and less than $5000 being subject to 5 per cent. tax, and the surplus income over $5000 being subject to a 10 per cent. tax. It may well be questioned whether the principle itself, and consequently this application of it, be soundly based. Certainly taxes ought to be laid on equal and equitable principles, but the difficulty of determining for different classes of citizens what would be an equality of burden is so insuperably great, that one hesitates before accepting it as the true principle of taxation. On the whole, I am clear that the best available guide in practical taxation are these simple principles, that property is essentially a power to render services, and that taxation should be as nearly as possible proportionate to the degree of this power.

If, then, taxes are to be laid on services, thus subtracting a portion from the gains which accompany them, the question now arises in what way are they to be laid? They are commonly divided into two classes, direct and indirect. A direct tax is levied on the very persons who are expected themselves to pay it; an indirect tax is demanded from one person in the expectation that he will pay it provisionally, but will indemnify himself in the higher price which he will receive from the ultimate consumer. Thus an income tax is direct, while duties laid on imported goods are indirect. There has been a great amount of discussion on the point whether direct or indirect taxation be the more eligible form; but the reader of penetration will perceive that there is not at bottom any very radical difference between them; each is alike a tax on actual or possible exchanges, with this main difference, that men pay indirect taxes as a part of the price of the goods they buy, without thinking perhaps that it is a tax they are paying, and consequently without any of the repugnance that is sometimes felt towards a tax-gatherer who comes with an unwelcome demand. Thus indirect taxes are conveniently and economically collected. Especially is this true of impost duties; since one set of custom-house officers collect easily and at once the government tax which is ultimately paid by consumers all over the country. The manufacturers' tax, the tax on keeping horses and carriages to let, and very many others levied by the present United States internal revenue law, are indirect taxes, whereby the government gets in a lump what is afterwards distributed over many subordinate exchanges. The countervailing disadvantage of indirect taxation, however, is, that the price of the commodity is usually enhanced to an extent much beyond the amount of the tax, partly because it is a cover under which dealers may put an unreasonable demand, and partly because the tax, having to be advanced over and over again by the intermediate dealers, profits rapidly accumulate as an element of the price.

Direct taxes are laid either on income or expenditure. An income tax, if the exact amount of income could in all cases be ascertained, would be a perfectly unexceptionable form of taxation. The only sources of income are three: wages, profits, rents. I do not think that gifts are legitimately taxable; they lie outside the field of exchange; they spring from sympathy, from benevolence, from duty; and while exchange must claim all that fairly belongs to it, it must be careful not to throw discouragements into the adjacent but distinct field of morals. Hence, it may well be questioned whether legacies, bequeathments, gifts to charitable and educational institutions, and gifts to individuals proceeding from friendship, gratitude, or other such impulse, are properly subject to taxation. The property is taxable in the hands of the donor, and may be in the hands of the recipient, but the passage from one to the other ought to be unobstructed by a tax. Gifts then excepted, and plunder, which is out of the question, the sources of income are few and simple, and there is no great difficulty in every man's ascertaining about what his annual income is. Fraudulent returns should be promptly punished by an additional assessment and collection. The income law at present in force in the United States has perhaps been subject to less complaint than the manufacturers' tax, and other forms of indirect taxation; and it is becoming more and more productive every year, as the forms are perfected, and as the memory and conscience of the payers are quickened by the action of a healthful public opinion brought to bear through the very proper annual publication of the list of their returns.

The other direct taxes are on expenditure of some special kinds, such as those on horses, carriages, watches, plate, and so on, kept for personal use. As the difficulty of a tax on a person's whole expenditure is much greater than one on his whole income, inasmuch as the items are more numerous and more diffused, it is only attempted to lay a few taxes on some peculiar items of expenditure, such as those above mentioned; but as these do not reach all persons with any degree of equality, they are so far forth objectionable. A house-tax, levied on the occupier, and not on the owner unless he be at the same time the occupier, would be a direct tax on expenditure every way unobjectionable.[1] Taking society at large, the house a man lives in and its furniture are probably the most accurate index attainable of the size of his general expenditures. They are open to observation and current remark; they are that on which persons rely more perhaps than on anything else external for their consideration and station in life; the tax could be assessed with very little trouble on the part of the assessor; and it is well worthy the attention of our national legislature, whether such a tax, if more taxes should be needed, would not be more equal and more easy of collection than any others now open; or whether it might not with advantage take the place of some of the com-

[1] Mill, Chap. III., Book 5.

plicated and objectionable taxes now laid. Direct taxes have this general advantage over indirect, that they bring the people into more immediate contact with the government that lays the taxes, and subject it to a quicker supervision and more effectual curb, whenever its expenditures grow larger than the people think it desirable to incur; they have this general disadvantage over indirect taxes, especially over imposts, that the number of officials required to assess and collect them is much larger, thus swallowing up a part of the proceeds of the taxes, with this liability also of bringing the people into an attitude of hostility to the government and to its contemplated expenditures. But whether the taxes be direct or indirect, or whatever be their form, except it be a polltax, which is questionable at best, they are laid upon exchanges, and are designed to withdraw for the use of the government a part of the gains of exchanges. From this point of view, which gives unity to the whole field of taxation, some practical hints may usefully conclude this discussion and this volume.

(1.) Taxes in general, in order to be most productive in the long run, as well as discourage as little as possible the exchanges which would otherwise go forward, ought to be low relatively to the amount of values exchangeable. A high tax not infrequently stops exchanges in the taxed articles altogether, and of course the tax then realizes nothing to the government. As the only motive to an exchange is the gain of it, the exchange ceases whenever the government cuts so deeply into the gain as to leave little margin to the exchangers. The greater the gain left to the parties, after the tax is abstracted, the more numerous will the exchanges become, and the greater the number of times will the tax fall into the coffers of the government. In almost all articles, consumption increases from a lowered price in even a greater ratio than the diminution of the rate of tax; so that the interests of consumers and of the revenue are not antagonistic but harmonious. Particularly is this true of duties on imported goods: I do not know as there is anything imported, except what the government itself imports, which should not pay a small duty. It is a tax on exchange, like all other taxes; why should it not be paid on everything? A free list in imports is of doubtful utility at best, and may become, as the Morrill tariff demonstrates, little better than a swindle. On articles of luxury and ostentation, and on those, such as liquors and tobaccos, whose moral effects are clearly questionable, very high taxes may properly enough be laid, because their incidence will hardly tend to diminish consumption, and it would scarcely be to be regretted if it did; but with this exception, duties and taxes should be levied at a low rate per cent., as well for the interest of revenue as of consumers.

(2.) Duties and taxes should be simple, and their amount easily calculable by the payer beforehand. The complication of specific duties with *ad valorem* duties upon the same articles is a decided objection to the present tariff. So far as is possible, taxes should be levied upon commodities once for all, and then an end. The opposite principle of taxing commodities every time they change hands throws an indefinite burden on exchange, whose weight cannot well be calculated beforehand, either by the consumer or by the government, through uncertainty as to the number of transfers. Exchanges indeed are the only legitimate subject of taxation, but not every specific and subordinate exchange. An attempt to tax all sales whatever was followed in Spain, and will be followed everywhere, by a sluggish indisposition to trade at all. Let the amount of the tax be definite, and let everybody be sure that when it is once paid government will produce no further claim, and industry will go along under heavy taxes better than under those nominally lighter to which uncertainty as to time or amount attaches. All the more advanced governments have been simplifying of late years their systems of taxation, and collecting their revenue at fewer points, and under more tangible conditions, in order to interfere as little as possible with a free industry and free exchange. England, for instance, has given up a great variety of taxes which she used to impose, and now collects her revenue about as follows: —

Customs, 35 per cent. Stamps, 10 per cent.
Excise, 25 per cent.   Miscellaneous, 10 per cent.
Taxes, 20 per cent.

(3.) Taxes and duties should be collected by the government in as economical a manner as possible, that is to say, the money should be kept out of the pockets of the people as short a time as possible, disbursement following quick upon collection. It is poor policy to gather taxes at the beginning of the year which will not be disbursed till the end of the year. Let the people use their funds till they are wanted at the treasury; and if the taxes do not then come in as fast as wanted, it is better to issue what are called in England exchequer-bills, and in the United States certificates of indebtedness, to be redeemed at the end of the year from the proceeds of the taxes, than to let the people's money lie idle in the treasury.

(4.) If the necessities of the State require it, government has the right to demand from all persons who are capable of making exchanges, and who do make them, something in the form of taxes. But it is every way better, when possible, that people of very moderate means should be exempted altogether from direct taxes; and the payment of indirect taxes is a matter wholly in their own option, since they are at liberty to buy much or little of those commodities subjected to an indirect tax. In this country at present, incomes not exceeding $600 are exempted by the law. If a house-tax should be levied, all houses below a certain grade of style and comfort should be exempted, and the tax pass up by easy gradations from those just taxed to the palatial residences of the rich. In the present age of the world, the well-to-do citizens of every country are able to bear without too great difficulty the burdens of the government; and nothing tests better the degree of civilization which a nation has reached than the care and solicitude it displays for the welfare of its poorer citizens.

THE END.

www.ingramcontent.com/pod-product-compliance
Lightning Source LLC
Chambersburg PA
CBHW022110300426
44117CB00007B/657